Writing
and the Experience of Limits

EUROPEAN PERSPECTIVES:
A Series of the Columbia University Press

Writing
and the Experience of Limits

Philippe Sollers

Edited by David Hayman

Translated by Philip Barnard with David Hayman

New York
Columbia University Press
1983

P
302
S 58
1983

The publisher gratefully acknowledges the assistance of the French Ministry of Culture in the preparation of this translation.

Library of Congress Cataloging in Publication Data
Sollers, Philippe, 1936–
  Writing and the experience of limits.

  (European perspectives)
  Translation of: L'écriture et l'expérience des limites.
  Includes index.
  1. Discourse analysis, Literary—Addresses, essays, lectures. 2. Written communication—Addresses, essays, lectures. I. Hayman, David. II. Title. III. Series.
P302.S58 1983   808'.00141   82-25258
ISBN 0-231-05292-8

Columbia University Press
New York   Guildford, Surrey

Clothbound editions of Columbia University Press books are Smyth-sewn and printed on permanent and durable acid-free paper.

49463

Contents

Translator's Note

IN PRESENTING THIS English version of *Writing and the Experience of Limits*, several features of the translation should be pointed out.

Because the typographical organization of each essay has a definite function in Sollers, no effort has been made to alter this, for example by breaking up long paragraphs. Paragraph breaks and the subdivision of each section of an essay—indicated by a spacing between paragraphs within the section—occur here as they do in the French. Although some lengthy citations have been set apart from the body of the text in keeping with American and English editorial practice (for example in "The Novel and the Experience of Limits"), this has not been done in "Lautréamont's Science." Since "Lautréamont's Science" addresses itself to, among other questions, the opposition of text and citation, to the manner in which citations are negated, transformed, or "reproduced" by their "host" texts, the ambiguous reciprocity of text and citation thematized in this essay's form has not been altered by typographically separating the citations from Sollers' text.

All notes from the French text have been retained. Translator's notes have been used to incorporate bibliographical information, a limited amount of explanatory material, and excerpts from interviews in which Sollers expands on problems being discussed in the text. I have utilized, but have not followed exactly, existing English translations of the texts Sollers refers to when these are available; these translations have been indicated in the translator's footnotes as well.

In general, the translation has aimed for a certain "clarity" in English, although this clarity has, it is hoped, not been achieved by smoothing over opacities or difficulties inherent to the original French. In dealing with problematic words and phrases I have sometimes given the French in brackets. Brackets have also been used to point out terms whose associations and resonance in French disappear when the terms are translated, for example the distinction between a textual "apparatus" (*appareil*) and literary "affectation" (*apparat*). If the translation has succeeded in "reproducing" the effects produced by the French text without resorting to an overly gallicized English, it should be remarked that this is in large part due to the patient attention and suggestions of David Hayman.

The text used for this translation is that of the "Points" edition of *L'écriture et l'expérience des limites* (Paris: Editions du Seuil, 1968), in which some of the essays differ slightly from the versions in *Logiques* (Editions du Seuil, 1968). The final essay in the present collection, "The Novel and the Experience of Limits," is not included in *L'écriture* and has been translated from the version that appeared in *Logiques*.

Philip Barnard

Introduction

David Hayman

FEW CONTEMPORARY WRITERS have been as active or as controversial on the French literary scene as Philippe Sollers. Mercurial, protean, gifted beyond most of his generation, he is much more than the sum of his parts, much more available in his public nature than any comparable figure. To understand the qualities that adhere to the critical text published in translation here, we must take into consideration the man and his moment, his career as novelist, editor, and thinker.

Sollers was born Philippe Joyaux in 1936 into a family of minor industrialists, brothers who lived with their families side by side in identical semidetached houses within a large parklike garden next to their factory, which produced enameled pots and household utensils. He grew up during the war in an anti-Petainist family with strong Bordelais, hence anglophile, traditions, which he has never lost. It was a time, as he describes it, of great if not catastrophic unrest, with influxes of refugees constantly altering the complexion of the community. He was nine at the end of the war, a sickly, bookish, precocious child accustomed to isolation. This much and more is attested to, obliquely, in the semi-autobiographical writings that followed at regular intervals his first novel, and directly, in the volume of interviews, *Vision à New York*.[1] There, he speaks of his intermittent ear problems, the asthma he suffered from during adolescence, his cultivation of isolation, his early (and quite natural) fascination with Baudelaire's erotica and later interest in the Surrealists and, through them,

Lautréamont. He describes himself as the class clown in the Jesuit school to which he was sent at seventeen and from which he was eventually expelled partly because of his tastes in literature. Nothing could be more characteristic than this irreverence and intransigence, traits that must always be allied in him with high seriousness of purpose and a near veneration of the expressive and creative word, what has come to be known as *"écriture."*

Several factors were crucial to his intellectual development, at least in his own mind. He mentions, for example, the ambiguous Bordelais setting that shaped him; his curious family situation, the twinned and intertwined families (a fairy tale context that "reenforces a certain sort of mythological imagination");[2] and the fact that his childhood was shadowed by "maximalized contradictions among the different established institutions," symbolized by his mother's Catholicism and his father's atheism, as well as his family's rejection of the Vichy government. Above all, there is the early history of health problems which he sees as a central factor in his education.

> Illness enabled me to build a primary personal observation post. Through sickness I can recover the most precise coordinates for my memory in relation to an ambient reality. I don't recall ever having an integral, closed body. I remember always having a body in some sense impaired, open, lacking, inspecting its own possible boundaries, limits, (for example) in relation to my ear, which played an enormous role in my development, for it is thanks to all my ear troubles that I ended up with a very good ear, or rather, I became aware that, in relation to the body, it all begins with the ear—which leads me to conclude that I provoked all those ear troubles to assert my own conception of the world by way of the ear. . . . Breath is another factor that, along with the ear, conditions essential structures— as a result, as they say, I am a writer. So, it seems to me from this perspective that, without actually writing, I was obliged to give shape to a body that would one day be the ground for a possible writing. It took enormous effort in later years to establish the awareness that, rather than being called upon to overcome my body, I could make use of it. But that particular dialectic is among my first conscious memories. One that allows me to hazard the thought that writing is a function of disease.[3]

Whatever the truth value of such assertions, we may see in these words echoes of the highly individual mindset that informs the essays

in the present volume and a persuasive rationalization of Sollers' novelistic procedures as well as his more recent dedication to the spoken
text, the text as a vehicle for voicing.

Sollers styles himself an autodidact, claiming that he had to re-
learn what he was taught in his various schools. Doubtless this is true,
but his years in Bordeaux *lycées* marked him as a French reader react-
ing against French reading just as his period among the Jesuits ("the
only true atheists"), while failing to make him devout, provided him
with a respect for method and seared in his mind the need to understand his own lack of belief. Both experiences, combined with the
prolonged engagement with Marxist dialectics and Maoism, Lacanian
psychoanalysis, and Derridian philosophy, have contributed immeas-
urably to his critical vision.

While still a student in Paris, at en elite Ecole Supérieure, Sollers won recognition from François Mauriac and received the Prix Fé-
néon for a short story, *"Le défi"* (1957), written when he was nineteen
and published under a (permanent) pseudonym, assumed for technical
reasons. (He was still under the legal age.)[4] At the age of twenty-one,
he published to critical acclaim a novel of initiation, *Une curieuse
solitude* (1958),[5] written in a fine Proustian manner with echoes of
Bataille and a hint of that earlier prodigy, Raymond Radiguet. Designed to please, it did. With these publications, Sollers began a
twenty-five-year association with Les Editions du Seuil, where he
published all of his novels and initiated (1960) the controversial but
remarkably influential *Tel Quel,* a cultural periodical that quickly became identified with Sollers and generated the prestigious *Tel Quel*
collection.[6]

None of this could have been predicted in 1958, when the jacket
of *Une curieuse solitude* displayed, along with the photo of a moon-
faced young man, the following statement:

Born 28 November 1936, at Talence in the suburbs of Bordeaux. He did
his secondary school work there. At seventeen he leaves [sic] for Versailles
to study with the Jesuits. Having enrolled in the Ecole Supérieure des
Sciences Economiques et Commerciales, he lives in Paris.

Never again would his jacket copy be so circumstantial and flat.

Tel Quel was founded by young Turks partly as an organ for the sort of revolutionary formalist literature being produced by the New Novelists. So it comes as no surprise that Sollers' second novel, *Le parc*,[7] published in 1961 and awarded the Prix Médicis, is a semilyrical nod in that direction. Set in the garden of his childhood home, *Le parc* is a study in elaborately simple absence and unresolved mystery. Sollers followed it two years later with *L'intermédiaire* (1963), a collection which combines personal recollection, art criticism, and atmospheric word-painting in a minor key, all written in a carefully modulated prose designed to approximate the indirection so characteristic of Henry James. Two moments in this text are particularly premonitory: the first, a dreamlike divagation on the twinned houses of his childhood, a guided tour through a semi-imaginary space ("*Images Pour une maison*"); the second, a jocular meditation on elimination called "*Introduction aux lieux d'aisance*" (Introduction to the Toilet Facility). A playful piece designed to lighten the texture of the book, the latter falls into a hoary subgenre of adolescent pastiche. But it takes on a different character when considered in the light of later concerns, of a growing interest in the work and paradoxical vision of Bataille, to say nothing of Lautréamont and of a reevaluated Mallarmé. It should also be seen in the afterglow of the startling array of antithetical subject matter and moods in the novels of what we shall call Sollers' third phase (*Lois*, *H*, and *Paradis*). If passages like the following promise more than they are yet able to deliver, the high camp irreverence is more than masterful persiflage. It is a studied homage in the meticulous *chosiste* vein of Alain Robbe-Grillet, with overtones of Francis Ponge,[8] subverted by and subverting images and citations from Mallarmé:

> This vase is *crowned* by a plumped up circumference whose waxed wood surface can deliver a surprise, adhering much too firmly to our skin. (At times our sweat assumes the function of the wax.)
>
> If I urinate, I take pleasure in the violence of my stream, in multiplying the white bubbles swollen with their emptiness [*néant*]* soon to form a creamy froth. The froth crackles [*pétille*],† bursts, stirs, whispers, glimmers

---

* These expressions draw upon Mallarmé's heavy artillery.

† The word *pétiller* has overtones of small farting sounds though it remains perfectly polite French.

with a thousand flames.* For a moment I meditate on the shrivelling rem-
nant [grésillante résille].‡ Finally, disappointed by its dissolution, I drown
it in a maelstrom.[9]

It is remarkable how many traits of the later, even the latest Sollers
are already in place here: the self-mockery and the formal irreverence, the precise ear of the mimic, the capacity to shift tonalities, the
fascination with multipurpose discourse, the ability to make minimal
subject matter vibrate. At the height of the New Novel's development,
Sollers is already sounding the death knell of its pretensions. Significantly, the appendix to *L'intermédiaire* features "Six Propositions Concerning Alain Robbe-Grillet."

By 1963, Sollers had embarked on a career that was to derive its
consistency in large measure from its nonconformist vigor and its rigorous honesty. He was emotionally attuned to Mao's mode of perpetual
revolution long before he became openly engaged in the radical Left.
His career can best be seen as marked by a series of ruptures, informed
by an internal logic that feeds upon its own substance, advancing and
elaborating upon impulses available virtually from the start. In 1965,
when he published his third novel, *Drame*, he was not so much finding a voice as modulating and regenerating a method established earlier in *L'intermédiaire*.

It can be argued that *Drame* continues Mallarmé's struggle for
the expression of purity and simplicity, a plenitude in absence. For
Roland Barthes, writing in 1968 and reviewing his thought in 1979,
Drame is something of a zero degree novel, an illustration of the as-
yet-unrecognized fact that "the oblique is a fundamental mode of
enunciation."[10] It is also to be approached as a poem, as "the indistinct celebration of language and the beloved woman, of their movement one toward the other, as was in its time Dante's *La Vita Nuova*:
isn't *Drame* the infinite metaphor for 'I love you.' "[11] But Barthes
asserts that, while we should "enter into the author's vertigo," we should
also "ceaselessly separate ourselves from the fine poem taking shape.
. . ."[12] That is, in *Drame*, we experience an exercise in Spartan discourse, a denial in the service of language that far outstrips that of the

‡ Literally, shrivelling net, but clearly chosen more for sound than sense.

New Novel, while evidently continuing its development. Barthes finds in it support for a number of his own positions, thus establishing a pattern to be followed by later critics and admirers like Jacques Derrida and Julia Kristeva. That is, all of them, while testifying to the qualities of Sollers' fiction, have found in it inspiration as well as reenforcement. But on the moment of *Drame*, and perhaps *Nombres* as well, Sollers should have the last word. In a statement that at once praises the accomplishment of the language-oriented fiction (the elimination of "a metaphysics which preaches that language is transparent"), he refers back to the time when "poets and novelists [attempted] to make language the area of enquiry (*problématique*)." He goes on to say "that that approach has been exhausted." [13] *Drame*, with its emphasis on the word emerging from the page to evoke a possible event surrounded by concrete but "undecidable" detail, was only the first step beyond the less subtle problematics of the New Novelistic revolt against fictional discourse. It records, enshrines, the elaboration of the text out of the material of textuality, language itself.

Sollers' next move involved a double experiment: the novel/text *Nombres* and the collection of critical essays he called *Logiques*, simultaneously published in April of 1968. The latter, composed largely during the gestation period of *Nombres*, constituted an elaborate program for reading based in the writing practice (one could say *praxis*, given the Marxist moment) of a number of marginalized writers. The reflection of and upon these writers, notably Sade, Artaud, and Bataille, but perhaps even more emphatically upon "le livre" of Mallarmé [14] is everywhere implied in the texture as well as the various 'actions' of the plotless and virtually characterless *Nombres*. In this highly schematic text with 25 numbered sequences of four frames (suggestive of a synchrony/diachrony reflected in its rhetorical procedures), the spirit of these forebears contributes to a vitality and vibrancy, a gestural power absent from the more sombre *Drame*. While still oblique and reticent in its procedure, *Nombres* is consequently almost lavish in its effects.

Repeatedly, the reader (though usually in the guise of the writer) is placed in, engaged by, witness to situations that can be described as erotically, frontally polyvalent. Early on we are exposed to a real/symbolic/manifest beheading which could be our own and the text's castration, an event first stated in a revolutionary reflection worthy of Bataille himself but portraying a magical verbal space appropriate to the New Novel and its forebear Raymond Roussel:

2.14 . . . 'so that we have there, under our eyes, within us, an absolutely impenetrable margin'[15]: I saw the hall, the audience, and the one who spoke standing in the central alley, turned toward the windows struck by the sound. . . . A picture was hanging on the wall and the bottom of that picture, in a deeper blue, was therefore the space for additions and divisions. . . . And I saw myself rise, open the window, and, turning, note that the meeting was proceeding behind the window where someone was speaking my name. . . . The street, the city were in fact those which I had left. Nevertheless, I saw them as street, as city, only through a transposition backward whose prospective elements could not be stated. Just like, now, this engraver who, one hundred years before the event, showed the beheading of a king even though the mechanism did not exist. . . . It was easy for me to relive the scene: the discomfort of the participants, the sense of confronting an unprecedented act, the unconscious crowd, conscious more than ever of belonging to the sky and air of this day, to the taste of crime in each throat, and the symbol of his majesty, the body of his majesty dressed in silk cut in two in the cold and crowded square, cut and drowned in blood and cutting time. . . . The drum roll that finally drowns out that voice before the blade sends the organ that produces it into the basket though not before the head has been brandished as proof of a sacrilegious diminution, soiled. . . . Unique act having no equal aside from the massacres of priests permitted at last, or again, the parading of that flayed head affixed to a pike through the shouts. . . .[16]

This text is less a poem than a self-generating (and self-reflecting) process, described in part when the narrative "I" claims,

1.13 . . . The account had begun abruptly when I had decided to change language within the same language, when the first knot of resistance imposed itself, when the repetitions had invaded their outlines.[17]

Any translation of this text is risky, removing ambiguities essential to its movement, but clearly Sollers' speaker is beginning a description of a textual procedure *and* a physical encounter both with war and with language as joy and distress. The movement is toward an identity of speaker with "procedure":

> 1.13 . . . By the completion of a procedure during which I had passed by disfigured flesh, skinless and speaking by ejaculations of blood, by the mashing of nerves and blood become [casualty] figures detached and devalued by the exchange, I became this overturning . . .[18]

In short the experience/text began/begins as decision/s and proceded/s as a self-established decorum in which language and activity (to say nothing of spaces and temporalities) become variously interchangeable. Repeatedly, the body of writing mingles with the body of the writer,

> 3.43 . . . I was therefore ordered to move about in my own shape knowing that I would end up losing it, deserted by it . . . that I'd end up losing myself in it. . . . Nothing could withstand the story thus released, and the other thus becoming a black fire imposing itself on a white fire, a visible fire on an invisible fire, and the curves and the points—vowels, consonants—bodied forth the mouth of the procedure, 'ink on parchment,' the lowest river, the spring. . . . Silence and activity. Production using me as its base, mirror, filter, thrust, me producing it, in my turn, in its permanent reserve of wellsprings. . . .[19]

By elaborating upon that translation, this text underscores and vivifies the result, a discourse crossing incessantly between the world of its processes and the *trompe l'oeil* of its consequences, engaging the reader in the double, triple, troubling ambiguity of Sollers' research. Simultaneously, it introduces into its very texture intellectual, aesthetic, and political concerns that make it, however obliquely, one with its time, placing it within history.

No wonder this intensely written text stimulated Derrida to write the difficult concluding section of *La dissémination*, an essay that should be read as yet another mirror text for *Nombres*. "La dissémination" (first published in 1969) opens with a classic derridian description of Sollers' method as it relates to the readerly presence:

> The text is remarkable in that the reader (here in exemplary fashion) can never choose his own place in it, nor can the spectator. There is at any rate no tenable place for him opposite the text, outside the text, no

spot where he might get away with *not* writing what, in the reading, would seem to him to be *given, past*; no spot, in other words, where he would stand before an already *written* text. Because his job is to put things on stage, he is on stage himself, he puts himself on stage.[20]

Derrida reads *Nombres* in the light of Mallarmé, a procedure that is especially congenial, given the Mallarmé essay in *Logiques*:

> If that which, once it is framed, appears to be an element or an occurrence of opening is no longer anything but an aperture-effect that is topologically assignable, then nothing will indeed have taken place but the place.[21]

After all it was Mallarmé who first and most clearly delineated the problematic of the book for our century. It is also fitting, given the *Tel Quel* connection, that Derrida sees *Nombres* as the deconstructive text that demonstrates deconstructability:

> That is where the story (history) will have taken place, if it takes place, where something will have been seen, recounted, summed up as the meaning or presentable substance of the book.
>   But these *Numbers* dismantle such a representation; they take it apart as one deconstructs a mechanism or as one disconcerts the self-assured pretensions of a claim.[22]

In the light of such comments, it is hard not to conclude that the complex interplay of *Drame, Nombres,* and *Logiques* mirrors its relation to the history of the sixties, the vicissitudes of *Tel Quel* and the evolution of the avant-garde critical theory, a poetics in progress. If, for Sollers, the concentration on language and form eventually became a lifeless game, this was a formalism carried to an immensely productive extreme and characterized by an unusual amount of internal energy. By the seventies, Sollers' oeuvre, combined with his work as editor, had established him as a pivotal figure, seminal not only for himself but also for the self-awareness of other thinkers during a long incandescent moment, one of the most fertile in the history of this century. It was the period that saw the emergence of a *Tel Quel* group and a post-structuralist vision through which Derrida, Barthes, Kristeva, Foucault, Lacan, along with Denis Roche, Maurice Roche, and Marcelin Pleynet became the intellectuals' equivalent for household words. It was the moment when the PCF (French Communist Party) became intellectually respectable through the writing of Althusser, and *Tel Quel* entered and left the camp, becoming a political as well as an intellectual trend setter. It was also a moment of considerable tension within the *Tel Quel* establishment, of defections and quarrels characterized by heated polemics and violent regroupings which remain to be dispassionately documented.

Within the constellation *Tel Quel* at les Editions du Seuil (and now *L'Infini* at Gallimard) Sollers has been and will doubtless always be a moving target, but his trajectory is best thought of in terms of the young James Joyce's definition of a true portrait. It is "the curve of an emotion," a curve complicated in this case by the many intersections of private and public action but suggestive still of progress in relation to a well-defined identity. Thus, his next project, *Lois* (1972) constituted at once a rupture and a prolongation. Prolongation results from its use of a freer, harsher, more lively, almost Poundian or Célinian rhetoric laced with obscenity and argot in furthering a program derived from *Logiques*. It too is characterized by the lavish use of the discourse of the Other and marked by the explicit movement from the square(d) structure of *Nombres* with its metaphor of the stage to the cube(d) structure of *Lois* with its use of the historical metaphor. This development added fresh complications to the rigid (but also highly plastic, ambiguous, and permutable) use of system to impose an aura of control on the macrostructure of *Nombres*. But according to Sollers' own account and demonstrable not only from the jacket copy but from internal evidence of several sorts, the most remarkable development had personal as well as aesthetic and historical roots.

In *Vision à New York*, Sollers tells of an earlier version of *Lois*, which extended the project of *Drame* and *Nombres*:

> to attempt to bring as closely together as possible the act of writing and the story; the action dictating the story and the story recounting that action. . . . My hope at that time was to construct a self-perpetuating movement, the book in process of becoming a world. . . .[23]

While still stymied in this quasimystical, materialistic quest, he was confronted with the events surrounding his father's death, a circumstance that paradoxically, though after a delay of several months, permitted him to rephrase his problem, that of the "voices that emanated from the writing" and finally to turn back to Joyce's *Finnegans Wake*. There, he claims to have rediscovered the impulse out of which *Lois* could be written rapidly and with unprecedented gaiety as a "concert of voices . . . of body-voices, of gesture-voices" which combined significant impulses from Joyce with a sense of Dantesque polyphony.[24]

What sets *Lois* off from the more programmatic *Drame* and *Nombres* is the openness of its play, the outrageous sexual and political reference, the language bubbling toward, at times capering toward the oral, toward the enacted word, the personal utterance spoken on the page. *Lois* self-consciously joins Joyce with Rabelais and Céline, mingling them with a blend of Freud, Lacan, Marx, and Mao, of sex, history, and politics. The result is a manifesto suggestive of mid-period Godard, endowed with an elaborate rhythm and texture and playing upon a cyclic development roughly analogous to that of *Finnegans Wake*, part of which Sollers was then cotranslating with Stephen Heath.[25] If the exuberance fails to carry the text, the experience liberates a suppressed clown persona which complements wonderfully the dedicated, if somewhat perverse, romantic lyricist of the early work. Also unleashed is the previously hobbled musician/rhetorician. *Lois* is the most overtly Maoist/Marxist of the novels to date, the most outrageously/joyously erotic, the most polemical and the most timebound. A transitional work, it acted as a purge and a stimulus for his next and in some senses most accomplished work, *H* (1973).

In *H*, the liberation process, aided perhaps by the use of hashish (though hardly bearing witness to drug-induced *écriture*), is complete, though the gains in freedom, rhythmic variation, rhetorical play, and voicing are brought under control, interacting to make this a deeply coherent and personal work in which the promise of *Logiques* is fully realized. It is also in *H* that Sollers achieves his identity as object/subject/body of narrative discourse, an identity connected to the problem of the names Philippe/Octave Joyaux/Sollers as well as to the unprecedented use of biographical (privileged in part) detail as the armature of this polylogical book so rich in ventriloquized voices, so naturally dialogical (to use Bahktin's term).

In this post-Freudian, post-Lacanian age when the *Nom du Père* is so highly valorized, it is important to recall that Sollers' family name was in the balance from the start. *Fils de bonne famille,* he chose to adopt a pseudonym when he turned creative. Stendhal comes to mind, but more particularly Lautréamont and the Daedalian Joyce (though not Céline with his terror of discovery). For whatever avowed reasons, he was writing himself a new identity, though without fully abandoning the old. As he puts it concerning the period of *Logiques,*

> I'd like to emphasize the 'spiritual exercise' aspect of *Drame* and *Nombres.* I really wanted to separate myself from my body, to become uniquely the interlace of syllables, letters. . . . I recollect coming back to myself while writing not in my identity but *in the page.* . . . It was the airiness and modulation of the sentence that lived me. [26]

When it came to the name itself, levity was not in order, not until after the death of the father and the *re*writing of *Lois.* In that flight from gravity, borrowing became a vital, playful, creative, liberating procedure almost obscuring the essential Sollersian idiom but contributing to a fresh novelistic mode reflected in the dynamic opening of *H* (1973). Here, not only the name, but the pseudonym come into *play* within a context of total *"écriture"* and the written/writing persona [27] takes on full effervescent unpunctuated verbal life:

> after all I have this phi floating on my lips like the other infancy/legitimacy [*infans*] [28] with vultures' tail and if the eight returns endlessly when I walk if I think readily of the liturgy if a sound always seems to me accompanied overcome that's the effect of the at once impossible and latinate prename of my father no you won't guess I write it out octave yes precisely as in in-octavo which led to his signing that o turning on itself followed by a minuscule dot right before the j elaborated embroidered gladioliform bell tower in the key of sol sweeping away oyaux musically o. joyaux with below the animated paraph doubled tossed short topspin of liquid diamond octave is also a trade term for jewelers perhaps an idea of one of the deviants in a family of whom one member they say was buddhist alchemist shut in amidst his draperies evidently the name itself sufficed to excite them why because one hears in it simultaneously *jeu joie juif jouissance* [play joy jew pleasure] for example this *joyaux* milords this *joyaux* [see a play on jewel-jewels] what did you expect isn't a pearl or else *joyal noyau boyau aloyau* or then without x but not *joyeux joyaux* [joyous jewels] with an x as in xylophone . . . [29]

There follows a Rabelaisian divagation on the name Philippe dragged (schlepped) back and forth through history, a tightly woven rhythmic fabric of associations and coincidences culminating in a Poundian treatment of the coin struck by Philip of Macedon followed by an equally outrageous passage on the name Sollers. Significantly, the latter introduces a sequence on childhood play and illness.

Beginning as it does with a baroque embroidery upon the question of an identity open to the currents of history, *H* quickly becomes a startling display of the presence of the revolutionary moment, a display characterized by a rhetorical control unmatched even by the animated high spirits of *Lois*. This novel can best be seen as an oblique, but dramatic and poignant reenactment of the period following May '68 in terms of the dominant intellectual and moral trends, reflected in the voices of the epoch.[30] What is so remarkable about this unpunctuated wall of words, this extremely active, if not "action packed" mass of language, this virtual rewriting of Flaubert's famous put-down of the revolution of 1848 in *Sentimental Education?* Perhaps it is the range of life it conveys without resorting to plot, character, or (except in the most minimal sense) setting, the almost effortless incorporation of so much thought, so many tonalities, so many distinct and various attitudes and modes, the ability to make farce rub elbows with pathos and banality, nostalgia and sensitivity, with evil. In all events, conscious or not, it is, from this perspective, a thoroughly modern and highly articulated book, resembling paintings done "after" Velasquez or Delacroix by Picasso and Matisse, elaborate translations within a long and honorable tradition of reproduction through change.

Sollers' text repeatedly displays a precise ear for rhythms, for pitch, for the literary and social traditions against which his practice reacts as it shapes itself. Above all it is breath or timing (rhetorical or rhythmic as well as structural: relating to the interacting but often blending parts) that makes this cultural/sentimental education a shapely as well as a boneless "novel." A dissimulated narrative, one featuring or foregrounding precisely those novelistic components we are led to overlook by conventional narrative practices, between whose lines the historical moment simmers but fails to boil over, *H* is a fitting match for Flaubert's portrait of a spineless age adrift on the waters of its discontents.[31]

The period between 1974 and the present is to a remarkable degree shaped by the process of Sollers' life-work, *Paradis*, an ongoing
reconstitution of the pre-apocalyptic world. If *H* can be qualified as
the global history of a disarticulated moment in terms of the rhythmic
identity of Sollers fictive/real "I," *Paradis* is a radical procedure through
which the history of the Christian era is reconstituted as a polylogical
presence within a culture recognizably of our time. It is Sollers' coming to grips with that immense past through its multiple and fragmentary remains, set in vibration by his mental processes, made immediate by a radical associative process in terms of an inescapable,
incomprehensible, self-perpetuating contemporary universe. The book
has been parceled out in *Tel Quel*, in a manner of a (mock) serial
buttressed by mini-essays on relevant topics, interviews, and carefully
arranged, or rather orchestrated, contributions by other hands. In short,
it is a work complete with a creative aura, a process of learning and
living intensely joined, a project that accumulates its commentary as
it elaborates itself as commentary. As the title suggests, the spirit of
Dante inhabits both the project and its pages, cohabiting with the
secret history of religions, moving Sollers in unexpected directions,
though along paths established by *Lois* and *H*, to say nothing of *Logiques*.

If the method of the recent work remains in some sense dialectic
and materialistic, the shadow of Marx is beginning to fade as we move
into the post-Mao, post-Vietnam, and post-Gulag revelation days.[32]
Sollers and *Tel Quel* have gone to America, Japan, Israel and the
Elysée Palace if only for visits. They have been accused of moving
right, but then they have never been accused or convicted of staying
anywhere. What is more important for the student of the French literary scene and of Sollers, however, is the fact that his development
seems predictable by infallible hindsight, that these developments are
all within the logic of the man and his progress. The politics of creativity and creative politics mesh very well and, at 45, Sollers, who has
always taken his word out into the world[33] has found in his latest (his
fourth) incarnation, a way to continue the curve of his development
while seemingly spiraling back into his own past.

The first volume of *Paradis*, accompanied by *Vision à New York*, appeared, italicized and free of punctuation, in January of 1981. More even than the highly rhythmic, subliminally (genotexturally) orchestrated *H*, it was meant to be heard. Sollers has recorded all of it on tape, broadcast it in Belgium, delivered parts of it in Paris and Israel, seemingly reversing his earlier Derridian stance toward the written word, but actually fulfilling it by giving voice to the scripted at the same time he returns to the aural roots of the tradition he is describing and embodying. Even as new passages, parts of the continuing project, were appearing, he began writing a major "realistic" fiction which is bound to startle those who have for so long placed him among the unreadable.

All of this seems to take us far from the collection of essays published in 1968, only a few weeks before the outbreak of the events of May which he was to qualify in *H* as *"notre révolution."* But the argument of this introduction has been the *Logiques* is a pivotal work, premonitory as well as reflective. Given its author's situation in the literary world of the sixties and the dates of these essays drawn from an evolving *Tel Quel*, 1962–67, we may read *Logiques* as a complex social, political, and critical document as well as an original statement about the role of textual monuments in the definition of the limits of conventional "literature." In both its approach and its choice of subject matter, it was an integral part of the revolutionary moment *and* a trend-setter.

The original version of *Logiques* was to constitute a primer for a new kind of reading, but the outline was somewhat obscured by its organization. The "program" for a "comprehensive theory derived from the practice of writing," one that demands a reversal of the current concept of "literature," was clarified when the collection was reissued as *L'Ecriture et l'expérience des limites* in 1971. This abridgment laid bare the ideational skeleton by eliminating essays dealing with topical matters, brief studies designed to reenforce aspects of the argument. Most of the excised pieces were book reviews (of James, Roussel, Ponge, Pleynet), though two were brief studies of Bataille and two more, "*Logique de la fiction*" and "*Le Roman et l'expérience des limites*," functioned as self-complementing apologies for Sollers' method. The latter, restored in *Writing and the Experience of Limits*, constitutes its most polemic statement, while capturing the spirit of the moment, clarifying Sollers' personal commitment to this revisionist literary historiography.

Though much has changed since 1968, this volume is still best rationalized by the jacket copy for *Logiques*:

> This collection functions as an apparatus. Systematically, it delineates a theory of writing [*écriture*], which used to be called "literature" but which today we had better call *textualization* [*textuelle*]. Linked as it is to a precise experience, this theory derives from a group of limit-texts, rejected or put aside by our culture, texts whose true reading could alter the very nature of our thought.
>
> Dante, Sade, Lautréamont, Mallarmé, Artaud, Bataille . . . chosen for an 'unreadability' that is not only formal but ideological . . . constitute through time a series designed to reveal a continuity other than the mechanical and idealistic one we are taught to accept, a plural and seemingly self-contradictory space, but one to which 'occidental history' holds the key. The decipherment accomplished here draws upon the *labor* that made possible the production of these 'limits,' upon modifications in the economic situation and the historical conditions that facilitated them, that is, upon the reasons for which they were censored (suppressed) and the power resulting from their transgressions.[34]

Thus *Logiques* and now *Writing and the Experience of Limits* embody a theory of language and writing linked to a theory of ideological expression. The implied reading of Marx is, however, highly original and the application of dialectics is informed by contemporary (Lacanian) psychoanalysis, (structuralist) linguistic theory, Derridian deconstruction, and semiology.

When he compiled *Logiques*, Sollers was engaged by the dream of the coexistence of two revolutions, one intellectual (cultural in the limited sense), the other political, a fact which gives his utterance a particular poignancy. Asked about the impact of May '68, in an interview published in 1981 under the title *"Pourquoi j'ai été chinois,"* he attributes the failure of that "revolution" to the lack of an interrelationship between "culture, language, and action." He continues,

> I had the utopian notion, which I no longer hold, that the revolution in language and the revolution as action should coincide absolutely. It's an

idea that derives in some way from the Formalists and the Surrealists. It's an allusion of the 20th-century avant-garde that should be totally abandoned because we are wrong to think that everything moves at the same pace.[35]

Just because one half of that impulse failed, we should not assume that the revolution in the perception of how language works has been abandoned or that the essays generated by that revolutionary fervor are no longer valid. Even today, they constitute a fresh, coherent, and abrasive statement of the view that literature begins with the censored word and that that word, ideally freed from the externally imposed formal and ideological strictures, is a rich source of otherwise inaccessible and perhaps ultimately unstable verities. His writers still suffer for telling us what we don't want to or have not learned to hear about the nature of the sign and our relationship to it:

> But we are nothing other than this nocturnal and diurnal movement of the legible and illegible, in us, outside us—and this is precisely what we would rather not know. We prefer to think Joyce committed a baroque error; we speak calmly of Mallarmé's 'failure'; we insinuate that Roussel pushed the joke a little too far, that Kafka liked his illness, that Lautréamont was mad, that Artaud should have been locked up. . . . Thus the *intelligence* these names designate, a *textual* intelligence, becomes the object of a sentimental indulgence. And always for the same reason: the inability of a certain mentality *to read what is written* . . . to see itself as radically compromised in its language and in the blind night it would impose upon us, thus reducing the *wakefulness* of writing.[36]

Sollers proposes to turn the fringe into the center in much the same way Michael Bakhtin turns the dialogic "low" genres into literature's greatest achievements by a shift of focus which *dis*covers aspects of writing obscured by habits of reading.[37] For Sollers this is frequently a deconstructive procedure. Moreover, this centering of the exception, the unacceptable, or the "limit" is both dramatic and logical, pointing up the subliminal underpinnings studied by Julia Kristeva, the "anamnesic role of the 'genotext' "; revealing writing/reading as an unveiling.[38] In the process, it also underscores a dynamic of reception, a self-exclusionary dialectic that characterizes much of the avant-garde.

xxviIntroduction

Given Sollers' own tendency to break limits, it is more than an apology; it is a song of praise dedicated to his role models: literary pariahs, or misunderstood eminences. Finally, it is a reading of the Sollersian self, fragmented as by a multiglass mirror. (This last factor accounts in some degree for the particular intensity of the rhetoric, this and the elusive nature of the subject matter.)

The "logics" announced in the original title is a significant pun on *logos*, fiction, writing, and reason, all of which Sollers clarifies in a lengthy footnote to *"Logique de la fiction"* with an elaborate etymological passage drawn from Vico's *New Science*. [39] Clearly, his stance is similar to the deadly serious playfulness which has characterized the discourse of Derrida, Lacan, Kristeva and even, at some moments, Marx. His object/subject is in each instance the inversion of conventional codes. With the possible exception of Dante, each study is devoted to a figure who has outraged the critical establishment by closing off readerly options, calling into play subliminal instincts, and questioning the very nature of reading/writing.

Even the well-disposed reader is bound to find the going difficult at times as Sollers fences with the seemingly unrecuperable, if not dangerous, aspects of these texts. It is one thing to discover in Dante, not the much-touted layered significations, but the figure of the writer presented *as* his writing and bringing on the foreclosure of the writing subject. We may not flinch when Sollers proclaims the *Vita Nuova* as a "temporal readingology" of the *Divine Comedy* or discovers there desire *in* language *through* language. Sollers' view of Mallarmé is equally fresh. The *chef d'école* of Symbolism is far bigger than that label, being central to the grammatological consciousness in literature dating from the second half of the nineteenth century and focused partly by Marx, Nietzsche, Freud, and the new "scientific, economic, and technical mutation." [40] A breaker of limits, he generated among other things a new theatrical and mythographical awareness of the unconscious. Thus the Catholic mass "interests him as a technique of gratuity, a symbolic ritual" for an abandoned religion that must conceal the intimate secrets of the "race." "The time has come," says Mallarmé "with the necessary detachment, to undertake its excavation."[41] Given the temper of the sixties, we need not be surprised to find Sollers demonstrating that the hermetic poet of "Literature and Totality" was a protorevolutionary.

If Dante and Mallarmé are misread or unread, Sade is still "unreadable," though his fictions function as the "sacred" texts of a forbidden but essential jouissance. The fact that sexuality is causeless because unmediated will hardly cheer true believers. Sollers' joyous and bold acceptance of the *affective* "message" of Sade, his enthusiastic exploration of its impact in language and bodies as well as culture, effectively pits "heroic perversion" against "normal neurosis." It initiates us into the realm of our own repressed "desire" where he proclaims "the absence of limits, the interminable and irresponsible energy without opposites" which Sade insists we face to the detriment of our pride and person.[42] This harsh message, this vision of overturned values, is mitigated only slightly by the declaration that "Sade's adventure occurs entirely *within discourse*."[43] For in this essay as in those on Bataille, Artaud, and Lautréamont, we are being called upon to face what is least acceptable in our mental climate and physical universe, in its least acceptable form: in a language capable of forcing the "return of the repressed." Sollers is not trying to sweeten the pill. He is proclaiming its indispensability as a specific for a sick society. This is manifest in the discussion of "madness" in his chapter on Artaud. If Sade depicts the heroics of "perversion," Artaud *lived* the heroic awareness of the repressed. For Sollers his struggle was to release what Kristeva would call the unmediated genotext and play it on the stage of life, hence his "madness" was a superior form of sanity.

The philosopher of this sort of procedure and of the special outcroppings of necessary violence and the antisocial is Georges Bataille, a figure whose prominence was more marked in the early *Logiques* and whose message has the ring of ritual truth. Bataille goes far beyond the relatively benign message of Karl Jung: for him prohibition and profanation are two sides of the same cloth. They are essential to each other and to the health of the society. Transgression completes prohibition. In this instance, as witness Bataille's rich and virtually unclassifiable writing of paradox, liberation does not imply the relaxation of rules. Quite the contrary, it demands their enforcement. The pill is far more bitter, and it is covered with spines.

Though chronologically the first of these truth-sufferers, Lautréamont may be Sollers' stellar example. His "Lautréamont's Science" is an elaborate defense and illustration, a post-surrealistic reading of the dialogic aspects of *Les Chants de Maldoror* and *Poésies*, perceived here as complementary texts. Through a meticulous inspection of the text's deliberate irregularities, Sollers shows Lautréamont to be an avant-garde writer of the first order, the inventor of an entirely new range of discourse, an "infinite text," discontinuous, nonlinear, spatial, capable of producing in its reader a new sort of writing. Perhaps paradoxically, the figure revealed by Sollers' carefully culled citations is closest to William Blake, another great precursor of the "modern." At any rate, this, the penultimate text in our volume, so predictive of Sollers' own practice, speaks with exceptional passion and directness of problems and concerns inherent in his own production while managing to give a rational account of Lautréamont's this-worldly vision, his science/system, his dynamic.

In relation to each of these authors, whose vision is exposed through examinations of the totality of their text, Sollers elaborates a contrary, unsettling but well-supported and complex argument that ultimately contributes to the development or establishment of his "Program" while drawing upon and projecting his own creative project.

It may be said that Sollers assumes a great deal in treating as familiar these writers from beyond the pale of writing. The American audience is hardly alone in being innocent of what is shown to be the essential content of most of their work. At times we are led to recall Stuart Gilbert's practice in his famous study of *Ulysses*, a book which presumed to present a sampler of the banned text of which it was the only available reading process. Then, as now, the reader aware of the original material is clearly at some advantage. But actually, Sollers, like Derrida, Barthes, and even Kristeva, to say nothing of Stephen Heath writing on Sollers, is writing *through* his subject toward facets of his own project. The reader is now free to turn back to the originals for a post-Sollersian reading, a *logic*-al one.

Notes

1. *Vision à New York* (Paris: Grasset, 1981).

2. *Ibid.*, p. 34 (my trans.).

3. *Ibid.*, pp. 47–48 (my trans.).

4. The actual reasons are, as we shall see, more complex. But he had been using this name since he was fifteen or sixteen, affixing it to the writings in his schoolboy notebooks.

5. *A Strange Solitude* (New York: Grove Press, 1959).

6. As I write these words that association is being dissolved and a fresh chapter in Sollers' career has begun at Gallimard where he will edit a new magazine to be called *L'Infini* and publish a long "realistic" novel.

7. *The Park* (New York: Red Dust, 1968).

8. Ponge was an early favorite to whom Sollers devoted a monograph: *Francis Ponge, ou la raison à plus haut prix.*

9. *L'intermédiaire* (Paris: Seuil, 1963), p. 40 (my trans.).

10. *Sollers Ecrivain* (Paris: Seuil, 1979), p. 26, note v.

11. *Ibid.*, p. 13, note 1.

12. *Ibid.*, p. 13.

13. David Hayman, "An Interview with Philippe Sollers," *The Iowa Review*, 5/4 (Fall 1974), p. 99.

14. Jacques Scherer's study, *Le "Livre" de Mallarmé* (Paris: Gallimard, 1957) with its painstaking documentation of the notes for that heroic project had a profound impact in the 1960s on the *"écriture"*-oriented *Tel Quel* group.

15. The interior quotation may be seen as providing the stimulus for the illustrative matter that follows. One thinks among other things of Roussel's description of his pseudo-aleatory method in *Comment J'ai Ecrit Certains de mes Livres*, where a misplaced letter, by rendering a simple phrase incomprehensible, could generate an entire sequence of false but entertaining rationalizations in narrative form. Here, Sollers seems to be giving point to what was otherwise a whimsical procedure by including the *"amorce"* while unveiling the way in which illusion is achieved and dispelled. An essay on Roussel, dating from 1963, was included in *Logiques*.

16. *Nombres* (Paris: Seuil, 1968), pp. 28–29 (my translation). Jacques Derrida includes some of this passage in his discussion of castration in "Dissemination" in *Dissemination*, trans. Barbara Johnson (Chicago: University of Chicago Press, 1981), p. 302 and *passim*. Like the essay, Derrida's book takes its title from the Saussurian concept of the anagram but it occurs in a phrase in *Nombres*: *"la dissémination sans images"* (p. 61), which refers as much to numbers (*chiffres*) as to words, or rather, reverses the field, turning a page of letters black on white into a column of numbers, an account of the war dead among whom *we* inevitably figure as does the writer, who donates himself to his words.

17. *Ibid.*, p. 27 (my translation). For another reading of this passage see *Dissemination*, pp. 325–26.

18. *Ibid.*, pp. 27–28 (my translation), see *Dissemination.*

19. *Ibid.*, p. 59 (my translation).

20. *Dissemination*, p. 290.

21. *Ibid.*, p. 297. Mallarmé punctuates his toss of the dice with "NOTHING WILL HAVE TAKEN PLACE BUT THE PLACE."

22. *Ibid.*, pp. 296–97.

23. *Vision*, p. 100 (my trans.).

24. *Ibid.*, p. 114.

25. Stephen Heath's study, *The Nouveau Roman*, includes a remarkably clear-headed appreciation of Sollers' accomplishment through *Nombres*. Heath's Marxist-oriented argument for "the practice of writing" still provides one of the best introductions in English to Sollers and the early *Tel Quel* (Philadelphia: Temple University Press, 1972), pp. 179–242.

26. *Vision*, p. 101 (my trans.).

27. There are earlier references to both Sollers and Joyaux. *Nombres*, for example, as Barbara Johnson has shown (see *Dissemination*, p. xxxi), cleverly conceals the double signature. However, this passage from *H* constitutes a new threshold.

28. A reference to Lacan's use of the term to denote the "mirror stage" (6–18 months) of the infant's development (see Jacques Lacan, *"Le stade du miroir"* in *Ecrits* I [Paris: Seuil, Collection Points, 1966], p. 90 and *passim*), a sign that Sollers is infinitizing his person and text in ways consistent with but in advance of the procedures described in "Lautréamont's Science."

29. *H* (Paris: Seuil, 1973), pp. 9–10 (my trans.).

30. Julia Kristeva, picking up on or retrieving a term from the novel itself, calls it a "polylogue" in her moving and provocative essay included in *Desire in Language*. (See "The Novel as Polylogue" in *Desire in Language*, ed. Léon S. Roudiez [New York: Columbia University Press, 1980], pp. 159–209.) The essay was first published in *Tel Quel* 57 (Spring 1977) and reprinted in the volume *Polylogue*. It seems paradoxical that we now have not only that essay but also *Writing and the Experience of Limits* while only tiny extracts from Sollers' fiction are available to English-speaking readers. (See Inez Hedges' fine translation of the Ezra Pound passage from *H* in *The Iowa Review*, 5/4 [Fall 1974], pp. 102–05; and Carl Lovitt's translation from *Paradis*, first published in *TriQuarterly* 38 [January 1977], pp. 101–106, and reprinted both in *Tel Quel* 77 [Automne 1978] and in David Hayman and Elliott Anderson, eds., *In the Wake of the Wake* [Madison: University of Wisconsin Press, 1978].) It is time that our reading public sees what the shouting is about and that, at the very least, a Sollers anthology appear to show us what it was that so visibly vitalized French critical theory through its revisionist novelistic practice.

31. This polylogical attack on the "reasons" of a period was followed by the most emphatically Marxist/Maoist/rationalist of Sollers' books, *Sur le matérialisme* (1974), one that Julia Kristeva saw as a complementary structure. Her perception appropriately relates the moment of *Lois* and *H* to that of *Drame/Nombres/Logiques* reenforcing the public/private/creative symmetry observed earlier. *Desire in Language*, pp. 183–190.

32. Writing in 1976, at the end of the era of Mao but in the middle of the process of *Paradis*, Julia Kristeva significantly juxtaposes Sade, the writer of jouissance, and Solzhenitsyn, the writer of horror. This allusion, matched by others in *Paradis*, marks a turning point in the development of *Tel Quel*. "Place Names" in *Desire in Language*, p. 271.

33. Even his first publication, the thirty-page *Le défi*, was published with a five-page explanatory addendum (*Ecrire* 4, Seuil, 1957), a response to critics that is as ironical in tone as the Bataille-like narrative with its rhetoric out of a Lautréamont passed through the water of Existentialism and Surrealism.

34. My translation.

35. *Tel Quel* 88 (Summer 1981), p. 13. In the same interview we find Sollers' view of Mao's failed opportunity, an opinion that, for all its romantic overtones, clarifies later developments at *Tel Quel* and illuminates the spirit that informs *Logiques*: "The true interpretation of Mao may be that he pushed Marxism to the point of incandescence in order to eliminate it. As for me, I was hoping that in 1968–69, Mao would convoke a mass meeting in Tian-An-Men Square and announce to the Chinese people the overextension of Marxism or its dissolution, and that would give rise to a gigantic crisis in Chinese civilization. Unfortunately, he died before that occurred, and naturally, the machine continued to function, he was embalmed, etc." *Ibid.*, p. 22.

36. See below, pp. 197–98.

37. See "Discourse in the Novel" in *The Dialogic Imagination*, ed. Michael Holquist (Austin: University of Texas Press, 1981), p. 273 and *passim*.

38. Julia Kristeva, "L'Engendrement de la formule," in *Semiotiké: Recherches pour une sémanalyse* (Paris: Seuil, 1969), p. 282 and *passim*. See also Léon S. Roudiez' introduction to *Desire in Language*, p. 7, and Kristeva's application of the concept to *H*, where Sollers "refashioned his 'I' and his language into a music adequate to the continuing, splintering times." In "The Novel as Polylogue," *ibid.*, p. 207.

39. *Logiques* (Paris: Seuil, 1968), p. 15.

40. See below, p. 64.

41. See below, pp. 80–81.

42. See below, p. 42.

43. See below, p. 51.

Writing
and the Experience of Limits

C'est de toutes parts et de toutes façons qu'un monde en mouvement veut être changé.

Prolegomenon

Writing and Revolution

Let us move on then, to *Logiques* and *Nombres*. Do you accept the conventional designations of *novel* for *Nombres* and *essays* for *Logiques?* Or do both these books constitute a single space, inside of which, nonetheless, two writings are in dialectical interaction?

LOGIQUES IS NEITHER an essay nor a collection. It is an apparatus, a kind of reading machine intended to historically situate a theory of exceptions. Thus, each of the texts must be read in terms of all the others, which implies that the formal organisms treated there are brought onto a terrain where in principle they should not be meeting: hence Dante and Sade, Mallarmé and Georges Bataille. In each instance an irreducible experience is at stake, yet each time a common problematic appears in all its complexity. What is shared is in fact the censure these texts have undergone at the hands of a single ideology, or rather a series of profoundly unified ideologies. We can, if you will, identify the common feature of these ideologies, all of them incapable of recognizing a text as text, as *linearity*. By means of the experiences explored and rewritten here, the outside of the library begins to be illuminated. And so one enters a kind of written immensity which

Excerpted from an interview with Philippe Sollers by Jacques Henric, in *Théorie d'ensemble* (Paris: Editions du Seuil, collection Tel Quel, 1968). *Logiques* and *Nombres* (Paris: Editions du Seuil, collection Tel Quel, 1968).

culture—a necessary agency of repression—has served only to bring back into line, to smother. As for *Nombres*—yes, it is a *novel*, in that the narrative process is at once X-rayed and carried beyond itself. A novel that aims to make novelistic exploitation and its mystifying effects impossible. *Nombres* and *Logiques* need to be read simultaneously and dialectically. In the first text fiction serves to open a scene whose animating principles are given by the second.

> What criteria made you select the "works" of Dante, Sade, Lautréamont, Mallarmé, Artaud, and Bataille for study? In "Program," the prefatory text that opens *Logiques*, you state that the resistances these *limit-texts* meet with "point up the existence of a textual writing as real history." What is the new type of *historicity* you attempt to lay the foundations for in the course of your *logical readings?*

Those texts function as hinges: on the one hand they "speak" to us, they haunt our discourse, which is compelled to make a place for them even as it deforms them; on the other, and in their literal substance, they are turned toward an economy other than that which we customarily employ to think history as *expression*, and so remain unreadable. Real—which is to say materialistic—history cannot do without a *semantic materialism* (hence the exergue from Lenin: "History of thought: history of language?") which, if founded, would open up a vast field for research. What is challenged here is the linear history which has always subjugated the text to representation, subject, meaning, truth, and which represses the enormous work done by the limit-texts in order to privilege the canonical categories of meaning, subject, and truth. It seems to me that these limits can be characterized by the names which linear history—that within which we are speaking—has given them: the mystical, eroticism, madness, literature, the unconscious. The time has come not to celebrate, as Surrealism did intuitively, but to systematically investigate these appelations, to call forth the thought which is enclosed and withheld there in the form of a convenient excuse. Now I think the distinctive quality of this thought is its multidimensionality, which is precisely what writing, as opposed to speech, discovers and entails. The history of this specific production remains to be articulated and integrated into the historical process in general. In fact, this *textual* history immediately deciphers the expressive (Christian) history that believes it can do without writing's deep resources [*la profondeur écrite*]. In all these texts, the theory of writing is immanent, demonstrably so; but it is generally perceived as delirium, fantasy, poetry, hermeticism, individual deviation, etc. Whereas, if the system of reading is changed, if reading is made into the gesture of the writing initiated [*mise en jeu*] by these texts, if they are no longer made to represent so that we may grasp both their articulation and consumption, then everything becomes clear. The decisive break [*coupure*] here—which acts both retroactively and on the future—is Lautréamont/Mallarmé, which corresponds to that of Marx/Freud. Thereafter, one might say everything re-commences, and commences.

Program

History of thought: history of language?
Lenin

1.   A COMPREHENSIVE THEORY [*THEORIE D'ENSEMBLE*] DERIVED FROM THE PRAC-
     TICE OF WRITING DEMANDS TO BE ELABORATED.

1.1. This practice is not to be identified with the historically deter-
     mined concept of "literature." It implies the overturning[1] and
     complete rearrangement of both the role and effects of this con-
     cept.

1.2. *From the practice*[2] signifies that it has become impossible, begin-
     ning with a rupture that can be precisely situated in history, to
     make of writing an object that can be studied by any means other
     than writing itself (its exercise, under certain conditions). In other
     words, the specific problematic of writing breaks decisively with
     myth and representation to think itself in its literality and its space.
     Its practice is to be defined on the level of the "text," a word which
     henceforth refers to a function writing does not "express," but of
     which it *disposes*. A dramatic economy whose "geometrical locus"
     is not representable (it occurs as play [*il se joue*]).

1.3. The theory envisaged has its source in the *texts* of the rupture and
     those capable of "announcing" and "pursuing" it. The choice of
     these texts is based on their coefficient of theoretical-formal con-
     testation (for example: Dante, Sade // *Lautréamont, Mallarmé* //
     Artaud, Bataille). Whence the definition of a before/after which
     must refer in fact and at the same time—through the disappear-

ance of discourse's position as "expressive" truth and the affirmation of a textual space—to an inside/outside defined by occasional reference to other cultures.

1.4.   This *textual* rupture, taken as a theoretical point of departure, is contemporary (in the sense that "X is contemporary with Y" means that sets are penetrated by the same unknown) with that manifested in Western thought and history by Marx and Engels, viz. by the elaboration of dialectical materialism. It is the crisis itself, the violent revolution, the leap, of *readability*.

2.   THE THEORY OF TEXTUAL WRITING TAKES SHAPE [SE FAIT] IN THE MOVEMENT OF THIS WRITING'S PRACTICE.

2.1.   It entails the setting up of an historical field that breaks with the pseudo-continuity of all "literary history" which is based on speculative thinking that disregards the role of the written economy as an *a priori* determinant of all thought.

2.2.   This historical field is *discontinuous*. It discloses, first, the exclusions by means of which "literary history" has made and continues to make its ideological profit, exclusions in the sense of "repression" or "negation" (Freud). Its strategic points, its *borders*, are designated by the words: "mysticism," "eroticism," "madness," "literature" (this latter taken solely in the sense that entails rupture). Normality of discourse is conceived of as need for a defense (ideology) vis-à-vis these points whose function is explained and defined historically.

2.3.   These past and/or present exclusions are those affecting texts which expressly challenge the concept of "history" postulated by expressive and instrumental idealism (which from that moment on becomes readable). Those texts excluded from systems capable of repeatedly integrating the process of language: myth / representation / writing (*myth*: hierarchy, divinity, "beyond," overlapping [*redoublement*], feudalism, religion, symbol; *representation*: exchange, identity, the picture, splitting, capitalism, idealism, sign; *writing*:

production, infinity, network, double, materialism, dialectics, space).

2.4.   The theory consequently aims first at challenging this concept of history and proposing the "history" of this concept as "literature" (fiction), just as the exclusions we have noted point up the existence of a *textual writing* as *real* history.

3.   THE THEORY OF TEXTUAL WRITING'S HISTORY MAY BE TERMED "MONUMEN-TAL HISTORY" INSOFAR AS IT SERVES AS A "GROUND" ["FAIT FOND"] IN A LITERAL WAY, IN RELATION TO A "CURSIVE," FIGURAL (TELEOLOGICAL) HIS-TORY WHICH HAS SERVED AT ONCE TO CONSTITUTE AND DISSIMULATE A WRIT-TEN/EXTERIOR SPACE.

3.1.   This multidimensional space (which assumes that of "cursive" history while consuming it) implies a principle of retroactivity (Lautréamont/Dante), long-range relations, heretofore unperceived [*in-édites*] (noncultural) *periods*, a duration conceived of as *language time* [*temps des langues*]. It puts itself in a position to think the termination of one history and its *transition* [3] to another level as well as the "entrance into history" of other dominant cultures.

3.2.   The theory is defined first of all as a reading. This reading is made possible only by a writing that recognizes the rupture. The rupture affects the concept of "text" in the following way: the real text is conceived of as the product of a duality that it *produces*. Thus there are always *two* loci in relation to *one* text existing purely by and for this "two" that radically divides it. The text does not "exist" outside this division (no "true," "first" or "last" text—fundamental): the process is thought through in this contradiction which simultaneously founds matter, play, the scene, and the dialectical transformation.

3.3.   Writing "that recognizes the rupture" is therefore irreducible to the classical (representational) concept of "written text": what it writes is never more than one part of itself. It makes the rupture the intersection of two sets (two irreconcilable states of language). As reading, it refers to the acknowledged act by which writing selects its fields of reading (its divisions [*découpage*], syntax, logic), the "surfaces" where it acts, where its *sliding* occurs.

3.4.   The role of the theory is to indicate that textual writing sees *science* alone as qualified to give it its reality and its "significations": its formulation *summons* that of science, its literality opens up to the formulation of science, it constitutes an object for science as well as an object for its own extension, it is in a dialectical relationship with itself and with science. It is no less a theory of ordered, infinite process, than a practice on its own of textual writing.

4.   THE THEORY, WHICH APPLIES ONLY TO *TEXTS*, IS THEREFORE, INSOFAR AS IT READS THEM [*LES FAIT LIRE*] IN THEIR "MONUMENTALITY," THE PUNCTUATION, THE SCANSION, THE SPATIAL DISTRIBUTION OF TEXTS. IT IS BY DEFINITION PLURAL. IT GOES BY THE NAME *LOGICS*.

4.1.   It demonstrates the decidedly contradictory status of textual writing, which *is not a language*, but, in each instance, *the destruction of a language*; a destruction that, on the interior of a language, transgresses that language and gives it the function of *languages*. This destruction, this negation, is explicated by the theory which is therefore the language of this destruction of language (of the group of operations necessary to posit, develop, and annul a language).

4.2.   It states textual writing's potential for subtending and verifying the developments of logic by presenting itself to them as "examples" (citations). It reveals that textual writing is the historical text recognized as text, insofar as its perpetual difference is the mark of every written text's historical limit and its "passage to the limit," or in other words of its inscription as part of "monumental history."

4.3.   It indicates textual writing's radical non-expressivity, its variable, plurilinear play, its function as an active and productive "integral" knowledge [*connaissance*] of the "real;" its relationship to "monumental history" as a contestation of "cursive" history.[4] It underscores the boundary between textual writing (multidimensional literal network, generative strands and their reciprocal transformations, empty sums of language's consumption through its own articulation) and nontextual writing (linear, expressive, causal, noninscribed and non-bound to "written space"). It shows how textual writing, by definition excluded from the "present" (whose function is to misunderstand [*méconnaître*] it), constitutes precisely the deferred history—and ideological exposure—of that present.

4.4.   The theory treats "literature" (and the whole of the culture within which it is located) as closed. It henceforth exposes the *form* of what has thought itself under this name. It elaborates textual writing's real (economic) conditions, its *a priori* systematic structures and the conditions of its effacement, while avoiding any fixation on the "work" or the "author" (on the cultural fetishization and the fiction corollary to a "creative subjectivity"). As "historical consciousness," it necessarily finds itself on the side of the revolutionary action in progress.

1967

Notes

1. Tr. note: *Overturning* translates the French *renversement*; the term implies a corrective redistribution of emphasis in dialectic, literally a "turning upside down/right side up," or an "inversion." Louis Althusser discusses the term's theoretical implications in the essays "On the Young Marx" and "The Materialist Dialectic," in *Pour Marx* (Paris: François Maspero, 1965); Eng. ed. *For Marx*, Ben Brewster, tr. (London: NLB, 1977). See also Sollers' note on *renversement* in his *Sur le matérialisme* (Paris: Editions du Seuil, 1974), pp. 98–99.

2. Tr. note: In Marxist terminology, *practice* is a process of social or economic transformation whose three primary forms (economic, political, ideological) constitute the social formation. Althusser views theory as a fourth practice in which ideology is transformed into knowledge. See L. Althusser and E. Balibar, *Lire le capital* (Paris: François Maspero, 1965); Eng. ed., *Reading Capital*, Ben Brewster, tr. (London: NLB, 1970). For *textual* practice seen from a semiotic and psychoanalytical perspective, see Julia Kristeva, *La Révolution du langage poétique* (Paris: Editions du Seuil, 1974). Kristeva defines this practice as the text's "essential dimension . . . challenging symbolic and social *finitudes* by advancing *new signifying fields* [*dispositifs*]" (p. 186).

3. Tr. note: The Marxist concept of *transition* (*passage*) describes a distinctive,

interim mode of production (as opposed to a simple shift from one mode to another, for example from feudalism to capitalism) which creates a specific dislocation between the economic systems in question, and which entails a transformation of the social structure on its various levels, for example on the level of historically determined forms of individuality as well as on that of economic production.

4. Tr. note: In a recent interview, *"On n'a encore rien vu"* (*Tel Quel* 85, 1980), Sollers discusses writing's relation to the real at greater length, and describes the sense in which his own writing might be viewed as realism: "I'm a realist. I deal with the real—which is not necessarily the same as reality. Reality is what newspapers talk about, what we observe but can be mistaken about. The real is what really takes place on the level of power relations which are not always evident, and this is why I write rather than taking part in politics. If I thought everything depended on politics I would simply go into politics. But I think the matter goes farther than politics, or in other words that politics itself is no more than a symptom of something more profound, more meta-physical—a word I do not hesitate to use in this case. And it's at this point that the real novel begins. For if, from the perspective of a strict metaphysics (metaphysics in the sense of a beyond of physics, of all physics), I begin to tell how physics is manufactured, then I undertake a work of realism; I show how bodies are engendered by means of illusions, how humanity *lives itself* as an illusion, speaks to itself with false representations of the world, speaks to itself with imaginary religions, dreams, and biographies; I do my work, which is also, you could say, of a theatrical nature (it's a metaphysical novel in the sense that Shakespeare's is a metaphysical theater), which simply means that it offers the best possible perspective on the real, the best possible realistic perspective on the society of my time" (p. 22).

1

Dante and the Traversal
of Writing

L'acqua ch'io prendo già mai non si corse.
Paradiso 2.7

The Book

FEW WORKS ARE as distant from us as *The Divine Comedy:* closer
in history than the *Aeneid,* upon which it is based, it nonetheless
seems farther away. It retains its mystery, despite commentaries and
readings characterized by excessive erudition. But no doubt this is because it is concealed in the depths of our culture like a blind spot, a
limitless enigma whose very proximity seems to render us inattentive
and verbose.

The question it raises is of such magnitude that its still problematic visibility is perhaps only now becoming apparent. Humanism rapidly immobilized it, reduced it to a cultural reference whose torpor
seems to have been disturbed solely by a painter, Botticelli. Despite
Milton, classicism has no idea of what is at stake in this great poem,
which seems barbarous to it. In the eighteenth century—with the exception of Vico, who elaborates the *Scienza Nuova* on the margins of
his era, using a title that pays homage to the man he calls "the
Tuscan Homer"—this text remains an unreadable, inhuman monstrosity (unreadable always means inhuman), a "hodgepodge," according to the *Encyclopédie.* It might be said without paradox that, for this
period, Dante is as invisible as Sade, whose achievement is probably

alone in rivaling that of Dante. The nineteenth century is less sure of itself, but no less blind: thanks to Schelling, Dante becomes part of a romantic mythology that, in France, will be perceived as a decorative and spectacular image; *Dante* and *Inferno* become synonymous terms, within the category of the visionary and the horrifying. Nevertheless, the rupture now traditionally marked by the second half of the last century will make of the *Comedy* a formal ("Homeric") presence, the background against which a decisive displacement and reversal will unfold, linked to the appearance of the signifier as such, to language as an increasingly radical question.

This presence is manifested in a contradictory manner: Joyce and Pound accentuate what might be called the microcosmic, globally linguistic project; Claudel, as usual, although finding in it an occasion for his best formulations on poetry (that "does not plunge into the infinite to find the new but to the depths of the definite to find the inexhaustible"), wants to reinforce the Catholic interpretation, which has no idea what to do with so embarrassing (so universal) an author. The fact is that Dante lends himself to whatever one likes: the university, academism, modernism, can all lay claim to him, and without great risk. But of course this is not the problem (no more than it is for Hölderlin, Lautréamont, or Mallarmé; clearly, our thought has long since deserted these superficial classifications). If there is a Dante "mystery," if this text's archeological upheaval can teach us something that has not ceased invisibly to determine our history, then it is neither its appearance nor its content that we ought to question, but the profound relationship Dante maintains with writing. *The Divine Comedy*—which, revealingly, has been called by that name only since the sixteenth century (Dante says simply "sacred poem")—will thus be for us a text in the process of being written, the first great book thought and acted integrally, as *book*, by its author.

The fundamental historical importance of the symbolism of writing and the book is becoming increasingly apparent.[1] An infinite metaphor substituting itself for itself across time, it represents, in each literature and even each system of thought, a kind of privileged point, a mirror, a referential limit where not only the space but also the key and the meaning of all expression would be granted to us. This constitutive symbolism, whose fate may be followed through its incessant reshapings, imitations, deformations, or reactivations—this hidden and dispersed common denominator, at times the more dissimulated because it seems to declare and expose itself in the light of day—finds its most complete Western manifestation in Dante, and designates the totality he confronts as author. As "author," but also as actor and as reader, which gives his appearance a crucial, exemplary reality, as if located at the intersection of two planes, one horizontal (historical), the other vertical (individual). Symbol of antiquity's resumption and herald of modern times, symbol of a singular adventure with neither precedent nor sequel, Dante is balanced both in the midst of time, of the temporal line on which we are located, and at the center of each particular experience: *"nel mezzo del cammin de nostra vita."* This, at least, is what he consciously aims for, making his text a total world designating itself, a comedy of language and of the path a subject may pursue through it in an attempt to exhaust it in all its dimensions, through an active unveiling.

Thus we must try to conceive of this double movement: on the one hand, the organization and construction of a book that will occupy the site where all books coincide—the bringing together of all that is (memory, thought, dream, acts, world, individuals, nature, material, history, culture, myths, texts, religion) referred back to the symbolism of writing—in other words a book in whose orbit all books (all phenomena) henceforth turn; on the other hand, the institution— the instruction—of this book's *subject*, that is to say the subject who becomes its sum and meaning. Or: the genesis of a language conceived of as the unique surface of all languages at last untangled and translated, as well as the role an operator, or more precisely a computer, would have to play in this language, possessing both its code and the capacity to use it effectively. Such a volume, in its endeavor to be *written* rather than ideal (in other words utilizing the symbolism of the book as the mechanism of its own existence: a book for which everything is a book, but which is alone in saying it—and consequently a *book* that is the contrary of *a* book), will consequently be conceived entirely from the reader's point of view. An essential trait,

and one that makes Dante, beyond all problems of erudition, someone
who speaks to us today in the most direct manner.

It is not enough merely to observe the *Comedy*'s perpetual appeals
to the reader (the most significant of these formulae is undoubtedly
the *Inferno*'s "*0 tu che leggi udirai nuovo ludo*" / "You who read, you
shall hear new sport [*jeu*]").[2] One must recognize that the entire poem
is turned toward this empty site that reads it, and to which it is addressed in order to become readable to itself. Such a site is no more
exterior than interior to the poem, nor is it its reverse side; this is not
some sort of site we have to imagine, moreover, but rather a resource
anterior to all possible localization. As we shall see, Dante found no
other words to describe it than those implying a double motive force:
passion and *action*. It is the reading of the text, but also its writing,
insofar as, from its first line to its last and according to the temporal
unfolding of a narrative that concludes with the end of every narrative
and the endless recommencement of a unique, anonymous poem or
language, it was nothing other than the scriptor's birth within this
language addressed to someone continually being born, as well as the
birth of the meaning that was making use of them for all places, all
times. Such is the experience the book demands of us—"total expansion of the letter," as Mallarmé was to put it.

To illuminate this play, we may perhaps outline a provisional
myth of language, an oscillation between two virtual, never-attained
poles whose constantly displaced limits would appear as their own effective reality and confusion: that of an unreadability, of an impenetrable opacity; and symmetrically, that of an absolute transparency.
Nothing is ever unreadable, nothing is ever completely readable. The
entire space of meaning, as well as its particularization in each of us,
unfolds between these two poles, two reflections of a single summit.
Thus the endlessly debated question of the arbitrariness of language or
its adequation to things (Dante takes up the formula: *nomina sunt
consequentia rerum*) would be implied by the division of a single given,
the basis of the disparity between the Same and the Other, the empty
and initial form of thought. It would be tempting, although perhaps
at the risk of some misconception, to imagine universal and individual

history as secretly resulting from this polarity, as if we could not avoid pursuing an elliptical path whose foci would be these two myths. A cyclical path, whose law of development and return Vico ventured to summarize by distinguishing three types of language (mute language of the gods, heroic language, vulgar language) and a repetition that would endlessly deploy these three signifying levels. We assert that the *Comedy* is the amplified description of this movement.

Vita Nova, Ars Nova

Two texts will serve us as keys: *De Vulgari Eloquentia* and *Vita Nuova*.[3] Significantly, the first is written in Latin and deals with the language (Italian) in which the second—which will prefigure the *Comedy*—has already been written. The importance of the rupture with the Middle Ages that Dante accomplishes (ten centuries teetering toward a new enunciation, and consequently a new world) is inscribed in this paradox: the singularity of language is juxtaposed to the affirmation of universality ("we whose country is the world, as the sea is to fish . . ."). Dante writes in the *Convivio* that the "vulgar" tongue "shall be a new light, and a new sun, which shall rise where the old sun sets, and shall shine on those who are in darkness and shadow for lack of the old sun which gives them no light" (and we know that for Dante the *sun* is a standard metaphor for arithmetic, for the unity from which other numbers radiate, and also for God, since it "falls silent" in Hell). This language will have to be pursued on three planes: first of all, as the living tongue in contrast to the dead tongue, it is what we would call the maternal language, "that to which children are accustomed by those who are about them when they first begin to form diverse sounds . . . that which we acquire without any rule, by imitating our nurses," and through it, subsequently, the two-fold dimension of the original language. This latter myth functions as the pivot of Dante's reflections: it is through speech that man occupies an intermediary position between animals and angels. While animals share the same acts and passions within the same species and do not communicate between species, angels are felt to communicate with one another directly or by means of the resplendent mirror of the divine (devils, by virtue of their previous state, are capable of making them-selves immediately intelligible to one another). In sum, we might say that the former are in an integral signifier, the latter in a pure signi-fied. The function of language, at once "rational and sensible," is thus recognized here: "For were it only rational, it could not pass from one man's reason to that of another; and were it only sensible, it could take nothing from reason nor give anything to reason. Now this sign is that noble subject of which we are speaking; for it is a sensible thing since it is sound, but rational insofar as it carries some meaning ac-cording to the pleasure of the speaker." What is the original nature of this sign? In the breath [*souffle*] of God, and in response to this breath-ing, instantaneous speech burst from Adam: God can make the air speak, but from the very start speaking belongs to the first man who addresses his speech to God and speaks in order to glorify the gift he has received (thus this point is a zero degree of signification, a speech for speech itself): "and therefore it is evident that the joy we feel in the translation of our natural faculties into orderly action proceeds from God." Paradise is none other than this site of a first speech, and this "first" undoubtedly indicates more than simply a dimension of time.

To this mythical language is opposed the real diversity of lan-guages, or in other words the impossibility of communication: "Since human affairs are carried on in very many and different languages, so that many men are not understood by many with words any better than without words, we should search out the language spoken by that man who had no mother, who was never suckled, who never saw either adolescence or youth." Dante insists on the fact that God cre-ated a certain form of language simultaneously with the first soul, and by "form" he means discrete vocables as well as their groupings and the manner in which these groupings of words are pronounced: it is this Adamic form, the form that "every tongue of speaking man would use if it had not been destroyed and thrown to the winds by the fault of man's presumption," that was preserved in the Hebrew "formed by the lips of the first speaker" after Babel and the confusion of lan-guages. For Dante, Babel is not only the image of our condition, but also the central myth of the Bible, of which it is the most obscure point—and in effect we will see that he writes from this mythical perspective (Joyce had a similar obsession and appealed to the *dream* in order to reveal the fusion of signifiers). The physical symbol of Babel is the giant Nimrod, who will occupy a precise location in the *Inferno*. But, then, which living language (as opposed to dead, like Latin) will Dante be able to speak (in which will he be able *to make himself*); and how, despite its shifting individuality, will it have access to the immobile motive force of all language? Among the three languages he is led to consider (the languages of *oc, oïl, si*), and which are defined by their manner of saying *yes*—recalling the great assertive function of language—he must consequently recognize the basic formal element, since "the fact that we agree on many words . . . is in conflict precisely with that confusion which was the consequence of the confusion that flowed from the heavens during the building of Babel." Thus, he says, the word *love* is shared by the three languages (the choice of this word as exemplary signifier is determined by the fact that, for Dante, it will be the most heavily weighted with "meaning"). The problem is thus the asymptotic gap between a language that was never made—the horizon created by the first myth of a stable and inaccessible language—and all other languages, which have been constantly remade since the initial confusion. It is notable that, for Dante, this confusion is marked by a *forgetting* of the first language, a forgetting that is at the root of what we might call that history which incessantly displaces usages, customs, and above all speech itself. If the dead who once walked where we walk now were resuscitated, says Dante, we would not be able to understand them. Moreover, this imperceptible change, a change that can be equated with physical growth, is a permanent source of blindness for us. We believe in the immutability of that which never stops changing (ourselves, our bodies, language): "the longer the time required for perceiving the variation of a thing, the firmer we suppose that thing to be." In this manner, the past is at every instant both closest to us (present in our speech) and farthest away, and language is our unconscious witness to this fact. Therefore a language "varies . . . successively in the course of time, and cannot in any wise stand still." Individuals are subject to the double determination of their species and language, within which the illusory comedy of their freedom is played out. Nonetheless, through *grammar*, which is "nothing else but a kind of identity of language, immutable in different times and places" (since it should not be subject to any individual's "whim"), we have access, beyond the "fluctuation" of languages, to languages different from our own, or in other words to the foreign and the past (to literatures, and we know that for Dante the *scriptures* [*écritures*] are both the Bible and ancient authors). Thus, for whomever would assume the responsibility of speech, Dante posits the necessity of an awakening to the history of speech, to the cartography, the current, the unrecognized actuality and endless novelty of speech, which must be reinvented by an act in some wise revolutionary. This is the explicit image of a sieve which will retain as much of the polyvalent and general (the polysemic) as possible, while sifting out singular and regional extravagances. At this point in his discourse, Dante indicates to us the threshold of the *Comedy*. In choosing a language "which is the most worthy of praise," we will attempt, he says, to net "this prey whose odor spreads everywhere, but is nowhere seen"; we will pursue it through the *Italic forest* (this is the forest of language and signs, the "forest of symbols" Baudelaire will speak of in the "Correspondances"). A multiplicity of the signifier beneath which the signified escapes us must be succeeded by a semantic unity [*unité de signifiant*] capable of bringing out the invisible multiplicity of the signified.

In the same manner, says Dante, "that in every sort of thing there must be some standard to which all things of that species may be compared" (measured in relation to what is simplest in that species: numbers to unity, colors to white, etc.), thus in our actions "however many may be the species into which they are divided, we have to discover the sign by which they may be measured." An anthropological postulate is clearly involved: thus the category man may be broken down into "absolute man," man the citizen, Latin man. . . . Language is to be pursued in the cities (these cities where, during Dante's era of continual savagery, Vico says that one lived as if in a forest), and we would also say among authors (in these libraries which are cities within cities, and contain their own hells). Dante views the whole of existence as a sort of scale on which all things find their approximate unit of measure. Thus we derive the following chains: ONE / ODD / EVEN // WHITE / YELLOW / GREEN //, as well as, in a manner which then appears strictly formal, GOD / MAN / ANIMAL / PLANT / MINERAL / ELEMENT / FIRE / EARTH. It is not difficult to observe how these metonymical series are subsumed by a single original fact, which is metaphor (which, for Dante as for Donatus, is the genus of which all other tropes are only species). Thus the "mirror of speech" we will have found—and to which we will be able to relate all things—will become our principle subject: an instrument for measuring man and the world, exempt from the divisions and limitations of the language it depends on, it assumes a synthetic function. Dante defines this language by means of four terms whose meanings he sets out precisely: illustrious, cardinal, royal, and courtly.

Illustrious: that illuminates and, being illuminated, shines forth; that teaches; that makes "the unwilling willing" by virtue of a force more powerful than that of kings and exile (that exile which is undoubtedly its direct consequence);

Cardinal: here are the "door and the hinge," the "gardener and the graft," what we might refer to as the *axial* side;

Royal: because this language "seeks welcome in humble shelters, since we have no royal court";

Courtly: for it is weight and measure itself (that which measures, not that which is measured).

To summarize, the members of this language's court of love (and of the language of love, as we will see), in contrast to the princely court, are "united by the gracious light of reason." (Quite clearly something other than a vague "republic of letters" is in question here; the meaning of this passage implicates not a superficial, academic, or eclectic theory, but rather a violent and secret experience that we will attempt to describe.)

To this language, which approaches a perfect reflection of the origin and of things, poetry is, for linguistic reasons, fundamental: it is through poetry that this language is *linked* [*liée*] (bringing out "the palpable aspect of signs").[4] It is this "*fictio rhetorica musicaque posita*," this fiction fashioned through rhetoric and music, that comprises a specific teaching, or in short, as Mallarmé will write—"human language returned to its essential rhythm." We should not forget that what we refer to as *music*, as a result of a significant convergence, is born at the same time as Dante: with the *Ars Nova* appeared isorhythm and proportional notation; the development of polyphony and the pursuit of a greater melodic and rhythmic independence of the parts; a revolution which is above all a revolution of *writing* marked by the emergence of *lines*. From another perspective, language and knowledge are in profound communication: "the best language will . . . be suited to the best thoughts." For this era, such a "best" is represented by prowess in arms, the flame of love, and the "right direction of will," that is, by what admits the highest degree of invention—and the troubadors are those who, moving from one place to another, make this free speech heard, as it seeks and repeats itself in the need to *find* [*trouver*]. Thus the *song* becomes its privileged form: it condenses and "embraces the whole art." The poet who is equal to this art must be equipped with a "courageous spirit, tenacity in his practice of the art, and familiarity with the sciences." Thus Virgil and the sixth canto of the *Aeneid*, thus the poets "beloved of Jupiter, raised by flaming virtue to the ethereal sky, and sons of the gods, though he [*Virgil*] is speaking figuratively." And here the image of the *eagle* is introduced, which will play such a crucial role in the *Purgatrio* (as a dream of transport) and in the *Paradiso* (as a metaphor of multiple writing).

An unfinished treatise, *De Vulgari Eloquentia* is largely concerned with technical considerations. The hendecasyllable (that of the *Comedy*) is defined as the most perfect odd-numbered line, "the stateliest as much because of the length of time it occupies as because of the extent of subject, construction, and language of which it is capable." Problems of construction and of information, as it were, become predominant: thus, from Adam acquiring language in Paradise to the hand tracing signs on paper, there are no more than a few pages. Dante divides style into the undistinguished, the savory and ordinary, the savory and ornate (superficial use of rhetoric), and the exalted savory and ornate (illustrious rhetoric). Among the poets, the models are Virgil, Ovid, Statius, Lucan; among prose writers, Livy, Pliny, Frontinus, Paulus Orosius. Words are classed as childish, feminine, masculine; or as sylvan, urban, combed and glossy, shaggy and bristly. The glossy and bristly words have a startling [*outrancier*] sound. The combed words are those which unite these qualities: trisyllabic, nonaspirated, without acute or circumflex accent, without the double consonants *z* or *x*, without doubled liquids or a single mute, flat, and leaving the lips with sweetness (*amore, donna, disio, vertute, donare, letitia, salute*). The shaggy words are monosyllables or interjections (*sì, no, me, te, se*) or those which are inevitably ornamental: *terra, honore, speranza, gravitate, impossibilità*. All of these considerations will form the bundle and arrow of the poem,[5] its interrelatedness and percussive force, which will therefore be all the more lively as it has *also* been thought as raw signifier (as devoid of signification). Thus it will be necessary to distinguish, within the song, between *action* and *passion*. "According to the true meaning of its name, the *song* can be either the action or the passion of singing, just as a lesson—reading—is either the action or passion of reading."[6] Thus Virgil's statement, "I sing of arms and the man," has a different meaning than a singer's statement [in reciting Virgil], "I sing." The song (the text) is sometimes acted, sometimes acting. To someone's action corresponds his passion (today we would use the terms *encoding* and *decoding*). Despite everything, a text is identified by its action, and this is why its author is not he who sings the song but he who composed it. The song is "the completed action of one writing words arranged harmoniously, that lend themselves to music," and this action will lead us to the stanza, which is "a spacious room where all art can be staged."

Thus, in this treatise that may be regarded as the crucible and microcosm of his great work, as its genetic fiction and formal matrix, Dante never ceases to refine the reader's critical gaze as it passes through his own. He unambiguously alerts us to the fact that the question is right here, beneath our eyes, in our voice; that it is rooted in our location within language; that the condition of our existence is exposed there without mystery, yet at the same time retains a kind of absolute mystery. Words—their relations, their disposition, their origin, their form, and their meaning—situate us in a field of experience we may be subjected to or desire. We have said that he was the first to posit the trio of actor, author, reader. The author's action is the reader's passion, but this action has no other source than the passion of the actor. It is to a *new life* that this profound actor of language corresponds, if, escaping from unconscious and mechanical codifications, he knows how to play and to play with [*jouer et se jouer de*] this continually enlivening newness. And thus we enter the scriptural dimension of the *Comedy*.

"Love"

How are we to interpret the *Vita Nuova?* Like all of Dante's writings: literally. The letter is the heart of his life and writings. We need to approach these writings as *names*—extended, varied, repeated, and forming the floating base of his texts: these are never expressive except in the second degree, as derived. Secondary significations—indefinite in number—are only the excess that flows from this extremely deep— or extremely superficial—level, a level attained through the imperfection of signification itself. Saussure was right in saying that an *attachment to the letter* lay at the mysterious origin of poetry (and above all of vedic poetry). Music may serve as a comparison here, although only indirectly. At issue is the subject's testing of *meaning* as the subject of his existence, of the corporeal experience—and the unknown space— in which his position as subject undergoes global reexamination.[7]

The *Vita Nuova* is comprised of three levels of enunciation: a narrative that provides a setting for poems that, in turn, elicit commentary. These three "lines" of notation (pretext, text, context), this *division* (in the sense of to describe, to recount, that makes this word, etymologically, the first element in the chain: division—distinction— detailed explanation—description—narrative—statement), give us a background for the persona who will be actor and author of the *Com-*

edy. First intersection: the *book* of the world (of language) joins that of the individual (the "book of memory"). And the point of encounter has a name: Beatrice, Love. A name, or rather a cipher, the 9 of which this name is only the verbal exponent (Beatrice *is a* 9, says Dante). The *New Life* is thus not only a life renewed and life anew [*vie neuve*], but life under the sign of nine [*neuf*] as well (in other words, both life being born, appearing at the end of nine month's time, and life situated in the rhythmic space of the Muses, who share this number). Their intersection—the linguistic birth of the subject— occurs within a dimension at once daily and cosmological. The "bolt of lightning" Dante receives, what today might be called the dramatic entrance and eruption of his unconscious, produces an organic distur- bance. He sees Beatrice greet him, nearly faints, returns home, dreams that Love is giving his heart to this woman as food and, straightaway, he writes. Here we find an impressive logical sequence. For if Dante is thus precipitated into writing, into a search, which will become infinite, for the point where language speaks (a site which is not that of automatism but a more complex, more perpetual and deeper move- ment), he does so with a single goal in view: that of communicating. From this instant on, as his life, withdrawn from ordinary limits, re- makes itself in writing (an event whose nature is to cut off whoever accepts its import), Dante posits the paradoxical equation he will never abandon: someone makes him speak, he speaks, he speaks for some- one. An equation in which he figures simultaneously as overwhelmed victim and translator, but also as addressee: a three-fold division of the unknown. Admittedly, this first speech is illustrated by a minimum of anecdote: Beatrice "exists," and the reader, who in fact answers, is his friend Cavalcanti. But what is important is this concrete and theoret- ical model of Dante's speech as a whole, which, let us emphasize again, is sheer movement, communication. The space discovered here is that of the body as primary signifier, the field of that symbolic de- termination attained in the trembling of desire. The complicated mathematics that, for Dante, consists in simultaneously veiling and unveiling the sign of this desire obeys the law of speech which "indi- cates" and remains enveloped within this indication as the site of its own modesty. As a consequence of this indirection, phenomena are arranged and linked together in unforeseeable ways; from dreams to "real" encounters, from obsession to physical disturbances, from sight to vision (the book opens with a greeting that effaces consciousness, bringing the body to the surface and provoking language; it closes with an apparition that brings this language to an impasse), all things hold, all things correspond. But Dante still remains on the outside of this activity that makes him its object: Love is a *circle* in which he does not yet participate. He addresses himself to its speech, but does not speak it. Undoubtedly he has already "become an other," undoubtedly the ecstatic experience has possessed him (an experience that is often the sole criterion permitting the reader to comprehend what is written): "That which I remember dies / Fair jewel, when I am about to see you"—("Eyes that long for their own demise"). He has not yet abandoned subjective expression, however, and it is for this that the "Ladies" encountered "as though he had been led by fortune" will reproach him, while nonetheless recognizing that his love "has a unique goal." The aim of writing must therefore change: from "Romanesque" lament, it must make itself mute, objective. Another project emerges here, and along with it, the true desire for writing, but also the fear of beginning. The beginning must occur on a deeper, more involuntary level, must happen without being decided or willed, as on the day when, walking near a "limpid stream," Dante can assert that: "Then my tongue spoke, as if moving of its own accord, and said: *"Donne ch'avete intelleto d'amore"* ("Ladies who have knowledge of love"). Dante has a predilection for this line, citing it twice in the *De Vulgari Eloquentia*, recalling it in the *Purgatorio:* he indicates the involuntary ground behind its form, its phonetic and unconscious layer, or in other words the language he belongs to and that he owns, that will support his existence and the development of a people. From this moment on, Beatrice becomes a universal signifier. Sheltered from the order of things, given up to an intimacy without limits, her mouth, eyes, smile, and gaze now act upon every individual. By the same token, she enters and makes Dante enter the dimension of mortality, of a continual consumption. This is the "straying," the "aberration": sickness, hallucinations, premonitions of disappearance, a chaotic eruption. Dante sees Beatrice dead and hears himself say that he will die, while the world is dying. Here we approach the point where contradictions reach the height of their intensity, establishing a theretofore unknown reciprocity between the interior and the exterior, a nondifferentiation that language carries to a state of impersonality and prophecy. Henceforth, Love comes and speaks within the heart, in the trembling that seizes the experimentalist in silence and solitude. One might say that, for Dante, the essential is never to be at rest, to be able to explain every phenomenon, every trait of his poems, but only so as to pour the comprehension and the provisional result thus obtained back into the perpetual movement of desire: creation and criticism become inextricably bound. Love possesses nothing, and desires to possess nothing: its sole (but infinite) truth is to abandon itself to death. In this sense, Beatrice's death is the key to Dante's language; far from the death of an other, this is his only means of living his own, and of speaking it. Beginning with this death, moreover, the commentary takes on the status of narrative, leaving the poem to end in silence (in order to show that the text, as Dante writes, is *widowed*: [8] the role of signifier assumed by Beatrice at this point could not be better indicated, the context taking on the status of pretext, permitting the text to appear as the only egress, as a last word: individual elements disappear or, rather, are given over to this region where "no language is capable of stating them").

Let us insist, without fear of repeating ourselves:

Humanistic and psychological conformism, with its concern for "biographical" vacuities, has always feverishly occupied itself with "identifying" Beatrice. An inevitable misunderstanding: it could be said that this effort epitomizes a certain exemplary misconception. This does not mean that Beatrice is in any sense an allegory, but that for Dante her reality is that which distance and death render certain. To the extent that the object of his desire is not simply a mortal object but rather comes to life only within a continual death, a luminous point made all the more fiery by the darkness in which it can only assert itself, the identity of this object (irreducible to the status of object, but a subject *other*, increasingly other) is posited as destroying the representation of social identities [*comme détruisant la mise en carte de l'identité social*]. This, it seems to us, is how the secret poetics (the "*trobar cluz*," the "*senhàl*") of the troubadours and the "*fedeli d'a-more*" is to be understood; not as the illusory idealization of a real being, but as the concrete, erotic relation maintained between the indestructibility of desire and death. In general, we can say that woman (whence we come) is the sole sign capable of eliciting a limitless desire. She is the site of the law (of reproduction), and at the same time she maintains the material (biological) power to recognize its transgression. It would seem that a man's death is open to recuperation and so may afford an impression of finality and necessity, a group of clear, definite sentiments. A woman's death, on the other hand, leaves us unsatisfied. It maintains a hidden, delusive side that summons. Whence the necessity of pursuing this death, of playing out its inexhaustible stakes, foreign to all reason, the source of an unknown writing and visibility. The other, insofar as it is linked to death, is the sign of this irremediable truth: death's head, says Quevedo, is death in the masculine [le *mort*] but death in the feminine [la *mort*] is a face, a most lively face.[9]

Woman is this passage through the mother, through the maternal language (the primary prohibition), toward the vision (the inverse of Oedipus), toward the fire that one *is*. She is what leads to the sight beyond the face and the repetition of bodies. Beatrice's death allows Dante, physically coming to life in the world of death, to call up this dead woman's life as the condition of his own, and, thanks to it, to see this world of death, to make "his entire vision manifest." Another inversion of the ancient myth: *Beatrice* is opposed to *Eurydice* in every respect. A deliberate transgression is substituted for the blind speech of antiquity, an accession to and consummation of sight (in the *Comedy*, once the paternal language—Virgil—has disappeared in the rebirth of an innocent language escaping the law, Beatrice compels Dante to look at her and to speak to her; she makes him return along the path he has followed, toward the earth, finally effacing herself in the writing she gives rise to).

Thus Beatrice's loss of identity is the sign of Dante's nonidentity, the space where his writing is deployed as desire, his desire as indefinite writing. An experience which necessarily became increasingly anonymous; an experience which was, perhaps, on very different and increasingly nocturnal levels, that of Hölderlin (Diotima), Nerval (Aurélia), Baudelaire, and, closer to us, Georges Bataille. Such an experience is transgressive by definition: nothing is more scandalous today (this word having become the emptiest in our language) than this decided, non-"romantic" rechannelling [*détournement*] of *love*. Bataille saw that one must henceforth seek the meaning of this word (which, perhaps, as he suggested, is the *affection* unveiled by the mortal pact behind chance and laughter, this affection beyond good and evil and all signification) in the night, in slippage, irregularity, defilement. But the essential is to see that in each of these cases, we are dealing with an experience that isolates and destroys the subject irretrievably, beyond any community, a naked experience of language that *atones* for itself, of its permanently diverted and hidden economy (whose two poles, here, are Eros and Thanatos: an Eros who, as Freud says, "holds all living things together," and whose cry implicates the "mute clamor" of his twin brother).

The *Vita Nuova* may thus be understood as the struggle to maintain desire on the level of death by means of language. This combat immediately results in the disappearance of the simple and limited subject, its splitting into a speaking body and a writing that comprehends this body. A text that states the code through which it is enunciated, it composes what is virtually a temporal "readingology" of the *Comedy*. In it the three rival lines—narrative, poem, and commentary—are concretely resolved. In a predetermined, arbitrary, numerical space that includes time in a circular manner, as simultaneity and return, the three panels of the "sacred poem," divided into an introduction and three times thirty-three songs measured in tercets, will unfold a narrative poem, a poetic narrative, a transmuted language that comprises its own "lesson" and refulfills itself from this lesson indefinitely.[10] The *Comedy*'s actor (passion) will be Dante's *body*, its author (action) his language, its reader (passion) the totality into which they are led by what moves, unveils, and burns the whole. In the *Vita Nuova* we learned to recognize the effects of Love (of meaning that compels speech), and how all things were seen under this sign which is communicated to others under cover of ordinary communication. Beatrice in "blood-colored robes" is henceforth the material of Dante's thought: "this thought of mine is entirely concerned with my lady." Yet this thought, he says, "ascends so far in measuring the quality of this lady that my intellect cannot follow." Thus the "marvellous vision" that closes the book remains, for the moment, unutterable; the narrative can approach no closer to it; language must be reconstituted "beyond the widest of the circling spheres," attaining this immobile and moving region where it will be able to account not for a singular experience, but for the entire world where it is written and lived. The relationship between two languages (Latin and Italian) had permitted the discovery of meaning as the passage of signs, of this law for which "the meaning of a sign is another sign by which it may be translated,"[11] of the exchange and metamorphosis of the signifier. The genuinely living (*nova*) language is found only at the moment when the dead language it contains is exhausted. Now, the language attained in its depth must double and answer itself, translate itself at every instant. An analogous and quite different experience will unfold later in the [Rimbaud's] *Saison en enfer*, whose technique oddly recalls that of the *Vita Nuova*. And in fact, in *Illuminations* we read: "I am a far more deserving inventor than those who have preceded me; a musician actually, who has found something like the key of love."

"Dante"

The *Comedy* is the passage into a third dimension. It may be understood both as the unification of the three levels of language within a book with the power to reapportion them by means of an "objective" writing, and as the necessary consequence of the triplicity of the writing subject. The author delegates himself as actor, and as this actor's guide. Dante will be Dante and Virgil (Latin), Dante and Beatrice (meaning), Dante and what happens to him, what he overlooks, what remains a question for him. This dissymmetry is essential: it permits the other to become manifest in relation to the same, while indicating that this other and same belong to a space that precedes their conception. Dante's *alter ego,* whose role as actor subjects him to a violent displacement, nevertheless designates a "Dante" situated beyond their distinction. As *other,* Dante already knows what he is learning from an other and by means of an other, because he writes it: but he is not what he is without speaking, without carrying this experience of speech and its subject through to the end. He himself engenders the generation whose object he is, but this "he," in a certain sense, does not "exist." Or rather, he only comes to be as our reading. In sum, this textual relation is an *unus ambo,* a dialectical relationship, and it is in this sense that we may say that *Dante situates himself as Dante's writing,* as a traversal of this limitless and endless writing.

As a totalized work, a work to which "heaven and earth have set their hand," the *Comedy* must thus draw together, in the language of an anonymous and mythical author whose operative double alone will henceforth be known to us, the maximum of contradictions, delineating an infinitely full and empty sphere at whose center every phenomenon and its opposite would coincide. One might compare it to a game played for zero stakes [*jeu à somme nulle*], since the result of this project can only be its disappearance (so that nothing remains save the whole as disturbance and return, the whole must be both accepted and consumed). The *reader* of the *Comedy* is confronted with an impossible totality: a totality that dies out in an ever more ample recommencement, along with the meaning that animates it and delivers it to this ever more active reversal. If, today, our truth has become discontinuous (a rupture bearing the historical name of Hölderlin, a turning from thought experienced as fragment of the writing that bears it, as the separation of a concealed rhythm, as summons to a new experience), then this is perhaps in order to effectuate, through the need to accommodate the metamorphoses, the meaning of this henceforth absent totality, divided by silences and upheavals. The great unitary form that was given us to read is gone, a star retreating into the night whose light reaches our gaze only long afterwards, herald of a dark return.[12] The *Inferno, Purgatorio,* and *Paradiso* have this in common: they all lose themselves in a fourth locus which is each and none of them, a locus not only of the poem ("made, being," as Mallarmé insisted) but of its subject as well, a subject that may be *as much* anything at all as its contrary—torment and ecstasy, nonmeaning and transparency, ice and fire. The Comedy is everywhere, is nowhere. Its circumference is everywhere, its center nowhere. While it may trace an irreversible path culminating in "the Love that moves the sun and the other stars," the point thus made refers *in fact* only to the meaning and words of the text, to what insures their permanent movement. The circumference proves the center insofar as nothing is excluded from it, as its contradictions and opening are affirmed, but it is by definition unlocatable: the everywhere *grounds* the nowhere. History and the individual are indissoluble, made legible against a single ground that does not suppress one in relation to the other, but makes them appear as reciprocal elements. Thus the scriptor and reader, while hardly reducible to one another, are related to a single exterior. The goal of the author's action is himself and yet other than himself, the passion of every possible reader. One might say that the *Comedy* includes and writes tragedy as *birth*, if we understand tragedy to be the Dionysian drama of individuation, as Nietzsche would have it, "when belief in the indissolubility and stability of the individual vanishes, when the earth trembles beneath our feet." Here Apollo and Dionysius incarnate this twofold dimension of language, its articulation and leap into the vocalic and consonantal systems of pleasure and pain. This paroxysm of the symbolic function (setting the entire body into motion), this violent dispossession of the self in some sense unleashed, this Apollonian "symbolic dream" that follows after Dionysian music (itself a function of pain and the primal contradiction)—all this is what the lyric poet represents, according to Nietzsche, through a "me that lifts the voice from the depth of being." The "I" that thus accedes to language is not that of the individual, but of language itself become other and "celebrating its redemption in appearance." It is on this account that he may be subject and object, poet, actor and spectator at once. Already in 1229, Ibn Arabi was saying: "The interior says no when the exterior says me; the exterior says no when the interior says me. The same follows for every antinomy; and yet there is only one who speaks, and he himself is his auditor." But we may note that

Kierkegaard, in *Either-Or*, also observes the structure so clearly effectuated by Dante:

> And truly, if one has the courage to lend himself to the aesthetic transfiguration; if one feels himself to be a character in the drama which the Deity composes, where the poet and the prompter are not different persons, where the individual, like a practiced actor completely immersed in his role, far from being disturbed by the prompter, feels that the word whispered to him is what he himself would say so that one might ask which of the two is the prompter; if one in the deepest sense feels that he is the poet and the poem, possessing at the moment of creation, spontaneous lyrical pathos, and at the moment of performance has the erotic ear which picks up every sound: then, and only then, one has realized the highest ideal of aesthetics. But this history which proves to be irreducible even to poetry is internal history. It has the idea in itself, and for this reason it is aesthetic. It therefore begins with possession, and its progress is the acquisition of this possession. It is an eternity in which the temporal has not vanished like an ideal moment, but in which it is constantly present as a real moment. When patience thus acquires itself in patience we have inward or interior history.[13]

This "interior history" that incorporates repetition and symbolically passes from speech to writing, or rather founds, through and in writing, the original speech that speech silences and dissimulates in the diversity of languages; this archeology of language and this *archeography* that rediscloses the three levels Vico distinguished within external history (which is thus restored to its perspective) bring us back to the myth of Babel explored in depth, then restored and finally transcended [*dépassé*]. A witness to contradiction and division, but also to their conversion, this language, at this extreme degree of symbolization, will at each instant designate and describe itself, will utilize all things as metaphors for itself. This is the biblical myth of the book written "within and without" (*intus et extra*), and we may illustrate it with the legend related by Benvenuto, which says that at the moment Dante decided to write the *Comedy*, "all the rhymes in the world (and we might translate: the world as rhymes, as signs) presented themselves to him asking to be admitted into that great work." "The book happily advances to its end, and not one shall be excluded."

The Comedy

Here is our reading of the *Comedy*:

1. a) first of all a proscenium—a threshold binding the work to the earth, a satellite song whose orbit is distinct from the 99 others—that explains why the comedy of language cannot actually be lived or seen. Because he has escaped death (escaped absolute determinism of the signifier, the dark forest comparable to sleep, unconscious night), a flesh and blood Dante will be able to speak, guided by the source of this language he has torn from silence (Virgil commanded by Beatrice, whom love—meaning—impels to speak). A book that resumes all books (the *Aeneid*), reactivated by desire, will thus be the cause and map of another book.

b) the *Inferno*, 9 reversed, is the matrix of the signifier, which it simultaneously constitutes and undergoes, element and arena of the second death, of repetition without reprieve: in the proximity of eternity, hell eternalizes itself. To be in hell is to be self-exiled from one's own language: this is the reverse side, the inversion where "the sun falls silent," the site of the antagonism and confusion of languages, of definitive metamorphoses, noncommunication and the illusion of identity. Nimrod is the giant who designed Babel and for whom "every language is . . . , as his is for others, incomprehensible." Here we are under the sign of the spectacle, or radical exteriority. Speech there is not only as diverse as hell's torments, but fixed once and for all, and increasingly aphasic. If, for Dante, the earth is the site of the book's dispersion, then the earth's interior, the infernal, represents the freezing of whomever has failed to reassemble these fragments, who takes the part for the whole and consequently becomes his own signifying limit, his own repetitive dumbness. Immense and heavy, Lucifer eats threefold, in the shape of living bodies, the bloody and frozen silence. By contrast, heaven will be where *liaisons* appear, and no longer *bonds* (there God, or love, or meaning, etc., writes the revolutionary volume of stars and signs).

Hell, then, is the corporeal prison in depth, increasingly solid, naked, solitary, limited, and colossal to the degree that it lacks speech:

degree zero of space and speech. Condensation takes the shape of a multiple *one* (Geryon, Lucifer) instead of *one multiple* (the griffin and the retinue of Purgatory) and the one *multiple* (the eagle of Paradise), the first and last being inverted images of totality. The language of the damned, who are outside time but granted a historical prescience that advances toward blindness (the future returns toward them), is imprisoned there to an ever greater extent: "having at first no course or outlet in the fire, the doleful words were transformed into the flame's language." Questioning proceeds brutally and at length (language is for them useless suffering, without interest, *heroic* in Ulysses, turned toward the past, the summation of their lives). We are in the constraining plethora of the signifier, which can be understood as the world's initial law. "Sins" are deduced from this position vis-à-vis meaning: action, money, and economy are metaphors for the signifier diverted from its free usage and bent toward a goal (usury, fraud, treachery, heresy, etc.). All things accomplished for self-interest become devalorized and overturned (talion). *Language turns upon and possesses he who believed he possessed it but in fact was only one of its signs.* Generally this condition is insurmountable (requiring the aid of a divine messenger), and Dante insists on the *exception* that allows the rule to be revealed (and likewise Virgil, in the *Aeneid:* "*Noctes atque dies patet atri janua ditis / Sed revocare gradum superasque evadere ed auras / Hic opus, hic labor est*"). As Aeneus was led to the underworld by the Sibyl (voice of the signifier), so Dante specifies that the language of Virgil is the key to his power over the lower world: the work (*opus*) assumes its full signification. Thus Beatrice (desire) searches out Virgil in hell but will appear to Dante-actor only after his archeological traversal of language.

Once past the deepest point of this mechanical silence (bottom of the universe, dark pole of language), a complete turnaround is effected, returning language to its present, in sight of the signifier (of the stars), where

2. we enter an extension of the signified and, in the mode of active participation (no longer that of terrified passivity), scale the inaccessible mountain of Babel whose summit is earthly paradise: a climb that

will become increasingly effortless as we better understand that the entire *Comedy* is an apprenticeship in thought, vision, and writing.

After the dark forest, verbal incoherence, and the funnel of frozen silence, here is the deserted island where "dead poetry" will be resuscitated. The ship of souls approaches, guided by an angel, a line of light on the water. A rediscovery of the voice and music takes place immediately. The *Purgatorio*, in fact, is a continuous image of the poetic condition: hearing and sight are continually summoned (spirit voices passing by; living frescoes on the walls and pavement). The meeting with Statius—another writer inspired by the *Aeneid*—indicates the new splitting of Dante-actor: his language walks between two languages, that of before his birth and that of after his death. We are in time regained and brought back to its source, in the time of genuinely progressive action. Suffering is no longer *of* speech, but *in view* of speech; the function of imagination and the dream becomes increasingly more subtle, sleep changes in nature and, as it were, in density, the body becomes lighter, increasingly *understood*, until the moment of its passage through the fire beyond which that light (its desire) of which it is only the shadow awaits it. Dante walks, questions (questioning is the *Comedy*'s main motive force; none of Dante-actor's thoughts can be hidden from Virgil and Beatrice, or in other words from the origin of his language and of his desire, so that Dante-actor experiences this origin twice over by obliging himself to interrogate it), passes through *"non falsi errori"* (errors which are not false), *"visible parlare"* (visible utterance), and the sight of thought's transmutation into dream (*"e'l pensamento in sogno trasmutai"*), while the letters the angel traced on his forehead, and which manifest an endured writing (sin), are effaced one by one. Continually speaking to the reader, whose empty and future form he sees nearby (*"pensa la succession"*), drawing ever closer to a spontaneous signifier opposed to that of hell as is song to lamentation, assimilated neither to the subjective nor the objective functioning of *"immaginativa,"* of *"l'altra fantasia,"* to the discontinuity that rediscovers the silence and otherness of a new language, he approaches, through successive ruptures, the *"umana radice"* (human root), approaches in other words the root of a language exempt from guilt. Here the great rotational form of the *Comedy* intersects with itself as it designates writing set into motion:

> . . . I' mi son un che, quando
> Amor mi spira, noto, e a quel modo
> ch'e' ditta dentro vo significando,[14]

musical, innate superiority; a dictation of meaning that allows him to "go signifying" and which only a few attain, as Bonagiunta recognizes:

> Io veggio ben come le vostre penne
> de retro al dittator sen vanno strette,[15]

an episode followed almost immediately, and not by chance, by knowledge of the soul and body's generation, and subsequently the crossing of fire (meeting Arnaut Daniel and Provençal, while Latin exclamations continue to be heard: the new language gradually embraces those that preceded it), until at last Virgil announces that he will speak no more, that Dante is henceforth free and his own guide. Now we enter into the heart of the poem's words, into *"la divina foresta spessa e viva"* (the inverse of the first canto's, the attainment of what was seen from a distance, inaccessible, atop a sunny hill, and approachable only after the crossing of hell), "the divine forest green and dense" where nature, renewed by fire, engenders itself, a myth of language as a perpetuity being born and inexhaustible, whose metamorphoses are indicated by the procession which then appears, dancing and singing, bearing the unique sign of desire (Beatrice). Nature is present only here, a condensation in which a single signifier receives ever more numerous significations—and it is at this point that Dante's *name* is written in its place, for the first and the last time, at the moment the task entrusted to him is revealed:

> . . . e quel che vedi,
> ritornato di là, fa che tu scrive.[16]

Having passed through fainting and forgetting; having seen, beyond sleep, the center of time and the signs in relation to which his verbal position has shifted, henceforth situated solely on the axis of his desire (which will allow him no longer to speak as if in a dream, but rather to undertake a "dark narration," herald of this text as return, completion of the past, visible present, a future of meaning unfolded for those whose life is a race to death:

> Tu nota; e si come da me son porte,
> così queste parole segna a' vivi
> del viver ch'è un correre alla morte),[17]

Dante has become a precise mediator for himself, a "brain . . . which does not change the imprinted figure," a thought that will be capable of understanding itself, a hand that writes, a body, renewed in his memory like "new leafage," that will be able to "*salire alle stelle*," to "rise to the stars," into the air of language where the most synthetic writing will be unveiled without reserve.

3. With the *Paradiso*, then, we find a plenitude of the signifier, a mode of repetition of signs opposed to that in the *Inferno*, outside of space and time, of the *where* and *when*, inside a transparent, spherical, and burning eternity (toward a ringing, vibrant 9). The text becomes a "tall singing ship" (as well as the meaning that races over waters "never traveled" and Jason's ship, which represented the earth and could speak). After having experienced spectacle and participation, here we find fusion achieved by means of the equilibrium Dante-actor / Beatrice, man / woman. This is the locus of writing writing itself, a state in which the actor and his feminine double (who become signs of this writing) occupy an increasingly central, revolutionary position. The passing beyond humanity (*trasumanar*), says Dante, cannot be signified in words (*per verba*)—by which we must understand: since this passage is effectuated at the breast of language, it cannot be spoken *by* it. An affirmation immediately contradicted (but that should mark language's overflow and excess in relation to itself), because the necessity for speech makes itself increasingly urgent: the shades that emerge like reflections desire to speak, ask to be questioned, and the actor—encouraged by Beatrice—must speak in order to draw ever closer to his desire and transform his speech into vision. It is a question here

of a direct experience of speech, of its consumption, of its indescribable rapidity (thought is related to language as arrow to bow, and this bow shoots all creatures toward the target that is their end). From this perspective, space and thought are *on the same side,* and from this point on appeals to the reader become increasingly urgent: only the reader (the other) can assume this truth, the truth of an unlimited communication. Torches, flames, songs, dances, concentric wheels of fire that present successive versions in their turning, answer one another, sentences becoming isolated before returning to an endless round—racing lights, musics, incessant language interrupted only in order *to speak* to whomever wishes to hear—a writing of laughter ("*l'affocato riso della stella*" / the enkindled smile of the star) attained through the interior, through silence, or rather through the language which is "one in all" ("*con quella favella ch'è una in tutti*"); a writing that reads in the "great volume where neither black nor white is ever changed":

> . . .leggendo del magno volume
> du' non si muta mai bianco nè bruno,[18]

where we may gaze into the mirror in which "before thinking, the thought is made plain. . . ." It is necessary to speak, not in order to express oneself, not to give this or that signification (which in any case is already known), but in order to draw desire to its extinction. Dante indicates that during his journey he thus passes back through his biological ancestry (his "root"), and this regression leads to an instantaneous mental progression, approaches the point for which all times are present, where the future comes into sight "as harmony comes from an organ to the ear." Thus if the text would be inscribed in becoming [*le devenir*], it must possess a redoubled rigor, without which, Dante says, "I fear that I no longer live among those who will call these times ancient": writing (the radical experience of language) is a question of life or death. For this reason it is essential to *see* one's language, to place oneself in the position that will allow one to observe how one writes onself, how the world we are in speaks and writes itself:

> Io vidi in quella giovïal facella
> lo sfavillar dell'amor che lì era,
> segnare alli occhi miei nostra favella.[19]

The language of the birds writes five times seven vowels and consonants, and Dante deciphers and notes (in Latin) what he reads in the
sky. Likewise the eagle whose beak resounds with "I" and "mine" while
in thought there is "we" and "ours" (thus it could be said that
throughout history there is never more than a single scriptor, and, if
we follow Christian mythology, a single man is actually responsible
before all of history and history before a single man—a unity that tests
its indefinite limits); this eagle has the power to condense signs: "O
perpetual flowers . . . all your odours seem to me but one." The
book of the universe sings and writes itself before us in Dante's heart,
and at every instant his speech releases a more fervent, more concise
speech at the heart of the multiplicity in which every thing becomes
what it is. The mind emerges from itself "as a fire breaks from a
cloud"—an inversion of the *Vita Nuova*'s bolt of lightning, after which
Beatrice's smile passes beyond all expression. Thus, Dante writes, the
"sacred poem" must "leap," must accept its lack, as if it had become
an integral element in a text of which it is no more than a fragmentary
apparition. And so the actor is again given over to the "battle" with
his "feeble eyelids." Changes will now take place in full sight, as the
transformation of seeing provokes that of the milieu in which it is
submerged (a structure opposed to that of the *Inferno*'s metamorphoses): the shining river changes to red, the line to a circle; knowledge is a writing of fire, a turning melody closing upon itself:

> così la circulata melodia
> si sigillava,[20]

while the spirits turn like spheres and shine like comets, and sight is
directed there where "all things are pictured." Dante is able to take a
place in this festival of speech that affirms the coexistence of the plural
and the singular (the trinity) insofar as he has ceased to be this or that,
as he is stripped of all singularity (Augustine: "Expand yourself so as
to be filled; depart so as to return"). Blinded, he must still speak in

order to recover sight of that which is beyond darkness: speech carries with it the light of the "court of love"'s boundless legibility—

> lo ben che fa contenta questa corte,
> Alfa ed O è di quanta scrittura,
> mi legge amore o lievemente o forte,[21]

(the good that satisfies this court is the alpha and omega of all that writing that love reads — teaches — to me in tones loud or low)— and at this precise point Adam repeats the argument of *De Vulgari Eloquentia*, after which—and now it is language that says "I"—the "laughter of the universe" manifests itself:

> Ciò ch'io vedeva mi sembiava un riso
> dell'universo.[22]

Beatrice disappears once more, and, passing through the play of angels, we arrive at the vision of the *volume* in its entirety, no more than a "gleam" of which is captured in writing:

> Nel suo profondo vidi che s'interna,
> legato con amore in un volume,
> ciò che per l'universo si squaderna.[23]

(Examples of atemporality: the "time keeps its roots in this vase and in the others its leaves"; of ubiquity: the reflection and the flame reflected accord with one another as "a song with its measure," and the gaze reaches any point in the immensity without hindrance; of multiplicity: "Every spark kept to its own circle of fire, and they were so many that their number ran to more thousands than the doubling of the squares on the chessboard.")

Henceforth, traversing the 9 circles that turn ever more rapidly as one moves farther from the periphery (a reversed image of the sensible world), language reaches its verbal end, tends toward the infinite, exceeds itself, is no longer pronounceable by anything particular; at the moment when Dante wishes to learn how our pattern unites with the circle, he will enter into the *wheel* that has always driven his desire and will. At the moment when he becomes what he sees, and when, perhaps, he realizes that from the very beginning he was what he saw (what he wrote), he ceases to be in order to make room for the text: *the Love that moves the sun and the other stars refers back to the constellation of meaning and words whose entrance lies midway along our path through life.*

4. In the *Convivio*, Dante distinguished four levels in the interpretation of a text: literal, allegorical, moral, and anagogical. The last, he says, "is the highest meaning; and this occurs when we expound spiritually a writing which, despite its literal sense, also gives intimation of higher matters belonging to the eternal glory." But we could, perhaps, call this last meaning *hyper-literal*, if, as we hope to have shown, concentric possibilities of examples and translations are determined by language (in terms of its widest reality). The *Comedy*'s concrete choices (narratives, figures, significations) are accomplished circularly, beginning with this final meaning that refers back to the first—from which it is nonetheless farthest removed. "The veil of strange verses" does not prevent their reduction to a clear, flat signification, their translation into a series of flat signs (a dead language)—but it does prevent us from seeing and living them (reading them) as they are. The "doctrine" thus hidden "under" this veil is a doctrine of meaning through [à travers] the multiplicity of signs, what we are referring to as a *traversal of writing* because it implies at once a reading and a writing. Unveiling is not reduction, but *passion*. Logically, the *Comedy*'s reader is Dante, in other words *no one*—he too is within "love," and here knowledge is only a metaphor for a far more radical experience: that of the letter, that in which life and death, meaning and non-meaning become inseparable. Love is meaning and non-meaning; it is perhaps that which, by allowing meaning to emerge from non-meaning, renders the latter evident and readable: lack or ultimate plenitude are equivalents leading us back to the movement of the world, at once revealed and freed [*livré, délivré*]. In this itinerary of the body toward meaning (of the body, in other words of the entire world taking the longest and most complex detour, by means of the most demanding thinking: "only man," says Feuerbach, "celebrates the festivals of theoretical vision"), language appears as the locus of totality, the path of the infinite: whoever ignores his language serves idols, whoever would

see his language would see his god. In its insistent scription, the *Comedy* is a most impressive argument against any idea of another world or world-behind-the-world, the contrary of the complicity of the idealism-mechanism opposition: the decisive negation it performs on itself, its dialectical affirmation, are shown to be unique in excluding nothing from our reality. With the *Comedy*, we are present at the founding of the form which announces the end of the individual. Literality is attained when the subject has become the sign after having only read, perceived, understood it. In so doing, he does not simply produce, learn, or translate the language of the world: within a permanent revolution, he *is* this language in the proper and nonfigurative sense, he is an irreducible term there, in other words, one that cannot be reduced to a simpler expression. All "significations" are inadequate here, failing to achieve their goal, which has always preceded them. We *are* the imbrication of the *Inferno, Purgatorio*, and *Paradiso*; we *are* the active writing of the comedy of love, meaning, and speech. Because he has been in Paradise, Dante was able to write Hell; but because he was able to write Hell, he revealed Paradise to himself.

In his serial translation of the *Comedy*, Botticelli understood that the text was a single body in a continual state of transformation, so that any one passage was never more than the herald, reply, annulment, or realization of another, by a continually verified law of reversibility under which the book had been composed and lived. Setting out from this space of numbers, he can only return to it. Landscapes and characters are words in an impersonal language where Dante saw and wrote himself as one word among others, accomplishing what this language was accomplishing in him: the journey of totality toward the "love" that destroys it and in which a new experience of the whole [*expérience d'ensemble*] is reborn. Botticelli, multiplying and varying its traits, extricating the text's geometry, its condensations and displacements, from an intense multiplication to a rarified and ultimately vanishing equilibrium, showed that the distance from one white page to another white page, from one side of a page to the other, could be that of the world explored in its largest dimension. And, to conclude, one also thinks of this sentence, by one of Dante's contemporaries, of this Dominican who disappeared after being condemned by the church—while Dante was exiled and then condemned to death by the Florentines—of this Eckhart whose sermons, rediscovered early in the nineteenth century, surprised Hegel: "There, I am what I was, neither believing nor disbelieving, for I am there, an immobile cause that moves all things."

1965

Notes

1. See E. R. Curtius, *European Literature and the Latin Middle Ages*, Willard Trask, tr. (Princeton: Bollingen Foundation, 1973)], particularly the chapter "The Book as Symbol"; see also Maurice Blanchot, *Le Livre à venir*, in particular "La Parole prophétique" and Blanchot's remarks on the "Book" of Mallarmé [pt. 4, ch. 5].

2. Tr. note: Citations in English are based on *The Divine Comedy*, John D. Sinclair, tr. (London: Oxford University Press, 1948); translation modified.

3. For these texts we refer to the translations of André Pézard [in Dante, *Oeuvres complètes* (Paris: Gallimard, Bibliothèque de la Pléiade, 1965)]; we have drawn on some of Pézard's commentary as well, along with Yvonne Batard's *Dante, Minerve et Apollon*. [English translations: *Dante's Convivio*, William Jackson, tr. (Oxford: Oxford University Press, 1909); *De Vulgari Eloquentia*, A. G. Ferrars Howell, tr. (London: Rebel Press, 1969); *La Vita Nuova*, Barbara Reynolds, tr. (London: Penguin Books, 1969). All translations slightly modified.]

4. Roman Jakobson, *Essais de linguistique générale* ["Concluding Statement: Linguistics and Poetics," in *Style and Language*, Thomas Sebeok, ed. (Cambridge: MIT Press, 1960)].

5. Tr. note: The "bundle" and "arrow" are described respectively as the "rough material" (the different sounds and types of words) that will be gathered together to make the poem, and the knowledge that will move it toward its goal. See *De Vulgari Eloquentia* 2, 8.

6. Tr. note: For the distinction between singing as "action" (the initial composition or creation of the text) and as "passion" (subsequent performance or reading of the text, which is not passive, but another form of activity), see *De Vulgari Eloquentia* 2,8. Sollers recalls this distinction on pp. 27 and 40.

7. For the problem of the *letter*, see two important texts by J. Lacan: *"L'Instance de la lettre dans l'inconscient"* and *"Le Séminaire sur 'la Lettre volée,' "* in *Ecrits*. [Tr.: "The Insistence of the Letter in the Unconscious," in *Yale French Studies* (1966), No. 36/37, and "Seminar on the Purloined Letter," in *Yale French Studies* (1972), No. 48.] The text by Saussure we are referring to has been edited by Jean Starobinski as "Les Anagrammes de Ferdinand de Saussure," in *Mercure de France*, February 1964.

8. Tr. note: See *La Vita Nuova*, ch. 31, and the *Convivio* 2,1.

9. Tr. note: See Quevedo's "*Visita de los chistes*" in *Los sueños, Obras completas* (Madrid: Aguilar, 1966), pp. 178–79; translated by W. Woolsen, "Visit of the Jests," in *Dreams* (Woodbury, N.Y.: Barron's Educational Series, 1976), pp. 134–35.

10. Tr. note: Besides the English sense of "lesson" as what is learned by a student or taught by a teacher, the French *leçon* has two additional meanings which are relevant here: a *leçon* can be a text or fragment of a text as read by an editor, and, by extension, a reading or variant, or a text drawn from the Scriptures or Church Fathers to be read or sung during Nocturns.

11. Charles Sanders Peirce. Tr. note: See "Logic as Semiotic: the Theory of Signs," in *Philosophical Writings*, Justus Buchler, ed. (New York: Dover, 1955).

12. Engels, 1893: "The close of the feudal Middle Ages and the opening of the modern capitalists era are marked by a colossal figure: an Italian, Dante, both the last poet of the Middle Ages and the first poet of modern times. Today, as in 1300, a new historical era has begun" ["Preface to the Italian Edition of 1893," in *The Communist Manifesto* (London: Penguin Books, 1967)].

13. Tr. note: See S. Kierkegaard, *Either-Or*, Walter Lowrie, tr., revised by H. A. Johnson (Princeton: Princeton University Press, 1972), p. 140; translation modified.

14. Tr. note: *Purgatorio* 24. 54–56: "I am one who, when love breathes in me, take note, and in that manner which he dictates within go on to set it forth."

15. Tr. note: *Purgatorio* 24. 58–59: "I see well how your pen follows close behind the dictator."

16. Tr. note: *Purgatorio* 32. 104–05: "and what you see, when you have returned from there, that you shall write."

17. Tr. note: *Purgatorio* 33. 52–55: "Take note, and even as these words are uttered by me, so teach them to those who live the life that is a race to death."

18. Tr. note: *Paradiso* 15. 50–51: "the reading of that great volume where neither black nor white is ever changed."

19. Tr. note: *Paradiso* 18. 70–72: "I saw in that torch of Jove the sparkling of the love that was there trace out our speech to my eyes."

20. Tr. note: *Paradiso* 23. 109–10: "so that circling melody reached its close."

21. Tr. note: *Paradiso* 26. 16–18.

22. Tr. note: *Paradiso* 27. 4–5: "what I saw seemed to me a smile of the universe."

23. Tr. note: *Paradiso* 33. 85–87: "In its depths I saw that it contained, bound by love in one volume, that which is scattered in leaves through the universe."

2
Sade in the Text

Matter . . . is definable only as the *non-logical difference* which represents in relation to the *economy* of the universe what *crime* represents in relation to the law.

Georges Bataille

THE QUESTION POSED by the seemingly unapproachable name of Sade may no doubt be summarized thus: why doesn't the Sadean text exist *as text* for our society and culture? For what reasons does this society, this culture, insist on seeing in a work of fiction, a series of novels, a written ensemble, something so threatening that only a reality could produce it—a reality that, by the very fact of its acceptance in the form of this occult sign, must necessarily be a sacred one?

Why, then, is this text, an immense, coherent, and meticulous text paradoxically declared to be monotonous and boring, though in fact one of the most varied and fascinating in our library; why should it be both read or edited incompletely and reduced to a few primary significations which are then said to be exceptional? More precisely, why should we feel compelled to posit a *Sadean thought* beyond his writing, a thought that—depending on whether one assumes the role of accuser or accused, in other words whether one submits to a juridical and consequently rhetorical mode of expression—would be inhuman and pathological, or, more profoundly, lucid, audacious, and explicative of the fact—*man?*

Why should Sade be both prohibited and accepted, prohibited as fiction (as writing) and accepted as reality; prohibited as a multifaceted experience of reading and accepted as a psychological or physiological reference?

Perhaps we can hazard an answer: because *we have not yet decided to read Sade*, because the reading we should be able to give Sade does not exist within this society and this culture; because Sade himself represents a radical denunciation of the type of reading we still perform and project indiscriminately. He does so to the degree that his undertaking—already fully active beneath the veil of discourse—is concerned not with thought as the cause of language, but with language without cause, with the writing of the signifier as pure effect.

For what makes its appearance with Sade is a violent, integral modification of the writing ceaselessly repressed by deified speech. What appears beneath the savage mask of Perversion is the exact inverse of the Neurosis instituted by a civilization based on the deification of speech. It is, very precisely, not anarchy, but the *cosmological level*, the destruction and reproduction of a whole that is subjected to elemental play; as such, it stands in opposition to any idea of completed or halted creation, of creation dependent upon definite intention.

If there is a burning center of Sadean writing, surely it is this: the rejection of all causality which, after using Nature to refute God, immolates Nature in a ceaseless movement of words which redoubles itself and culminates in its own designation: "we are no more dependent upon God than upon Nature," says Sade; *"perhaps the causes do not determine the effects."* [1]

That the world should finally be reabsorbed into material discourse, that nature should thus be shown to have always been the dialectical contrary of culture, that at some point we can calmly affirm: *nature is a hallucination of culture*—this may be the ultimate unacceptable premise. Whatever society claims us, the mere existence of Sade's text is enough for a hidden contamination to take root and emerge, for a silent mockery to continually unmask the foundations of our knowledge, for the support of the *natural*, and *norm*, to be forever shaken and undermined. Thus we have a warning of the limit within which we are resigned to survive. This warning we must now examine.

Causality

Of necessity, we are born into a culture, and this culture, which functions to constrain and bend us to its ends, is entirely based on the
notion of *causality*. We are forced to accept as external to us, as judge,
measure, guarantee, supreme identity, paternity, law, truth, Being,
and finally God in all forms, a cause that is inculcated in us by education and fear. Consequently, we project this cultural formation as
reality, and without recognizing that we ourselves are necessarily its
authors, we abdicate, we prostrate ourselves before it. We become the
creations of our own creation. Wherever a nature presents itself as
fundamental, as nondialectical (determining interpretation *a priori*
rather than allowing interpretation its own self-determination), it becomes a function of nihilism, of a neurotic idealism that may in fact
take on the appearance of a pseudo-materialism or inverted idealism.
The human spirit thus falls prey to a singular and inevitable deviation,
a specific illusion we may refer to as the *hypostatic*, recalling that
hypostasis consists in making a fiction into a reality. The clearest form
of this deviation (at work in the very concept of origin) is of course
religion as a general form of neurosis: but religion itself—and every
belief, every mythology, and *a fortiori* every "humanism" founded on
a normality—becomes possible only by virtue of this causal thrust,
which draws its strength from a position adopted vis-à-vis language, a
position that may be stated thus: I make one word the master word of
discourse, the law writes me, I am only its provisional metaphor, a
particular case of the general "it is said," and thus I have only to
repress and deny what I find written within myself—"in my soul."
Now what does this writing teach me, if I haven't tricked it out as the
"voice" of my conscience? Desire. Desire, or in other words the absence of limits, the interminable and irresponsible energy without opposites which must be diverted and directed by every society. Sade
reveals this moment of sexuality's transmutation into God, Law, and
Conscience; the moment when man makes himself a servile animal
whose cruelty will be justified by the cause he gives himself:

> From time immemorial man has taken pleasure in shedding the blood
> of his fellow man, and to satisfy his urges, he has sometimes disguised this

passion under a cloak of justice, sometimes under one of religion. But let there be no doubt, his purpose, his aim was the astonishing pleasure killing procures for him.

Divinity . . . this fine machine is always needed to take responsibility for man's every iniquity.

This alliance of throne and altar—of power and belief—is thus the basis of human organization, which must either disappear or censure desire by cloaking it with causal speech. Sexual repression is first of all a repression of language: creed and culture are in strict complicity here. The human animal thus takes itself for a supremely privileged sign, the fundamental and central metaphor for a meaning that guarantees it: "of all the extravagances into which man's pride was to lead him, the most absurd was probably the precious case he dared make of his own person."

Whence an indefinite series of dualities, the most active of which will be that of spirit and matter, in other words of contained and containing, meaning and form, and, above all, good and evil. Collective neurosis is what automatically cuts us off from the possibility of contradiction; that is, right from the start the individual is denied the possibility of living his own language, of living himself not as a sign of something else (finding his identity in this relation), but as sign of himself (therefore non-identical to himself): his only choice is between communal neurosis and perversion, between neurosis and what will be referred to as "madness."

Since Sade is attempting *reasonably* to strip the constitutive neurosis of humanity down to the roots, and on the other hand writing only to tirelessly indicate this fold within which language escapes us, he must therefore inscribe himself under the sign of the perversion that functions as the operative negative of this neurosis and this fold. Here we must preserve the originality of what we are referring to as Perversion, and say that, on the level we understand it, it exposes the simple perversion-neurosis reversibility.[2] Just as Nietzsche saw in perversity the concrete realization of all "spirituality," so theoretical thought—that which is capable of modifying the real conditions of thought—appears to us essentially perverse. Perversion is theoretical thought itself, or in other words that element of thought which is the principle of all practical achievement. Nor is there any question, for Sade, of practicing on the one hand what he theorized on the other: this would be to accept precisely the dualist division he aims to destroy. Because the locus of neurosis is where fiction is transformed into reality, he will clearly demonstrate, by recourse to an uncompromising fiction, the fiction within which we confine ourselves, depending on the level on which we think and live.

As we have said, this level is that of neurosis, of established speech, of the "it is said," or, in other words, for Sade—and here is his first reversal—of madness ("As long as there are men, there will be madmen; and as long as there are madmen there will be gods, a heaven, a hell, etc."). The good-evil opposition may be schematically described as follows:

(+) good (the norm) is what places signs—which we ourselves are—under cover of a cause: we are the signs of this cause that guarantees our reality.

(−) evil (the anomaly) becomes the unconscious of the good: it is everything that, being repressed, menaces this substantial reality.

The "pervert," who does not accept this dissimulation of signs, is thus reduced to affirming evil in order to liberate the signs and attain the causeless effect of desire. To this end he is obligated to confront the most concrete and irrefutable duality, that of pleasure and pain. If he is able to show, through his life as well as through his thought—since his role is to prove their indivisibility, their reciprocal writing—that the other's pain as well as his own may be changed into pleasure, into an unlimited pleasure capable of overcoming every repulsion and of turning every negative sign into a redoubled positivity (as if less and less produced endlessly *more* for him), if he is able to accomplish this seemingly impossible and senseless task (senseless because sense, for us, is always the good), he will have undone the dualist series at its base and in all its density, while discovering that his task is indefinite repetition, his search a literal search for a kind of perpetual motion. The pervert is therefore continually menaced by weariness and fear of the semantic indefiniteness [*indéfinité signifiante*] he has thus brought to light; at every instant he runs the risk of yielding, of weakening, of converting to the communal neurosis and, consequently, to insignificance. He must then counter the evanescence of speech with a sort of hieroglyphic function, an irreducible force capable of going all the way to the end (thus Sade's "characters" either function as signs of life or are relegated to their deaths). The pervert's existence is thus a continual double or nothing, for to retreat or lose once is to lose all, to accept neurosis at all is to accept it in its entirety. Such a situation is danger itself, since whoever crosses the limits of prohibition risks more than the punishment of the law: he risks not being able to tolerate the loss of precisely what the prohibition functions to preserve: the subject's *reality*, that which allows him to be known by others and thus to know himself. Granted, the struggle against neurosis is hopeless; yet this struggle must be carried to such excess that it becomes victim as never before, an excess that ordinary "perversion" can never achieve, insofar as it becomes fixated on a few fragmentary aspects of the neurotic legislation. In fact, the problem is not simply to violate that legislation, but also to substitute oneself for the Law. The first is only one form of the second, just as the criminal—even the perverse one— elicited by society is more often than not only the most evident form of a movement he fails to comprehend; and it is from this incomprehension that virtue and the good most effectively draw their reinforcement and guarantee. However far the pervert may go in deed, he is soon halted and—height of irony—his act of counterbalancing the adverse system only serves to consolidate it. And this is because he has followed his tastes (his passion) instead of continuing up to the point of "reflection" and "apathy" Sade calls for, a point where complete monstrosity will communicate with something entirely other—which is, precisely, an economy of language that continually reverses the language of neurotic organization and its *falsehood* (taking this word not in a moral, but rather in a *technical* sense).

So long as crime is not explicitly associated with *jouissance*, it remains under the sway of causality. The crime of sexual expenditure, however, that which cannot be motivated (sexuality is not a cause, since it lies at the unconscious foundation of the causal process), *demotivates* virtue, unmasks and sterilizes discourse down to its roots: in this case, the reaction is sheer horror. Virtuous discourse—and ultimately discourse in its entirety, since all discourse retains a link with virtue—depends upon the connection of cause and effect, upon motivation (value). But for Sade, as soon as pleasure comes into play, all things have equal value, or, more precisely, only that which procures pleasure is justifiable as provisional value, as an object that becomes one figure in the algebra and grammar of pleasure's active counterdiscourse: "there would not be the slightest wavering, were the choice even between a gumdrop and the universe." Thus the least sensation, from this point of view, is worth more than any representation: this becomes evident if I treat bodies as raw signifiers, which is only possible if the signifier is first posited as object, as external to its signification, in its radical materiality. For just as the law demands that an individual be responsible for himself in relation to a text exterior to him, that he be identical to himself *for an other*, or, in sum, that he coincide with his representation—so virtue assigns a representative role to discourse. For the good that becomes unconscious evil in positing the exclusivity of conscience, any contestation of discourse's representative role amounts to non-sense. But we can understand, then, how Sade's adventure occurs entirely *within discourse:* if one is to avoid a state in which discourse is always and by definition justified against the threat to motivation crime represents, then this discourse must be reduced to silence by discursive means, crime must find its voice in discourse and be utterly justified in its protest against it. Not only as official speech, but also as the uninterrupted thought of each individual in his own body, discourse must be entirely permeated by crime, and crime must become a sort of blind spot within it.

Narration

What Sade has never been pardoned for is perhaps less the explicit apology for the crime of pleasure, than for having dared make discourse permeable to that element which was supposedly, according to an internal rule of language, unutterable. It is perhaps for having shown clearly, once and for all, that language has "nothing to say" and that expressivity in all its forms depended on the neurotic economy: we continually extract our "something to say" (our something to think) from a fundamental dissimulation and repression where, just as in the case of our every action, "there is little doubt that the sentiment of lubricity almost always directs these matters." The narrative of our life is thus at the disposal of the cause to which we dedicate ourselves, the thought that we serve, the authority that will justify our actions. However, Sade remarks, "I will gladly commit crimes to indulge my passions, but not a one to serve those of others." The predominance of the "something to serve" and that of the "something to think" are in fact corollary. These two come together in the hypostasis that, as we have seen, transforms fiction into reality—a hypostasis that contaminates the real by rendering it metaphoric, a product of our illusion that, from the moment it is fixed by a cause, this real is stable, familiar, self-identical. At every instant we possess a ready-made idea, an answer, an explanation for every phenomenon—and thus we believe in a universal meaning that allows us to dismiss its form by means of a sort of incessant *a priori*:

> One readily perceives that the superiority accorded to spirit over matter, or to the soul over the body, is based simply on our ignorance of the nature of this soul, whereas everyone is more familiar with matter and flesh and fancies that he understands them to the point of knowing precisely how they work. And yet, any contemplative mind must be aware that the simplest workings of our bodies are enigmas as hard to comprehend as a thought.

Sade's absolute atheism and materialism in this matter are exemplary. In our culture they constitute one of these limits that must be rigorously recalled—and all the more rigorously since this atheism and this materialism must be *fanatical* if they would reveal the unconscious, repetitive fanaticism of neurosis itself. For, in order not to be neurotic in turn, they must be supported by an active perversion of discourse (a semantic materialism) that mirrors the whole of reality. In this sense, the Sadean monster—which, let us recall, is a *written* monster—appears as the embodiment of an integral literality: this monster is that which says what it does and does what it says—*and never anything else*; that which has no *clothing*, and whose nudity refers exclusively to a written [*tracée*] thought. This monster is, in fact, more of a locus than a character, a locus where extremes meet and are neutralized in a kind of black explosion whose interior is ecstatic *jouissance*, whose exterior is irremediable destruction, but which *taken as a whole* is something that no longer corresponds to the interior-exterior distinction—an intermediary milieu between solar eruption and the consumption of bodies, the *lens* that concentrates pleasure's rays on a precise point, that lends them a power as murderous as it is delusive, and this with a calm equal to the crisis to which it abandons itself unto death. The "heart" of the pervert is thus unfathomable: there is nothing we can compare him to, for he is what explains, he is what kills. He is incomparable, an absolute subject, one who has conquered the narcissistic mirror and, consequently, belief in fraternity with his fellow men. He has nothing in common with anyone else; and if he massacres innocents, his pleasure will not be diminished in *also* massacring perverts, or in other words objects as well as subjects, devoted as he is to reaching that limit toward which he is drawn, beyond all paradox, in an ever-increasing series of sudden turnarounds, of *"coups-de-théâtre,"* where in every scene his role is to effect the play's reversal, deriving pleasure from this reversal itself. This perversion of discourse, this perversion in the second degree, is naturally enunciated from the body. If the body has become a real continent for language, and if, on the other hand, language has become *real* for the body, then this is thanks to Sade's writing, a writing designed to traverse us bodily just as it traverses the bodies it destroys, inaugurating a sort of generalized and terrible radiography. We can understand, then, why our judgments on Sade judge us, why his books remain a permanent and sure snare: unreadable by virtue of their clarity, forming a perfectly visible and indecipherable jungle of signs, the complete and blind faith we unquestioningly maintain in what they show us is here a proof that we evidently take these books' details for the books themselves, and, as if compulsively, mistake the part for the whole. Judges and defendants, continual victims of our own revulsions and fantasies, we risk releasing the prey of writing for the shadow of representation, and thus—as virtuous individuals ignorant of our own nature, perverts nostalgic for virtue—becoming the shadows of Sadean writing. There is neither a final meaning nor a last word on Sade's works or his person; nor is there any cold-blooded reading of Sade that would culminate in this or that key to knowledge. And yet this cold-blooded reading can exist if we recognize what it is that toys with us in this writing's every word, if we cease to privilege this to the detriment of that, if we accept the entirety of what takes place at the hidden and visible center of these active pages. Sade's goal was a writing of fiction (of the novel), a writing that would accompany us ceaselessly and thus totalize our life, a rigorously organized writing with a logic permitting its own precise unveiling. Distinguishing three planes of organization: that which is narrated as exploit, as individual legend; that which is replicated and practiced by those who hear the narrative; that which is reasoned out by way of theoretical justification—situating three signifying levels where speech, gesture, and thought are imbricated within a global theater based on the writing of the unspeakable—Sade creates what he refers to as a *philosophy*, whose law and rule, formulated with manifestly didactic intent, will be to "tell all."

"Lorsange"

This narrative system, developing a triple interconnection (narrative in the narrative, narrative that confirms the narrative, narrative of what thinks the narrative), is realized in *Juliette, or The Rewards of Vice*, whose plan may be summarized as follows:[3]

A neutral and empty sign—a young girl—learns the negation of appearances (of the sign as representation, as effect of a cause) from a sign that is consciously the opposite of what it appears to be (a nun who is a whore). Through her cumulative participation in every crime and every pleasure, she successfully traverses, by way of prostitution and alliance with other signs that have already reached every extreme, the figures of religion, the family, marriage, incest, parricide, infanticide, theft, sodomy, murder, sacrilege, scatology, cannibalism, and massacre, and thus gradually pupil becomes teacher, her conscience having undergone the appropriate "twisting" and she having become expert in the annihilation of all virtue and the fortunate, supremely happy fulfillment of vice and *jouissance*. The narrative omits nothing:

not one form of treason, torture, ignominy. Everything has been reversed: opinions, beliefs, sentiments, sensations. The narrative closes with the death of the sign that has been associated with the sign-narrator, her double (Justine, Juliette's sister, virtue, neurosis), who as we know has been over the same path, only in another book and in the opposite direction.

Now in this text where the narrative figure, a woman, becomes the filter of totality and of the general movement of pleasure and destruction; where the *anti-cause* and absolute effect find their operator (desire, sex, a body cathected to the very blood) and their foundation (writing); in this text with an inexhaustible theatrical materiality, which we will simply attempt here to present for a reading, we can make four observations that will serve to underline the fact that Sade is attempting a global formulation of the question of communication:

a) *history* is deliberately changed into fiction: there is no genuine, objective, historical narrative. Rulers, kings, the Pope are all described in their assumed duplicity, official representatives of neurosis, perverts in hiding; all discoursing in public for virtue, in private for vice. The generalized figure of the Law (of causality) is neutralized. From the same perspective, the names of "characters," if they belong to figures who take an active part in the narration, are largely of a mythological nature and as if elicited by language itself—thus demonstrating, with occasional irony, that this is in fact what undertakes the disposition of the real:

> Noirceuil (*noir-seuil:* black threshold, who introduces us to the heart of monstrosity)
> Saint-Fond (*fond-sacré:* holy bottom, who will speak of hell)
> Clairwil (*clair-vouloir:* clear will, who will instruct Juliette)
> Durand (what endures, the sorceress possessing the secrets of duration)
> A financier: Mondor [world of gold]
> A brigand: Brisa-Testa [head-breaker]
> Olympia (dies in a volcano)
> Lorsange (*l'or, sang, ange:* gold, blood, angel)
> A nun: Delbene (with a heart black as ebony, *de l'ébène*)

Nor is it beside the point to remark that Justine and Juliette share the same initial, and that both have feminized masculine names—the one infallibly evoking right and justice, the other appearing as a coun-

terpart not only to *Romeo and Juliet,* but to Rousseau's *Julie ou la
Nouvelle Héloïse* as well; Rousseau the inventor of Education, of Natural Origin, Good, Sacred Interiority, Discourse, Individuality, and
Belles Lettres in all their glory, in short the representative of Neurosis
itself (thus Saint-Fond corresponds to Saint-Preux, Clairwil to Claire):
literary history is thus unmasked in turn.

b) *money* plays an essential role here: Sade does not resort to the
fantastic, but situates his narration at the very heart of actual values.
Economy and interest stand behind behavior, beliefs, systems of neurosis. Perversion must take this fact fully into account, neither affirming nor doing anything that will not cynically unveil this level of value
(Juliette will remind the Pope, in passing, that the wealth of the Vat-
ican and poverty of Christ seem to be two contradictory realities). The
pervert applies faultless logic: the discourse of good must be shown to
be entirely determined by bad faith.

c) *society* is located at the center of all ideology. Sade insists that
society is a fact of "language," an arbitrary organization of beliefs,
prescriptions, and customs contradicted by other societies (the number
of examples cited takes on an anthropological precision and amplitude). As universal—and atemporal—project, the Encyclopedia of Sade
annuls that of the Enlightenment, which is limited to a mechanical
and naturalistic mode of reading.

Moreover, projects for inverted or secret societies are elaborated.
A total subversion is fomented within the brothels and lost chateaus
where the narrative of perversion unfolds: the perverse text, confined
to prisons or books by neurosis, in turn surrounds and encloses the
latter by the sheer force of its narration. Hell becomes a lived paradise,
and prison: the world, the book: reality.

d) *science:* the Sadean text must destroy every superstition, and
so appears as an ally of science. Yet without realizing it, science may
remain imprisoned by superstition, as part of society (the scientist is
often an infantile puritan). This is why the only "scientific" figure in
Sade's narration is, in a strange and paradoxical manner, *magic* (represented by the go-between Durand); magic is a practical awareness of
"nature's secrets" (in other words of the fact that there is no nature),
and these too are attained through a correlation of knowledge and

sexuality. Combinations of bodies and their transformations occur in both the brothel and the laboratory. This is one of the most striking passages in the Sadean text,[4] its most central, most transparent, and most vulnerable moment: philosophy's voyage to the heart of matter and crime passes not only through the transgression of social and "natural" laws, but also through a kind of hidden, interior *physics* that leads us, by a sudden activation of the metonymy of desire—not a sequence that is not murderously obscene; not a word that does not take on the force of a spasm—into an analogical vertigo where the cause-effect texture unfolds, accelerates, and writes itself in what is practically a drunken fashion (the word that makes the sylph appear, raising a cloud of smoke; the impersonal sex that is "God"; the apparition and bloody or poisonous destruction of bodies whose fictionality or reality, within the narration, we can no longer determine; the release of women who tear out their victims' hearts and wallow in their organic debris; the powder that opens and overturns the earth, revealing a cemetery of skeletons; in sum, the respiration of a life and a death that have become twins): "mystery and diversion," says Durand, "are here at their center."

Thus, at the end of the narration that closes upon itself—and at this moment announces that philosophy "must tell all," a narration that, as we have seen, obeys the following schema:

1. Narrative → narrative—practice—theory
2. Writing → speech (individual narrator)—scene (bodies, gestures, a community of writing)—commentary (thought, impersonality, universality, culture)

(a structure that manifests a fundamental dissymmetry, since the narrative is always already a narrative, writing always a new writing displaced in relation to an indefinite body of signs), reality finds itself entirely at the disposition of the fiction that has incessantly manoeuvred it off the stage and into the wings. The *Voice* of conscience has given way to the WRITING of desire. We have passed, as Sade intended, citing Lucretius, "into the backstage of life."

Crime

This "transition" demands that the Sadean hero never lack the force
necessary "to forge beyond the furthermost limits." Strengthened by
the most uncompromising of theories and examples, he must overcome each of his revulsions in a practical manner (and not content
himself with an intellectual admission that would leave the repression
intact), he must comprehend that the supreme *jouissance* is both conscience and its loss.[5] We find the enigma of Sade, an enigma both
evident and secret, in this sentence from *Juliette:* "conscience is distinct from all the other maladies of the soul in that *it dwindles away
to nothingness as more is added to it.*" This work can be identified
with that which consists in reestablishing contact with an elemental
force of language to the degree that death—that death whose vanishing
point is neurosis—cannot turn it back. Initially identified with a "nature" that, as Sade points out, "lives by death"; having made sensation
a mode of judgement ("I judge all things by sensations"), the action
of the Sadean hero becomes a figure of willful repetition, a continual
transition from the unconscious to the conscious by way of a pleasure
principle constantly opposed to the reality principle of causality. The
goal is to reach "the invisible chain that links all beings together," the
indifferent heart of the perpetual movement of sex-language. The reign
of causality is thus stripped bare and destroyed. This reign is in fact
that of unconscious repetition, a repetition that, in the form of the
propagation of the species, prevents "nature" from creating "new figures," misunderstanding the basic creative power that maintains itself
in the same forms indefinitely. For Sade, who thus exhibits the most
radical atomism, the combinations we result from were simply
"chanced" [*hasardées*] and "cast" [*lancées*]; the figures that we are are
therefore, from the moment they were shaped [*figurées*], detached and
distinct from their ground. Having been "shaped" by a culture, man
is absolutely separate from nature, and what he aims to conserve is an
arbitrary representation [*figuration*] that makes him no more than a
simple walk-on [*figurant*] in the universal theater whose existence he
then denies by inventing himself a causality, by imagining that he was

"willed" and consequently that, *except for sexuality*, his existence is a good, his death an evil:

> Always remember, said the Pope, that there is no real destruction, that death is itself nothing of the sort, that, physically and philosophically viewed, it is only a further modification of matter in which the active principle or, if you like, the principle of motion, acts without interruption, although in a less apparent manner. Thus a man's birth is no more the commencement of his existence than his death is the cessation; and the mother who bears him no more gives him life than the murderer who kills him gives him death; the former produces some matter organized in a certain way, the latter provides the occasion for the rebirth of some different matter; and both create.
>
> Nothing is essentially born, nothing essentially perishes, all is but the action and reaction of matter; all is like the ocean billows which ever rise and fall, like the tides of the sea, ebbing and flowing endlessly, without there being either the loss or the gain of a drop in the volume of the waters; all this is a perpetual flux which ever was and shall always be, and whereof we become, though we know it not, the principle agents by reason of our vices and our virtues.

Here we touch upon what we were referring to in Sade's text as the *cosmological level*, precisely what our culture has wanted to abolish and forget. In a cyclical manner, this level reminds us of the chaos from which all order has emerged, that anarchy fatally precedes all law, the profanation of every system that takes root in initial disorder, the very irresponsibility of the world's play. Here, in principle, culture rediscovers its arbitrariness, its originary stammering. An insupportable thought for our thought, one that thus appears as an absolute profanation. But what Sade's profanation aims at, quite clearly, is not the sacred, but rather the sacred already desecrated by anthropomorphic sanctification, the sacred left destitute by its very institution (Being, God, Law, Reason: *capitals*). And in such a way that this profanation constitutes the sacred act *par excellence*, the questioning of everything that presents and establishes itself as cause, the destruction of this *halting of signs* that pretends in terms of identity to complete self-coincidence—a halting and torpor whose occurrence is inevitable, since necessitated by the very nature of our profane existence. This affirmation of divine Evil is opposed to a sacred justified by Good; Saint-Fond's function is to recall this, as a corrective to the slightly complacent and over-hasty atheism of Juliette. Nevertheless, this divinization of evil is only one necessary moment in the atheological act that aims at becoming a sacred impossible to sanctify. Being the sacred act *on condition that it never appear as such*, traversing the sacred by a kind of semantic archeology, an anamnesis that consists in recreating the conditions for sanctification in order to transgress them (which is why atheism, rather than adopting a ready-made negation, must remain as close as possible to the possibility that produces "God"), this act is ambivalent, producing the misfortunes of expression (of causality) on the one hand, the prosperities of writing (of the causeless effect) on the other. If whenever we posit cause, we refuse to recognize [*méconnaissons*] desire, then we have to choose between the good conscience of a fictive reality, and the extinction of a conscience that makes a reality of fiction and changes conscious reality into fiction. In relation to virtuous and unfortunate codification, vice is the index of a metamorphosis of the signifier, of a genuine polysemy of the real; and it is the feminine sign, *the sign without a voice in the world and the Law*, that must transmit its inverting energy. In fact, if woman were not the figure for the disruption, it would not be inscribed within the order of things, and it is precisely at the deepest point, at the very heart of this order, that this operation must manifest itself. The judgment by lightning that kills neurosis, in other words Justine, at the end of *Juliette*, closes the Sadean narrative and fixes it in a mythical atemporality. The lightning bolt is the paraph of writing, putting an endless end to the duality of good and evil, announcing the resolution to "tell all" that Perversion has finally recognized as its task.

For Sade writes. If he stages the division of virtue and vice and grants the victory to vice, there comes a point where this victory has so well compensated for the inevitable repression of virtuous discourse that the primary crime, the text, refers us to a guilt so intense as to become innocent and "divine." In the end, the text alone (a crime against causality) is the *nonsymmetrical* resolution that escapes both duality and contradiction. To summarize, we have the following development:

—virtue assigned a representative role to discourse;

—vice challenged this role but could still act as compensation;

—transgression was attained only by writing which becomes the site of a limitless affirmation; or in other words, a writing that (like desire) refers only to itself and accomplishes this primary crime (superior to the crime that, in a certain manner, recognizes the law) that consists in changing reality into an active fiction whose virulence lays bare the world of good and evil:

I would like, Clairwil answered, to find a crime which, even when I had left off doing it, would go on having a perpetual effect, in such a way that so long as I lived, at every hour of the day and as I lay sleeping at night, I would be constantly the cause of a particular disorder, and that this disorder might broaden to the point where it brought about a corruption so universal or *a disturbance so formal*, that its effect would be prolonged even beyond my own life.

(Emphasis added.)

One of the rare aesthetic principles Sade seems to advocate, moreover, appears in his modification of a passage from Aristotle:

Aristotle, in his *Poetics*, would have it that the aim of a poet's efforts is to cure us of fear and pity, which the philosopher considers the source of all the ills which afflict man; one might add that they are the source of all his vices as well.

To write, solely in order incessantly to destroy the rules and beliefs that conceal the writing of desire, not in order to represent or express (otherwise it's the chain of superstition, of "causes," of "literature" in the neurotic sense, literature pretending to refer to a real or imaginary world exterior to it, a truth that would correspond to it, a meaning that would precede it), but to destroy virtue and vice in their complicity, through a crime which is cause and effect of itself to such a degree that it may no longer be characterized; to write is then a crime against virtue and crime alike.

1966

Notes

1. Tr. note: Citations from Sade are drawn, with modifications, from *Juliette*, Austryn Wainhouse, tr. (New York: Grove Press, 1968), and *The Complete Justine, Philosophy in the Bedroom and Other Writings*, comp. and tr. by Richard Seaver and Austryn Wainhouse (New York: Grove Press, 1965); cf. D.A.F. Sade, *Oeuvres complètes* (Paris: Cercle du Livre Précieux, 1967).

2. "I am toying with the idea that in the perversions, of which hysteria is the negative, we may have the remnants of a primitive sexual cult, which in the Semitic east may once have been a religion (Moloch, Astarte)." Freud, *Letters to Fleiss* [letter of Jan. 24, 1897].

3. Sade's two principal "sequences" are *The 120 Days of Sodom* and *Juliette*, the first functioning as the signifying matrix of the second. In the *120 Days*, time and space are closed, predetermined, and systematically exhausted in the body. To this (theatrical) *condensation* correspond *Juliette*'s extension and *displacement*, a dialectical effect of the *narrative*.

4. Tr. note: Juliette's first meeting with Durand, in Book Three; see pp. 527–48 in the Wainhouse translation; in *Oeuvres complètes*, 8: 505–26.

5. Tr. note: It is worth noting that the French *conscience* signifies both "conscience" as a moral faculty and, more generally, "consciousness" or awareness. Translation of the word as "conscience" loses sight of this ambiguity and masks the passage's relation to the wider question of the status of consciousness and of its distinction from unconsciousness. Sollers takes up this question below (see p. 60) and in other essays, for example, "Thought Expresses Signs" and "The Roof."

3

Literature and Totality

He can advance because he goes in mystery.
Igitur

The Rupture

IF WE INQUIRE into the history of literature over the last one
hundred years, what strikes us first is the complexity and ambiguity of
that adventure, qualities most evident in the fact that a new literary
space, a profoundly modified understanding and communication, is
combined with a reflexivity [*réflexion*] within certain texts that renders them somehow indefinitely open in and of themselves. How can
we define this situation? As the development of a "new rhetoric"? Or,
if rhetoric implies a bimillenary, Greco-Latin culture—a shared, juridical, proprietary speech—as the appearance of something radically
other, something that would be linked to an increasingly urgent med-

Originally delivered in Roland Barthes's seminar at the Ecole Pratique des Hautes Etudes,
November 25, 1965.
Tr. note: In light of the particular difficulties of Mallarmé's writing, many of the long
citations will be given in French, with corresponding English versions below. To follow
this procedure with all of the citations would be counterproductive, but the compromise
adopted here will give some taste of the factors involved in reading Mallarmé. The
following translations have been used as references in rendering some of the citations:
Mallarmé: The Poems, Keith Bosley, tr. (London: Penguin, 1977); *Mallarmé: Selected
Prose Poems, Essays and Letters*, Bradford Cook, tr. (Baltimore: Johns Hopkins University Press, 1956); and *Stéphane Mallarmé*, Grange Wooley, tr. (Madison, N.J.: Drew
University Press, 1942).

itation on *writing* that a philosopher like Jacques Derrida, in a recent
and important text, proposes to call *grammatology?* In any case, it
would seem that the birth of the concept of *literature* as we know it
(which may be precisely situated in the second half of the nineteenth
century, at the turning point of the romantic movement, and by names
such as Flaubert, Poe, Baudelaire) remains largely inexplicable for us
today. In a constellation of names that includes Lautréamont, Rimbaud, Raymond Roussel, Proust, Joyce, Kafka, surrealism and everything related to it, Mallarmé occupies a key position, seemingly equidistant from all the rest. Nor is this constellation so incoherent as it
might initially seem: it unfolds against a philosophical and aesthetic
background overthrown by Marx, Kierkegaard, Neitzsche, and Freud
(and later linguistics); by Manet, Cézanne, Wagner, Debussy—a background itself referring to an unprecedented scientific, economic, and
technical mutation. Mallarmé occupies a particularly illuminating position for us, because we believe his experience of language and of
literature, of their mutual questioning, as well as his exposition of this
experience, to be the most *explicit* one this movement produced. We
will try here, as Roland Barthes has put it, to give the verb *to write* its
intransitive function, bringing an absolutely literal sense to the act of
reading;[1] in sum, through a series of practical and theoretical gestures,
to define a coherent myth that would correspond to the reality of our
situation today.

The experience of Mallarmé, at once similar to and the opposite
of Dante's ("Destruction was my Beatrice," he writes in one of the
letters), may be briefly defined as a creative [*productrice*] and critical
activity bearing on the symbolism of the book (of the end of the book
and its absence) and of writing: with Mallarmé, this long-eclipsed symbolism seems to reemerge in a new and reversed form. This does not
mean that the term "symbolist," a term generally reserved for a category of minor French poets, would be in any way appropriate here.
"Symbolist" has taken on a pejorative meaning, being a matter of literature, and, not unjustly, immediately evoking the literary in the
worst sense of the word: an obsolete, constricting, idealizing element,
an aesthetic decadentism, in short precisely what some, by a sort of

willful misunderstanding, still attempt to impose on Mallarmé by isolating fragments of his poems in which these shortcomings may be
found. Clearly, this attitude is not without a certain amount of bad
faith, a bad faith openly shared, moreover, by those who insist on
reducing Mallarmé's position to the "poetic," making him a poet—
tormented no doubt, but a poet nonetheless. But Mallarmé does not
seem reducible to the type of culture that still flourishes in our society
and benefits from outdated classifications. Quite the contrary, he is for
us one of the experimenters in "this impetuous, insistent literature that
no longer tolerates distinctions between genres and seeks to burst their
limits,"[2] an insistence whose significance and goal, whose enigmatic
means and end we must attempt to understand; a bursting and overflow that speak to us, provided we give up trying to fix them in a mode
of thinking that their very appearance transformed and denied. There,
where some would see a "failure," an end, something exhausted, precious, and crepuscular, we sense a recommencement, a summons,
something inflexible, the unknown, risk. Today, the "Mallarmé question" designates both a past and a future, or rather this point in time
where the past-future distinction dissolves, where the past seems accessible from every direction and the future appears to flow back toward us; this historical turning point that presents itself as the end of
history; this *beginning of the return* whose unforeseeable effects, whose
organic animation, regrouping and redistribution of final and fundamental elements we are only beginning to decipher: as if a bottom had
been touched and a limit attained which would confront us with an
absence of time, an ungraspable space, an endless but *finite* totality,
another logic, another function of the perhaps still empty pronoun we
have just employed: we.

Significantly, Mallarmé initially presents himself as consciously
continuing the work of Poe and Baudelaire, from whom he borrows a
still classical letter and an already revolutionary spirit. But very soon
everything changes. During the well-known crisis of 1866–70, he condemns his early, Baudelairean poems and states one of the essential
postulates of his thought: the necessary impersonality of the author. In
writing *Hérodiade*, in "hollowing out verse," he has, he says, encoun-

tered nothingness and death. An event whose import is stranger than one might be led to believe. For this nothingness, this death (this absurdity and this madness) constitute the kernel of the most difficult of his writings: *Igitur*. *Igitur*, meaning *therefore* in Latin, is thus substituted for another *therefore*, that of Descartes's *cogito* (Descartes who, along with Shakespeare, is Mallarmé's continual reference). With Mallarmé, the "I think, therefore I am" becomes, in a manner of speaking: "I write, therefore I think of the question 'who am I?' " Or: "*who* is this *therefore* in the phrase 'I think, therefore I am'?" This therefore, this name, this *Igitur*, will function as language returned to its ultimate role, to its own resumé; a locus of negation and absence, but also of self-consciousness in death where one becomes "absolved from movement," locus of an impersonality seized from the "race" (i.e., from history and the individual's biological ancestry)—an experience that will also entail a grave and unsuspected risk (Mallarmé will speak of "very disquieting symptoms brought on by the mere act of writing"). From this point on, an indissociable theory and practice of literary totality will be elaborated through him, a totality that will be the only possible totality of *meaning*: "this subject where everything is interconnected, literary art." "Yes, that literature exists and, if one likes, alone, to the exclusion of everything." "Everything, in the world, exists to end in a book." How should we understand this *everything* (and the exception it provides for)?

Literature, as Mallarmé discovers, is a great deal more than literature (he will go so far as to speak of theology). Or rather, it would seem that the violent crisis in which literature dissimulates and reveals itself, disappears and is defined, confronts us with the indefinite question of meaning itself. Claudel saw Mallarmé superficially as the first writer to have placed himself before the exterior as before a *text* (and not a spectacle) and to have asked himself: "What does it mean?" But that is not the question: it does not "mean," it *writes itself* [*ça s'écrit*]. This distinction is decisive, in that it questions not only the habitual order of literature, the rhetoric already shaken by romanticism (and the various types of utterances it implies, from narrative to eloquence), but also thought itself (since "to think is to write without accessories") and simultaneously the *economy* of this thought in the world, the economy of the world *along with* thought and, consequently, social organization. In other words, Mallarmé posits, through writing, a principle of interpretation which is both singular and universal—*a meaning to be made*—and his writing, in order to designate this co-incidence between production and interpretation, will be forced to undergo a transmutation that situates it in a clear position of rupture vis-à-vis the discourse of the preceding era. This era could be summed up in a single name: Hugo. Hugo had "reduced" all *prose* (philosophy, eloquence, history) to *verse* and, "as he was verse personally, he prac-tically confiscated from him who thinks, discourses, or relates, the right to express himself [*s'énoncer*]." Thus Hugo made it clear that the unconscious phenomenon: *verse* (what Mallarmé refers to as the *per-fect line, general sign, total word*—thus the exemplary sentence) is the symptom of the fact: literature. "The form referred to as verse is simply itself literature; verse there is as soon as diction is accentuated, rhythm as soon as is style." After Hugo, verse breaks with itself: "All of lan-guage, adjusted to metrics, recovering its vital divisions there, escapes itself, according to a free disjunction possessing a thousand discrete elements; it is, I insist, not dissimilar from the multiple cries of an orchestration, which remains verbal." In sum, under the sign of his individuality, Hugo drew all literary forms together in verse, and ef-fectively brought about the disappearance of orthodoxy and commu-nity of signification. From this point on, given the break in verse, each individual is obliged to seek and elaborate himself within his own language: "Anyone, with his individual play [*jeu*] and hearing is able to construct himself an instrument as soon as he breathes, brushes, or strikes it artfully [*avec science*]; to make his own use of it and also to dedicate it to language." "Every individual produces a prosody, new, attuned to his own breath." "For me, a true condition or possibility, not only of expressing oneself, but of modulating oneself at will, arises late."

A major revolution, then, and one that confronts each of us with our responsibility toward a practice that must, no longer metaphori-cally (*belles lettres* were hiding literature, rhetoric was hiding writing) but literally, "recreate everything":

Sait-on ce que c'est qu'écrire? Une ancienne et très vague mais jalouse pratique, dont gît le sens au mystère du coeur.

Qui l'accomplit, intégralement, se retranche.

Autant, par ouï-dire, que rien existe et soi, spécialement, au reflet de la divinité éparse: c'est, ce jeu insensé d'écrire, s'arroger, en vertu d'un doute—la goutte d'encre apparentée à la nuit sublime—quelque devoir de tout recréer, avec des réminiscences, pour avérer qu'on est bien là où l'on doit être (parce que, permettez-moi d'exprimer cette appréhension, demeure une incertitude). Un à un, chacun de nos orgueils, les susciter, dans leur antériorité et voir. Autrement, si ce n'était cela, une sommation au monde qu'il égale sa hantise à de riches postulats chiffrés, en tant que sa loi, sur le papier blême de tant d'audace—je crois, vraiment, qu'il y aurait duperie, à presque le suicide.

[Do we know what it is to write? An ancient and extremely vague but jealous practice, whose meaning lies in the mystery of the heart.

[He who achieves it, integrally, is strengthened.

[So much so, it is said, that nothing exists and (the) self, especially, in the reflection of scattered divinity: it is, this mad play of writing, to arrogate to oneself, in pursuance of a doubt—the drop of ink related to the sublime night—some task of recreating everything, with reminiscences, so as to confirm that one is indeed there where one ought to be (because, permit me this apprehension, an uncertainty remains). One by one, each of our prides, to rouse them, in their anteriority, and to see. Otherwise, were it not this, notice served on the world to make its obsession equivalent to rich numbered postulates, as its legislation, on the paper pale of such audacity—I believe, truly, that there would be dupery, almost to the point of suicide.]

Dupery, suicide: we can see that for Mallarmé the literary engagement is absolutely earnest. He is supposed to have said: "I believe that the world will be saved by a better literature." If authentic, this statement is in no sense a witticism. As for suicide, he rejected it ("Victoriously fled the grand suicide") precisely because of the dupery it illustrates: genuine suicide can only be literary. He implies the *sacrifice* of he who writes, a sacrifice "in relation to personality" and unique in its kind. In truth, there is no subject in itself (and thus it cannot be suppressed by killing it) since the subject is the *consequence* of its language. This language must therefore be pushed to its limits in order

to know what is at stake, *who* is at stake in us. A most difficult enterprise, given the extent of the unconsciousness we immediately discover buried deep within us.

Science

First of all, we must face the multiplicity of languages:

> Les langues imparfaites en cela que plusieurs, manque la suprême: penser
> étant écrire sans accessoires, ni chuchotement mais tacite encore l'immor-
> telle parole, la diversité, sur terre, des idiomes empêche personne de pro-
> férer les mots qui, sinon se trouveraient, par une frappe unique, elle-
> même matériellement la vérité . . . —*Seulement*, sachons, *n'existerait pas
> le vers:* lui, philosophiquement rémunère le défaut des langues, complé-
> ment supérieur.

> [Languages imperfect being several, in the absence of the supreme one: to
> think being to write without accessories, not whisper but still tacit immortal
> word, diversity, on earth, of individual languages prevents anyone from
> pronouncing words that would find themselves, by a single stroke, truth
> itself materialized . . . —*Except,* let us realize, *verse would not exist:* this,
> philosophically, pays us back for the failure of languages, a superior com-
> plement.]

We may then translate, since verse is "literature," it is "literature"
that, philosophically, makes up for the shortcomings of languages (and
not philosophy that would be able to do it by means of literature).
This is the "purer sense given to the words of the tribe" insofar as
these words correct one another through the death—the negativity—
that speaks there and leads us toward a sense of a single language. But
by the same token, this process also opens onto *science.* Mallarmé is
foretelling here, quite precisely, the science that literature can be and
whose image, as science, is none other than linguistics, whose historical development is based in a sort of "return" of the Middle Ages.
"The Middle Ages, for all time, remains the incubation as well as the
beginning of the world, modern." Literature and science are henceforth in close communication for Mallarmé (the second now having

to pass into the first, permitting an originary rediscovery). Philology ("yesterday's science") finds in Mallarmé an attentive observer:

> Si la vie s'alimente de son propre passé, ou d'une mort continuelle, la Science retrouvera ce fait dans le langage: lequel, distinguant l'homme du reste des choses, imitera encore celui-ci en tant que factice dans l'essence non moins que naturel; réfléchi, que fatal; volontaire, qu'aveugle.

> [If life nourishes itself on its own past, or on a continual death, Science will rediscover this fact in language: which, distinguishing man from the remainder of things, will still imitate him, insofar as he is no less factitious than natural in essence; thoughtful than inevitable; willful than blind.]

(We may observe, in passing, the remarkable precision here of the distinction between nature and culture, between conscious and unconscious, or rather the announcement that this distinction is only one historical moment whose oppositions will be resolved by the dialectic of language.)

> La Science ayant dans le Langage trouvé une confirmation d'elle-même, doit maintenant devenir une CONFIRMATION du Langage.

> La Science n'est donc pas autre chose que la Grammaire, historique et comparée, afin de devenir générale, et la Rhétorique.

> [Science, having found in Language a confirmation of itself, must now become a CONFIRMATION of Language.]

> [Science is thus nothing other than Grammar, historical and comparative in order to become general, and Rhetoric.]

Mallarmé sees grammar, moreover, as a "latent and particular philosophy, as well as the armature of language." He further carefully distinguishes *speech* from *writing*, *verbal* value from *hieroglyphic* value, and develops his thinking around an autonomous manifestation of writing that, by providing a basis for diction, music, and dance, leads us to the most essential of his contributions: the great statements on the *Book* and the *Theater*. Whence the necessity of distinguishing between two states of speech: the one immediate and raw (associated with monetary circulation: "speaking only relates to things commercially"), also functioning as *universal reportage*, the press, the era's system of informational exchange; the other declared essential—and here we find literature as a generative writing recovered from mechanical and unconscious writing, from vain and self-interested speech. This distinction leads Mallarmé to a startling proposition, a statement that accurately describes our situation today: "Everything is summed up in aesthetics and political economy." Aesthetics is a phenomenon of linguistic economy, and thought itself is comprehensible only in economical terms ("mental commodities"). Political economy may thus be understood in light of language, and we will see how Mallarmé's reflections on the notions of theater, festival, and fiction are altogether precise in this regard, denouncing the poverty of a certain variety of economy that remains incapable of organizing its own play and expenditure.

Before we get to the book and theater, however, we must proceed to a critique of literature, and above all of its pretentions and claims to realism and expressivity. The fundamental aesthetic error—the political-economic error—consists in believing that language is a simple instrument of representation. To naive expression that would, for example, introduce the forest as forest into its description, Mallarmé opposes *suggestion*, or in other words a writing that will situate itself on the same side as the world, insofar as the world is a writing that only a writing is able to bring to light and carry forward:

> La Nature a lieu, on n'y ajoutera pas; que des cités, les voies ferrées et plusieurs inventions formant notre matériel.
> Tout l'acte disponible, à jamais et seulement, reste de saisir les rapports, entre temps, rares ou multipliés; d'après quelque état intérieur et que l'on veuille à son gré étendre, simplifier le monde.
> A l'égal de créer: la notion d'un objet, échappant, qui fait défaut.
> Semblable occupation suffit, comparer les aspects et leur nombre tel qu'il frôle notre négligence: y éveillant, pour décor, l'ambiguïté de quelques figures belles, aux intersections. La totale arabesque, qui les relie, a de vertigineuses sautes en un effroi que reconnue; et d'anxieux accords. Avertissant par tel écart, au lieu de déconcerter, ou que sa similitude avec elle-même, la soustraie en la confondant. Chiffration mélodique tue, de ces motifs qui composent une logique, avec nos fibres.

> [Nature takes place, one will not augment it, except for the cities, railroads, and several inventions forming our material.
> [The whole available act, forever and only, remains to seize relations,

between times, scarce or multiple according to some interior state and, willfully, whimsically, extend, simplify the world.

[Equal to creating: the notion of an object, escaping, that fails to appear.

[A like occupation suffices (us), to compare aspects and their number such that it brushes against our negligence: arousing there, for decor, the ambiguity of a few fine shapes, at the intersections. The total arabesque, that binds them, makes vertiginous leaps in a barely recognized fright; and anxious resolutions. Alerting by such variation, rather than disconcerting, to its similarity with itself, withdraws it while confounding it. Melodic ciphering kills (or: silenced, *tue*), with these motifs that constitute a logic, with our fibers.]

For Mallarmé, who appears to be the first to have undertaken this radiography of the text of phenomena, a landscape, for example, becomes "rural page," where even if writing is limited to a few mental abbreviations, he can assert that "nothing violates the figures of the valley, the meadow, the tree." The complete text will thus appear as a space twice removed, or as the mirroring of an ideogrammatic and a phonetic writing. Given the profoundly negative function of language—which never names particular things, but rather the absence of that which is named—the *mise en scène* we find here comprises an opening, a renewed virtuality and a paradoxical confirmation of the concrete by means of its evocation (thus we pass from a dual dimension—one thing is equivalent to another, one thing represents another, the sign combines a signifier and a signified—to a *volume of meaning*, a trinitary system that overturns and transforms [*qui révolutionne*] the totality of signs):

> Au contraire d'une fonction de numéraire facile et représentatif, comme le traite d'abord la foule, le dire, avant tout, rêve et chant, retrouve chez le Poëte, par nécessité constitutive d'un art consacré aux fictions, sa virtualité.
>
> Le vers qui de plusieurs vocables refait un mot total, neuf, étranger à la langue et comme incantatoire, achève cet isolement de la parole: niant, d'un trait souverain, le hasard demeuré aux termes malgré l'artifice de leur retrempe alternée en le sens et la sonorité, et vous cause cette surprise de n'avoir ouï jamais tel fragment ordinaire d'élocution, en même temps que la réminiscence de l'objet nommé baigne dans une neuve atmosphère.

[As opposed to a facile and representative numerical function, such as it first receives from the crowd, speaking, above all, dreams and sings, rediscovers in the Poet, by the constitutive necessity of an art devoted to fictions, its virtuality.

[Verse that from several vocables remakes a new, total word, foreign to language and as if incantatory, achieves this isolation of speech: denying, with a sovereign stroke, the chance that adheres to terms despite the artifice of redipping them alternately in meaning and sound, and gives you this surprise at never having heard this particular ordinary fragment of elocution, while the reminiscence of the named object bathes in a new atmosphere.]

In such an economy, silence becomes one element of language among others, since we must constantly "deny the unutterable [*l'indicible*] that lies." Here again, the error stems from the fact that we instinctively believe in the unutterable, in the inexpressible—and it is precisely to the degree that we do so that we become convinced we must *express* ourselves. Silence, in writing, is clearly the white, the blank, or in other words a "distance copied mentally," the internal and intelligible slope of music, itself "the sum of relations existing in all things":

qu'une moyenne étendue de mots, sous la compréhension du regard, se range en traits définitifs, avec quoi le silence.

[let a medium stretch of words, beneath the comprehension of the gaze, be organized in definite traits, with which silence.]

Mallarmé formulates a particular technique whose "guarantee" will be *syntax*, a technique intended to short-circuit the wastage of meaning that surrounds us. It becomes necessary to intervene continually in this play, to act upon it so as not to be acted upon. To this end, the scriptor distinguishes himself from the speaker's *bavardage* by means of a reversal that consists in *not expressing*, or in other words making his discourse objective, by means of a sort of ritual (and at this point we abandon our fascination with "truth"):

Le sot bavarde sans rien dire, et errer de même à l'exclusion d'un goût notoire pour la prolixité et précisément afin de ne pas exprimer quelque chose, représente un cas spécial qui aura été le mien.

[A fool prattles without saying a thing, and likewise to talk on and on, except for a marked taste for prolixity precisely in order to express nothing at all, represents a special instance that will have been my own.

To unmask the truth-falsity duality that governs the expressive economy, we must reach that point where what counts is no longer *me*, but rather my language:

Je réclame la restitution, au silence impartial, pour que l'esprit essaie à se rapatrier, de tout—chocs, glissements, les trajectoires illimitées et sûres, tel état opulent aussitôt évasif, une inaptitude délicieuse à finir, ce raccourci, ce trait—l'appareil; moins le tumulte des sonorités, transfusibles, encore, en du songe.

[I demand a return, to impartial silence, so that the mind may attempt its reconciliation, of the whole—shocks, shifts, limitless and dependable trajectories, a certain opulent immediately evasive condition, a marvelous inaptitude for finishing, this abridgement, this line—apparatus; minus the tumult of sounds, yet transfusible into dream.

We arrive, then, at the consciousness of writing, at this "reciprocal contamination of the work and the means," where that which speaks is writing itself:

Ecrire—
L'encrier, cristal comme une conscience, avec sa goutte, au fond, de ténèbres relative à ce que quelque chose soit: puis, écarte la lampe.
Tu remarquas, on n'écrit pas, lumineusement, sur champ obscur, l'alphabet des astres, seul, ainsi s'indique, ébauché ou interrompu; l'homme poursuit noir sur blanc.
Ce pli de sombre dentelle, qui retient l'infini, tissé par mille, chacun selon le fil ou prolongement ignoré son secret, assemble des entrelacs distants où dort un luxe à inventorier, stryge, noeud, feuillages et présenter.
Avec le rien de mystère, indispensable, qui demeure, exprimé, quelque peu.

[To write—
[The inkwell, clear as a consciousness, with its drop, at the bottom, of shadows related to the fact that something is: then, remove the lamp.
[You noticed, one does not write, luminously, on a dark field, the alphabet of the stars, alone, thus indicates itself, sketched or interrupted; man pursues black on white.

[This fold of somber lace, that curbs the infinite, woven by a thousand, each according to the thread or unknown extension his secret, assembles distant interweavings where sleeps a luxury to inventory, vampire, knot, leafage, and to present.

[With the nothing of mystery, indispensable, that remains, expressed, somewhat.]

This is what Mallarmé refers to as *restricted action*, which for him is the only action based in reality; all others collide with the absence of a genuine *Present* (the present is the illusion of whoever lives within the field of truth), an absence that makes suicide and abstention impossible, since we can never declare ourselves to be our own contemporaries. An action that, on the contrary, deliberately and lucidly addresses itself to the future by means of a radical operation.

Economy

At the same time, the author's necessary disappearance in writing, which after all has produced him, takes place in anticipation of a *reading* which is no ordinary one. Reading, for Mallarmé, is a *practice*, a *desperate practice*. First of all, rather than abandoning himself to representations, the reader must have direct access to the language of the text (and not to its images, its "characters"), he must understand that *what he reads is himself.* The crowd is manipulated by its unconscious—and this is why, in one sense, the crowd is musical. But within this crowd (and made possible only by it), the individual who reads communicates with his own language, rediscovered in what he reads. "Myth, the eternal: communion through the book. To each a total part." "A solitary tacit concert is given, through reading, to the mind." In sum, the book is the locus of a double movement: on the one hand, a suppression of the author (Mallarmé frequently compares the book to a *tomb*), who abandons speech for writing and thereby lends himself to the transformation of time into space:

> L'oeuvre pure implique la disparition élocutoire du poëte, qui cède l'initiative aux mots, par le heurt de leur inégalité mobilisés,

[The pure work implies the elocutionary disappearance of the poet, who surrenders the initiative to words mobilized by the clash of their inequality.]

and on the other, the development of the reader that confirms the victory thus obtained over chance and silence:

Et, quand s'aligna, dans une brisure, la moindre, disséminée, le hasard vaincu mot par mot, indéfectiblement le blanc revient, tout à l'heure gratuit, certain maintenant, pour conclure que rien au-delà et authentiquer le silence.

[Then, when aligned, in the smallest, scattered breaks (on the page), chance has been vanquished word by word, the blank unfailingly returns, recently gratuitous, now in certainty, to show that nothing lies beyond and to authenticate silence.]

The reader's confirmation and recognition of himself, however, collides here not only with the conditioning he undergoes socially, a conditioning in which "the horizon and spectacle are reduced to a middling gust of banality" by current habits of consumption, but also with his unconscious, which, by a sort of inevitable transfer, causes the text he has only just seized from the unconscious to seem obscure, unreadable. Rather than coming to terms with his own unintelligibility vis-à-vis himself, he accuses the text of hermeticism—without realizing that, as always, he thus does no more than to speak of himself and the criteria that have been imposed on him. Mallarmé writes: "There is surely something of the occult within us all; I certainly believe in something abstruse, a closed and hidden signifier [*signifiant fermé et caché*], that resides in the ordinary, for no sooner does the mob pick up some trace of it [*sitôt cette masse jetée vers quelque trace*] than it becomes a reality, existing, for example, on a sheet of paper, in a piece of writing—although not in itself—(in) that which is obscure: the mob becomes agitated, a hurricane anxious to attribute its darkness to whatever it can, profusely, flagrantly." "Faced with aggression," he adds, "I prefer to reply that some contemporaries do not know how to read." Perhaps we can see these remarks in a fresh light through a consideration of the basic postulates of psychoanalysis, particularly the more recent one, that the unconscious is structured like a language.[3] This *closed and hidden signifier* that Mallarmé judges to be in each person has now, so to speak, been *proven* scientifically. To such an extent that the seemingly unproblematic question of *knowing how to read* may be posed with all its virulence. Mallarmé's writing, with its abridged and multiple space, its twists, its latent relations, its internal and visible intersections, confronts us with a question for which we generally have no more than a ready-made answer, our language being in general a ready-made and received one: we fail to realize that to think is to write, that to read is to read what we are—and thus the play of language escapes us, we continually misunderstand the nature of literature insofar as we disregard the impersonality of its play:

> Impersonnifié, le volume autant qu'on s'en sépare comme auteur, ne réclame approche de lecteur. Tel, sache, entre les accessoires humains, il a lieu tout seul: fait, étant. Le sens enseveli se meut et dispose, en choeur, des feuillets.

> [Impersonalized, the volume, inasmuch as one is separated from it as author, requires no reader's proximity. As such, know, among human accessories, it takes place alone: made, being. The buried meaning stirs and arranges, in concert, the leaves.]

The book as "spiritual instrument," the book that would correspond to this necessity of the book, to its meaning, would be written by means of *transposition* and *structure* (Mallarmé's terms). We have already seen the necessity of transposition (the impossibility of "realism"); as to structure, Mallarmé remarks that "ordering [*ordonnance*] is necessary in order to omit the author." It is necessary, then, that the line's location in the (theatrical) play, as well as the play's in the volume, be meditated—in order to go beyond the volume, toward a new space (an intertextual space) where books would read, clarify, and write one another, where books would ultimately be replaced by a real text that would be the permanent interpretation of the world, "the orphic interpretation of the earth," the ongoing letter of meaning [*la lettre courant du sens*] at last formulated and brought into play. "All books fuse together a few esteemed old saws." The book that would truly be *the Book* (that which delivers and delimits everything [*qui nous livre le tout*]) "is written in nature in such a manner as to allow only those intent upon seeing nothing to shut their eyes"; "it has been attempted, unawares, by anyone who has written." This book must consequently be *feasible*; and the object of literature, the completion of its history, will be nothing other than its culmination: "nothing that is not asserted [*proféré*] will endure." If Hegel saw the end of History in the form of a closed book, Mallarmé, for his part, opens, disperses and *overturns* it [*le retourne*], situating it within the space where we undertake to live, to write and read ourselves, and to die.

Mallarmé knows he will not be able to accomplish *the Book*: but in any case, he assigns the *impossible* to all subsequent literature as goal. Furthermore, he attempts to make its fragments conspicuous, to give instructions for its composition, to ensure that our thought moves irrevocably towards it:

> Le livre, expansion totale de la lettre, doit d'elle tirer, directement, une mobilité et spacieux, par correspondances, instituer un jeu, on ne sait, qui confirme la fiction.
>
> —Les mots, d'eux-mêmes, s'exaltent à mainte facette reconnue la plus rare ou valant pour l'esprit, centre de suspens vibratoire; qui les perçoit indépendamment de la suite ordinaire, projetés, en parois de grotte, tant que dure leur mobilité ou principe, étant ce qui ne se dit pas du discours: prompts tous, avant extinction, à une réciprocité de feux distante ou présentée de biais comme contingence.
>
> [The book, total expansion of the letter, must draw from it, directly, a mobility and, being spacious, through correspondences, institute a game, who can say, that confirms the fiction.
>
> [On their own, words rise up and reveal many a facet recognized as the most rare or precious for the mind, center of vibratory suspension; which perceives them separated from their ordinary sequence, projected as on grotto walls, so long as that mobility which is their principle endures, being that part of discourse which remains unspoken: all quick, before dying away, to an exchange of fires that is distant, or obliquely presented as contingency.]

One of these fragments (the deferred return of *Igitur*) will be the *Coup de dés*, in which writing orchestrates its new powers (no longer the transcription of a meaning, but the virtually spontaneous upheaval of the written surface; no longer the recording and comprehension of a previous word, but an active inscription in the process of forging its own course; no longer the truth or secret of one person alone, the usual humanist reference, but nonpersonal literality in a world based on a dice throw):

> Tout se passe, par raccourci, en hypothèse; on évite le récit. Ajouter que de cet emploi à nu de la pensée avec retraits, prolongements, fuites, ou son dessin même, résulte, pour qui veut lire à haute voix, une partition.
>
> [Everything takes place, through foreshortening, as hypothesis; narrative is avoided. Add that this naked use of thought with recesses, extensions, leakages, or its very arrangement, produces, for whoever would read aloud, a musical score.]

This new semantic space [*espace significatif*] is presented vertically, upright [*debout*]; as if the uniform surface of discourse had been straightened out and torn, as if the coffin of rhetorical speech had been forced open, as if language were undergoing a rape whose mark was a deep—written—rupture of the sentence. The *Coup de dés* is a single sentence: *Un coup de dés jamais n'abolira le hasard* (A toss of the dice will never abolish chance). Subjected to an atomic disintegration and dissemination, to an incessant effervescence, the sentence, which we have previously experienced only as surface, is thus presented as the most complex of organisms, as the summation of all complexity (*as a name*)—the figure and limit of the world's henceforth manifest imbrication, of chance, play, and the thinking in which "man" produces himself—whereas the surface of discourse, ultimately, can refer only to an unresolvable man-world duality. Within this space, no longer unified and horizontal, but vertically divisible— which *a priori* presupposes a new physics, a new topology—what emerges is no longer the usual situation, in which one person addresses another, but rather a double structure based in the text. Scriptor and reader are situated on the same side of the fictive screen; their operations become simultaneous and complementary. The same and the other speak themselves together [*se disent ensemble*]; when the same speaks, the other falls silent—but this silence remains an active and accentuated speech. The fiction is *confirmed*, or in other words continually written and played out at its source. The book is nothing other than the transition between the world and the theater, the world-as-text's theatrical appearance, the "naked use of thought," the *operation*: not simply one work [*oeuvre*] among others, but the dramatization [*mise en oeuvre*] of everything that exists.

Myth

The fundamental problem is therefore the theater, the three-dimensional book. But Mallarmé's texts have functioned in this manner since *Igitur*: "This tale addresses itself to the reader's intelligence, which itself stages the play." For Mallarmé, meditation on the book—since it concerns the unveiling of totality as writing and as meaning—cannot be separated from all other concrete problems. The book is not made simply to be read and closed again, but to be utilized [*opéré*] and consumed, so that it can *take place* in *reality* which, in its absence, remains an inorganic fiction. *Fiction*, for Mallarmé, is a central term. To define a "domain of fiction," a "perfect comprehensive term" (i.e., one that would comprehend all human activities), he proposes, for example, the relation:

thus indicating that the circulation of money providing the conditions for technology corresponds to the circulation of language that determines the forms and development of [*innervant*] "art" (music, dance, theater). The totality of these operations, unveiling and echoing one another even at the level of the *letter* that rules them all, is referred to as *fiction*, and the book—interpreted, completed, put into practice—is what gives this fiction *meaning*, in other words, reality. We thus move into a new mode of understanding: phenomena are returned to their figures [*chiffres*] and to the cycles that clarify their reciprocity. Mallarmé sees clearly that the decadence of religion is linked to the fact that *expenditure* is no longer conceivable within our society. The *mass*, for example, interests him as a technique of gratuity, a symbolic ritual that could serve a particular function: "it could not be that in a religion, even in its subsequent abandonment, the race has not placed its unknown intimate secret. The time has come, with the necessary detachment, to undertake its excavation." Writing will therefore operate on the level of *myths*—and the theater can become the mode for this setting down and fixing of myths seized from the unconscious of an obscurantist society dominated by money. Mallarmé is fully aware of the obstacles: the theater is in an unprecedented state of debasement and servility—and the foundation of the modern popular Poem, "which will be marveled at by a suddenly invented reading majority," is not yet possible. Nothing but limited works, narrow mythologies, and "representations" are being put forward; we are incapable of seeing things "themselves," or in other words of seeing "the play written in the folio of the sky and mimed by Man with the gestures of his passions." The theater, which for Mallarmé is of a "superior essence," is the "moment when the horizon shines within humanity, the opening of the chimera's maw that has been misunderstood and carefully frustrated by the social order." Taking up Gautier's ironic comment that "We should have nothing but vaudeville—they'd make some changes from time to time," Mallarmé adds, more seriously: "Replace Vaudeville by Mystery, a multiple tetralogy deploying itself in parallel to a newly begun cycle of years and insist that its text be as inviolable as the Law: there you have it, almost!"

What is called for is a theater based on the Book and in which the "mental milieu equalizing stage and audience" can appear. In truth, says Mallarmé, "the mental situation is much like the meanders of a drama"; the theater consists in making this process, hidden by time, manifest in simultaneous, spatial terms: "a dramatic work shows the successive development of the action's externalizations, without any one moment achieving reality, and without anything, in the last analysis, ever happening." The Theater would be the reading of the Book, its writing operating "within the labyrinth of anguish art elaborates [*que mène l'art*]." The most precise theatrical approximation to this myth is Hamlet, who, "reading from the book of himself," "externalizes, on the boards, the personage of an intimate and secret tragedy," "the latent lord who cannot become"—for "there is no other subject, you may be sure: the antagonism between man's dream and the fatalities bestowed upon his existence by misfortune."

The *stage* which is "our only magnificence"—the only place where the Book's envisioned totality may appear to us—is in some sense the painting of the text, where "everything moves according to a symbolic reciprocity between types or in relation to a single figure." "Mime, thinker, the tragedian interprets as a plastic and mental sovereign of art." The world becomes intelligible, then, as a writing at the intersection of the Theater and the Book—and this intersection is the Dance: the dancer has only to trace out her corporeal writing in order for the entire company, assembled around the *star*, to mime the writing of the constellations, the inverse of that which traces itself on paper. *Choreography* reveals the role of figures which themselves supply the key to *characters* or human types. The story is a drama, and ballet an emblematics, a hieroglyphic grouping; the whole constitutes a milieu of fiction in which reading becomes a "notation of sentiments in unspoken sentences." The dancer "delivers [*livre*], through the final veil which always remains, the nudity of concepts and silently writes [the] vision, like a Sign, which she is." It is important to note that Mallarmé points out here, in passing, the kinship between this writing and that of the *Dream*.

Through reading we may perform any play for ourselves, "inwardly." If we want to become aware of the writing that this reading is, however, we must appear on the stage (experience life). This is the point at which the latent drama is manifested by a tearing that affirms "the irreducibility of our instincts." So we come to "a musical celebration and also a figuration of life, confiding its mystery to language alone and to mimetic evolution [*l'évolution mimique*]."

Thus Mallarmé posits the existence of a "theater proper to the spirit," by virtue of which the poet "awakens, by means of the written, the master of revels in each of us." WE MUST THEREFORE REALIZE THE POSSIBILITY OF THE TEXT AS THEATER ALONG WITH THAT OF THE THEATER AND OF LIFE AS TEXT if we want to take our place within the writing that defines us: "knowing that in the spirit of anyone who has dreamed all of humanity in himself [*a rêvé les humains jusqu'à soi*] nothing exists but an exact account of the pure rhythmic motifs of being, which are its recognizable signs; my pleasure is to decipher them everywhere."

The language that rediscovers the totality of fiction is consequently the "foundation" of all possible art:

> Aux convergences des autres arts située, issue d'eux et les gouvernant, la Fiction ou Poésie.
>
> [At the convergence of the other arts, emerging from and governing them, is Fiction or Poetry.

This fundamental fiction reveals its own status as an orchestration of myths; for it is directly linked to the functioning of that thinking which dissolves myths in order to *remake* them. We may thus imagine a global, theatrical, theoretical, practical, and mental activity devoted to "the expansion of symbols or their preparation," an activity based not upon fable or legend (which, for Mallarmé, is Wagner's error), not in this or that particular myth, but on the unveiling of Myths and their unification:

> Le Théâtre les appelle, non: pas de fixes, ni de séculaires et de notoires, mais un, dégagé de personnalité, car il compose notre aspect multiple.
>
> [The Theater summons them (myths), no: not established, or secular and well-known, but one, removed from personality, since it composes our multiple aspect.]

Concerning this condition, Mallarmé may still write that "Man and his authentic stay on earth, exchange a reciprocity of proofs."

"The Interregnum"

We must now specify the precise role of one who in writing, in accepting death through literature, is more the less compromised within his society. This existence is initially experienced as an inconvenience: "Literary existence, except for one, [the] true, which is spent in arousing presence, within harmonies and significations, occurs, with the world, only as inconvenience." And further: "Literature, which has this in common with hunger, consists in suppressing the Gentleman who remains in the writing of it. What function can he have, in an everyday sense, in the eyes of those around him?"

The writer or, more precisely, the scriptor, whatever he may do, is therefore entirely cut off insofar as his work is directed at the unconscious functioning of language, insofar as this work constitutes a continually renewed and mute solitude which Mallarmé describes as "the derogation of destiny, at least, socially." Nevertheless, the consequences of this retreat are paradoxical: if he forbids himself all links and all ownership, if he forces himself to "satisfy some singular instinct, to possess nothing and simply to pass by," if he thus defines someone desiring to be nothing and to have nothing in particular, someone "infinitely alone on the earth"—he also discovers an unforeseen coincidence with the most alienated individual, the proletarian. It is of him that Mallarmé is thinking, as he writes: "How sad that for these my production remains, especially, like clouds at dusk, vain." "The constellations," he writes, "are beginning to glimmer: how I would like, in the darkness that steals over the blind herd, for some points of light, such as [were] thought just now, to become visible, despite these sealed eyes that do not pick them out—to establish this, to give it precision, to give it voice. [*pour le fait, pour l'exactitude, pour qu'il soit dit*]."

To establish this, to give it precision, to give it voice: the life of whoever writes is an "interregnum," and the seemingly useless work or play he pursues is linked to that future we know to be the locus of all symbolic work. Literature belongs to the future, and the future, as Mallarmé writes, "is never anything but the flash of what must have been produced previously or near the beginning." By virtue of a strange circularity, the man who *is* nothing and the one who *has* nothing are thus profoundly joined, vis-à-vis those who possess and consequently believe themselves to be something. Mallarmé's thought, then, is neither betrayed nor distorted if we affirm that his work was ultimately directed toward a single thought, a thought we might refer to, moreover, as the *formal thought*: that of revolution, in its most literal sense.

1966

Notes

1. Tr. note: See Roland Barthes, "To Write: An Intransitive Verb?" in R. Macksey and E. Donato, eds., *The Structuralist Controversy* (Baltimore: Johns Hopkins University Press, 1970).

2. Tr. note: See Maurice Blanchot, *Le Livre à venir* (Paris: Gallimard, 1959), p. 164.

3. Tr. note: See Jacques Lacan's *Séminaire, Livre XI: Les quatre concepts fondamentaux de la psychanalyse* (Paris: Seuil, 1973), pp. 137, 185; Eng. ed., *The Four Fundamental Concepts of Psycho-Analysis*, Alan Sheridan, tr. (New York: Norton, 1978), pp. 149, 203.

4

Thought Expresses Signs

We find that the strongest and most constantly used faculty at all stages of life is *thought*—even in the least perception and apparent passivity! Evidently, it thus becomes the most powerful and most demanding of the faculties, and in the long run it tyrannizes over all the others. Ultimately it becomes the "passion-in-itself."

Nietzsche

THROUGHOUT HIS WRITINGS, from the beginning to the end of his life's flawed trajectory, there is no word that Artaud pronounces more often, or with greater insistence, than *thought*. The immediate effect of his passage near us seems to radiate darkly around this word, and only around and through it can we try to question his silence. To a world in which mechanical processes of reduction expand ceaselessly, Artaud poses the limitless question of thought in no uncertain terms. And indeed a great deal more: affirming himself, through writing, as being this question, as having no part in the "pus of beings decanted from ontology,"[1] Artaud introduces the abrupt presence of the *body* into what he calls thought. Now of course, we don't have bodies anymore. This is what ideologies are supposed to teach, repeat, and dictate to us whenever necessary, and this is precisely where they are least inclined to give way. Thought without bodies, bodies without thought: let us look around and inside us and listen. But how could we see there without eyes, hear without ears? Or rather—how could we see with *these* eyes, or hear with *these* ears? Since they are not our own? Since we have not, as Artaud would have said, *come out* in ourselves [sortis *en nous*]? Since first of all it is a matter, still and always, of our difference, of our nonappurtenance to ourselves; or to put it another way, as much a matter of our social alienation as our continually misunderstood [*méconnue*] relation to the unconscious? Thought, the body, the unconscious: these are the three controlling figures of Artaud's broken language, which come together in a single figure that we can refer to, without excessive imprecision, as life. A new or final possibility of speaking is constituted here in an organic manner, moreover—a possibility of speaking not at random or in dream, but literally beyond chance and the dream. A possibility of speaking as if we were the same as our speech, rather than subjected to it. As if, in the unity of a heretofore unknown space of speech, we had at last ceased being double.[2]

In retrospect, what strikes us most about Artaud is doubtless his extremely acute and enigmatic timeliness. The things he was opposed to seem to us today more and more demystified, tentative, or senseless. The paths he indicated are becoming increasingly well-defined; not "openly," of course, but in a covert manner, firmly. A recent book like Michel Foucault's *Madness and Civilization* confirms this tendency. If Foucault can write that "man, in our day, finds truth only in the enigma of the madman he is and is not," it is because this enigma is henceforth that of a ceaseless contestation, an area at once present and absent, in relation to which the world must experience its limits, and the subject must face an image of itself which is no longer the mirror's falsely distorting one. Imagine a space that would contain only subjects: no more spectators, only actors, all similarly compromised, with no possible exceptions. It is this space of thought, abolishing all duality, that language (being itself this nonduality) imposes on us, and this is the space whose meaning Artaud lived and suffered. There, perhaps, where "one walks from the equinox to the solstice, shouldering one's own humanity." There, from where he could write: "I say / from above / time." A singular, manifest, and elusive space, a space that awaits those for whom the body has become an endless journey without the protection of communal unconsciousness, a body refusing to acquiesce (to be a *third*) in order to occupy its very surface. This, then, is the point at which thought becomes a visible and real scene [*scène*], and demands to be played out [*jouée*].

Thought is precisely what has been denied Artaud. This is what he says, at least, with a persistence and precision that are for us his most striking qualities. "It seems to me that I have even forgotten how to think."—"The thinkable whirls inside me like an absolutely detached system, and then returns to its shadow."—"I lose myself in my thought, actually, the way one dreams, the way one suddenly slips back into one's thought."—"I can truly say that I am not in the world, and this is not merely a mental posture [*attitude d'esprit*]."—What he is describing, what he shouts, is precisely the absence of body that should have been this thought, its deterioration and the torment this subjects him to. From the start, there is no compromise for him. He knows, with a strange and unfailing knowledge, that he was born to go to extremes, to challenge the reign of the unconscious which is precisely our society and logic. There where culture is content to record or question this unconscious—continually referring back to a "normality" of reasonable thought—where at best a kind of recognition of duality is established, but a recognition which does not fundamentally change this life or its boundaries [*cadres*], there he maintains himself in "fierce abstinence." He wants the total experience of the double that attacks the most accepted notions of reality. Psychoanalysis? He is aware of it, and speaks of its limited benefits. But: "From the very depths of my life I continue to flee psychoanalysis, I shall always flee it as I shall flee every attempt to circumscribe my consciousness with precepts or formulas, with any kind of verbal organization." In his violence and his refusals Artaud affirms the congenital impossibility he experiences—and that all men consequently experience with him—of compromising with thought, of accepting it as a *means*, as something to *express* and not to be. Everything elaborated in thought is true and real ("all dreams are true"), and for him the dualist division is unintelligible: "I do not separate my thought from my life. With each vibration of my tongue [*ma langue*] I retrace all the pathways of thought in my flesh. . . . There is a spirit in the flesh, but a spirit quick as lightning." This question (this language [*langue*]) and the impossibility it discloses explode all the antagonistic pairs that so reassuringly balance anonymous discourse, the discourse each person agrees to speak in accepting the supplementary illusion that one will find and understand oneself within it. A mythology is a terminology, and we yield to mythology the moment we separate thought from life, language [*la langue*] from its flesh. Always more or less idealistic, Western ideologies could ultimately be summed up in that well-known monstrosity: "*mens sana in corpore sano.*" Which is why one could say that they are all part of the obsession with the *father* (the law, utility) against which Artaud wanted to take radical action. In this respect his position could not have been more perilous, more transgressive or incomprehensible to his contemporaries (and it remains so today). Nevertheless, the essential was doubtless not this demand for a new, concrete, individual stance vis-à-vis thought, this lucid and tortured descent into thought ("there is a knife I do not forget"), this passion for thought whose purpose was to elaborate a true "sieve" for experience rather than any kind of method or system. The essential point here is the affirmative (nonnihilistic) extension and generalization that Artaud will subsequently achieve. The disarray and impotence of his language in relation to his thought (his ex-centric position as victim in relation to that thought which he nonetheless *is*) will in effect lead Artaud to this conclusion: "there are signs in thought"—and his own position of forced acceptance [*acceptation violentée*] was the best way to demonstrate it. He who will later say, "The question for me was to know not what would manage to insinuate itself into the structures [*cadres*] of written language, / but into the warp [*trame*] of my living soul," will achieve this decisive reversal that finally consists not in producing and writing, but in *writing oneself* and producing oneself, of entering the sole reality of signs where one is a sign—a reversal that will give his life (and his writing considered as that life's significant instant) an overwhelming scope and meaning. Where formerly there was a dialogue of thought to be endured, now "the discussion becomes an immense theater." The most obscure and distant point of thought unfolds before us here in broad daylight, confounding our distinction between inside and out. And the theater is precisely the place where thought must find its body.

The theater addresses the "unconscious" directly, whereas "life" represses it. Life is the theater's double, and the degeneration of the latter (the generalization of psychology, of the simple *reflection* that is cinema) shows well enough to what extent we are lived by a life that is not our own. We are, in fact, still "drawing thoughts from our acts, instead of identifying our acts with our thoughts." We have not yet understood that since all things are signs and these signs force us to think, we should, if we want to think, act out precisely these signs. To speak of Artaud's "failure" in the theater is senseless. That failure is inevitable (given our society, our culture), but the fact that this theater can be described makes a great deal of sense, since the undertaking it stands for concerns every person's life. Artaud's persistent description of the "true" theater (as he recognizes it in its oriental forms) undoubtedly means this: *that life should lead thought in order to lead life.* And why, in life, should I not be like this theater? If I belong unknowingly to the thought that I am, this is exactly what cannot fail to occur. To describe the corporeal life of thought is to be on an equal footing with the theater. Eroticism, for example, is the immediate possibility—I can draw on the "black liberty" of the unconscious at will. By successively comparing the theater to the gestures of "nature," to the plague (as manifestation of a generalized mentality [*psychisme*]), to painting (as formalization itself), and finally to alchemy (which is the "materialization or rather the exteriorization of a kind of essential drama"), Artaud unambiguously indicates that the theater he is describing is not different from life, but the detailed, concrete, precise, and compromising life of thought; or in other words a *continuous creation*, a *metaphysics in action*. Metaphysics: "I am very reluctant," writes Artaud, "to pronounce that word." It must be understood that he uses it constantly, in the non-Western, "non-Greek" sense (his references are sufficient proof of that). Theatrical activity is therefore that which must reveal the omnipresence of the language we bathe in. Not a language that is already accessible, codified, and contained by the spoken or written word, but one that comes from and occupies everything, simultaneously overtaking our body and coming from our internal night, at the intersection of space and thought where non-sense becomes sense, and where, properly speaking, we actualize our signs. Gestures, lights, objects, words, etc., everything must be articulated [*s'inscrire*] so as to make us think, everything must be "hieroglyphic," "an intense liberation of signs." For the actor (which we are) and anyone who must think "with his heart," "the body is supported by the breath," "the breath that nourishes life enables one to retrace its stages one by one." The passage through the dream must be accomplished with open eyes: "The events of the dream, directed by my deep inner consciousness, teach me the meaning of the events of the waking state through which naked fatality directs me. But the theater is like one long waking state in which it is I who direct fatality." It is a "dream that eats away the dream," where "ON BOTH SIDES OF THE DREAM / I make my will prevail." And further: "Just as there will be no unoccupied place in space, there will be neither respite nor emptiness in the spirit or sensibility of the spectator" (understood as one who lives and sees that which he thinks). A sentence from one of Artaud's later texts is of interest here, since it underlines the extremely uncommon nature of what we referred to as the space of thought (where we no longer distinguish between fiction and reality in order to remain within a generalized scheme of signs): "Why is the front, which is the only place, envied by the back, even though it is the indefeasible surface whose only state is fullness [*l'inaliénable surface dont le plein est le seul état*]" (and isn't this what painting tells us, when it has a "double meaning"?). This view is stated earlier, moreover, in *The Theater and Its Double*, where it constitutes a practical program: "And in man, [the theater] will bring back not only the recto, but also the verso of the spirit; the reality of the imagination and of dreams will be on an equal footing with life." Henceforth one can say that this global language (whose entry point is gesture) that "aims to contain extension, in other words space," "poetically retraces the path that leads to the creation of language," and that its "source will be tapped at an even more deeply buried and remote point of thought," since words now have their true and partial place, with "something of the importance they have in dreams," as if they have come from "a preverbal state, one which can choose its own language."

    This is not a matter of a derivative activity—as literature, for example, almost always is—or of a complacent irrationalism. It constitutes a demand addressed directly to the unconscious, to have done with what we call the "dream" (as opposed to "reality"), to seize and utilize our thought before it escapes us. Whence the indispensable idea of *cruelty*. Artaud insists on this point: he knows the monumental force of dispossession that one must enter into through one's fear in order to dominate it. Crime is a banal act in that it accomplishes no more than a discharge of force, the production of a blind transfer. As Georges Bataille points out, true violence is mute: the executioner makes no apology for his act, and Sade's revolutionary accomplishment is to have brought about a betrayal of violence through writing at the same time as a breakdown of writing through violence. As a result of this emphatic contradiction, Sade's language can be considered "honesty itself." "Violence and blood having been placed in the service of thought's violence," Artaud can add: "There is no cruelty without awareness [*conscience*], without a sort of applied awareness. It is awareness that gives life's every act its blood-red color, its cruel nuance, since it is understood that *life is always someone's death*." Or again, this sentence, in which we can, in effect, hear the word "thought" beneath the word "play" [*pièce*]. "A play that lacked this will, this blind appetite capable of overriding everything else, visible in every gesture and in every act, and in the transcendent aspect of the action, would be useless and a failure."

The only successful example of integral theater, of the life of authentic thought, will thus be the Balinese theater. It shows us what it means to enter the "mental forest," what it is to be a spirit "ceaselessly trying to take its bearings in the maze of its unconscious," a "purely interior combat," by means of "perpetual allusions to the secret and devious postures of thought."—"The drama does not develop as a conflict between feelings, but between states of mind, which are themselves ossified and reduced to gestures—to structures [*schémas*]."—"From a gesture to a cry or to a sound there is no transition: only correspondences, as if bizarre canals had been etched into the spirit itself."—"Even the least movement of the eye seems to belong to a kind of studied mathematics which governs everything and through which everything happens." Here it is impossible not to mention another description of thought lived fully in a state of "innocence," another protest, however brief and discreet—that of Kleist in *On the Marionette Theater*: "All the limbs are as they must be. They are dead, mere pendulums obeying the simple law of gravitation." Such phrases indicate that here we are beyond and yet *before* particular significations, as it were, that we are in what states itself through and between words, and thus initiates the appearance of *writing*: "This intellectual space, this psychic play [*jeu*], this silence molded of thoughts that exist between the members of a written sentence, is here traced in the spaces of a stage [*l'air scénique*]." In spite of (or thanks to) Artaud's necessary condemnation of the written and above all of the superstition surrounding it, this latter proposition helps us imagine a writing (a "literature") that would enter the theater of thought as a body of *traits*, that would be a "poetics of thought." We are then led to see it as a contemporaneous, fragmentary, fully conscious projection of the space described in *The Theater and Its Double*, as a state of writing in which the material presence of the page, of words and of their relations would be willed and would in a sense belong to the *still to be thought*, would produce a genuine nondistinction between scriptor and reader (who are in the same space). Breaking with a psychology that continually "reduces the unknown to the known," it would then, literally and briefly, open onto the limitlessness of living thought. It would simultaneously be sheer calculation—being elaboration and apprenticeship, invention, of a language, a syntax, a rhythm—and sheer liberty (it would be able to say "from above time"). For if "the gesture that emerges from a noise is like a plain word in a sentence," a plain word in a sentence can indicate the trace of a gesture which for us has just emerged from noise. Henceforth this much is clear: writing is what obliges one to live *in a certain manner*, or it is nothing. To live in a state of ceaseless communication. When Mallarmé addressed "the reader's intelligence" as a function of the text's *mise-en-scène*, when he concluded with "Every thought expresses a toss of the dice" (and if there are signs in thought, all thought expresses signs), he did nothing other than state the principle of this writing. In *Literature and Evil*, a book whose title seems to rhyme with *The Theater and Its Double*, Georges Bataille suggested that this notion of "fundamental communication" defines literature in its voluntary guilt and its sovereignty. Such an option is in no way "abstract," it is rather the

contrary of an idealism, basing itself on a perfectly rigorous and coherent conception: that of *consumption*, which makes "economy the
basis of morality, and the basis of poetry." Likewise for Artaud, reject-
ing the sterile myth of our culture: "To be cultivated," he says, "is to
burn forms, to burn forms in order to achieve life." A communication
with oneself and with an other insofar as this "other" is the unconscious. Now consider Bataille's definition: "A fundamental opposition
exists between *weak communication*, the basis of profane society (of
active society—in the sense in which activity is confused with produc-
tivity), and *strong communication*, which abandons consciousnesses
that reflect one upon the other, or one the other, to that impenetra-
bility which is theirs 'in the last analysis.' "[3] In this context, we can
see how the accusation of "madness" brought against Artaud is quite
simply displaced. The only person who can definitively be said to be
nonalienated is one who in one way or another *communicates* (since
we are obviously in a world of signs, a fact which is daily becoming
clearer—thanks largely to linguistics—on every level). Neither the
"normal man" nor the "madman" actually communicates: they are,
more precisely, communicated, informed, spoken (from without and
from within). In other words, they do not undertake that conscious
transgression of the prohibited (which *wants* to be transgressed), of the
prohibited which is within us before it is outside us—a transgression
which is thus the very definition of strong communication.

Artaud rightly observed that "poetry is anarchic insofar as it calls
into question all relationships between objects and between forms and
their meanings." But at the same time, if it would pursue this questioning, it must bring the full rigor (the "cruelty") of thought into
play. The theater is a "projection and an instigation of conflicts," but
"it is by intellectual paths that it leads us to the reconquest of the signs
of that which is." Like alchemy, it maintains an awareness of "the
philosophical states of matter" in order to "reattain the sublime, but
with drama, after a meticulous and relentless pulverization of every
insufficiently refined, insufficiently ripe form." The Balinese theater,
for example, concretizes "a sort of ultimate note, seized in its evanescence, that would be like the organic aspect of an indescribable vibra-

tion." But the economy of poetry, beyond all system, is surely nothing but this, as it enters this region of dramatic experience where its literal meaning (its consumed meaning) is found.

The strange individual whom Artaud lived to begin with, the being who felt "a kind of pain, a knot at the point where the spirit calls itself forth," who was not and did not want what it thought, who did not want and was not its thought—this being marked out for permanent suffering, "a sort of cyclical and fundamental martyrdom," thus discovers the global and cruel play of all thought in the world, and knows that he is called on to communicate it, to struggle against even the least discernable alienation thus unmasked. From the deepest current, where his spirit froze and was lost, where he could ask himself why red is actually found to be red, why judgment is perceived as judgment and not as pain, where life appeared to be nothing but "an acceptance of the legibility of things and of their connection in the mind"—here he is now on stage, knowing that the destiny of all men and all thought is being played out in him. The change—and the dimension it designates—turns on this word: *acceptance*. An acceptance equivalent to radical rejection (for here it is plainly a matter of a kind of agony lived as an approach to the key of language: "words are a slime that is not illuminated from the direction of being, but from the direction of its agony"). "I struggled," writes Artaud, "to try to exist, to try to accept the forms (all the forms) with which the delirious illusion of being in the world has clothed reality." He writes this just before Europe seizes him and shuts him up—in the wings of an asylum which is what the false theater refuses to allow to speak. He returns from Mexico, where the principle phase of his struggle to revive a body in thought, to live his thought integrally and write himself in it, seems to have taken place. There he saw the dance of the peyote priests, that "lasts throughout the night, from dusk to dawn, but it takes all the night and gathers it, the way one sucks the juice from a fruit, drawing out the very source of its life." He believed that in this dance he saw "the point at which the universal unconscious is sick." In peyote he recognized "the entire trajectory of the neurotic self [*du moi nerveux*]." Artaud's language was never more precise, more decisive, than in the *Tarahumaras*. "On the side near my spleen, an immense void took shape, painting itself in gray and pink like the seashore." Artaud is at the point where for "one who pushes the mental side of things with all his heart . . . every perception unfolds crosswise like cloth," where "each thickness is an idea and the idea a spiritual state [*état du coeur*]." He accomplishes this "emergence into oneself [*sorti en soi*]" in which the unconscious communicates directly with the body, and where, in fact, while "the spleen is the physical echo of the infinite," "the liver seems to be the organic filter of the Unconscious." This *emergence* is precisely what we refuse to accomplish: "Man, / one fine day / *stopped* / the idea of the world / Two paths were open to him: / that of the infinite without / that of the infinitesimal within / and he chose the infinitesimal within." In peyote, in what Artaud's thought understands and translates of peyote (being used not for itself, or as an "experiment," but solely for its energy, which serves to wash a false world from us, to disalienate us, to "whip our innateness"—all functions that belong to the limitlessness of thought, however little one *emerges* from it), the cosmogonic dimension is tangibly rediscovered: "For the Rite of the Ciguri is a Creation Rite and explains how things *are* in the void, how the void is in the Infinite, and how they emerged into Reality and were made." Just as he described the Tarahumara as somehow being conscious of their own unconscious, or in other words of their "other," just as in his "long and interminable battle with the occult" he reaches a life hidden from the surface of life, a life of ciphered signs—now he situates himself in an Adamic experience, or rather in that of the "uncreated man" who no longer has organs as a result of the unveiling of organs. He will later turn this experience back upon European society in the form of an implacable, scatological condemnation indicating his permanent nonappurtenance to this society that functions through repression and exclusion, and that refuses to think itself through to the end in certain areas apparently considered insurmountably foreign. "There where it smells of shit, it smells of being," Artaud will say. Now in our society, does there exist a single thought that does not go out of its way to avoid mentioning *shit*? From good taste to ontology, by way of the flights of pataphysics, everything is done to stop us from thinking our body, and it is precisely this fissure in our digestive, not active, thought that Artaud finally wanted to emphasize with the greatest seriousness and the most good sense. Stigmatizing this society's prohibitions, he dared inform it of its non-existence: "To exist one need only let oneself be, / but to live / one must be someone, / And to be someone / one must have a BONE / not be afraid to show the bone / and to lose the meat in the process." In Mexico he had seen the internal possibility of "making thoughts mount thoughts," of *giving birth to himself*, of simultaneously being himself, his son, his father, and his mother, a claim that could only appear "insane" to familiar (familial) reason. But this familiar reason is linked to organic death, and "one can say that what the mind's reason looks at is always death." "Learning [*science*] has petrified reason." But the body that experiences itself in thought clearly sees other things. It sees, for example, that sexuality must "be put back in its place," that "if there had been no doctors, there would never have been any sick people," and other truths dangerous to state—or which it is better to pronounce in a "scientific" tone of voice if one would maintain one's freedom to come and go. Now given the fact that Artaud indeed said all this, given the fact that in our theater that bestows the title of reality upon itself Artaud passed through what we refer to as "madness," how is it possible not to see the doubling and denunciation that result? Artaud denounced both madness and the society that pronunces the word madness. What we call *madness* is doubtless never anything but what reason refuses to face, what reason itself arouses whenever necessary in order to change itself. In this sense reason is cruel, and Artaud lived it as such within himself, like the very adventure of reason. In so doing he unmasked an attempt to halt thought and language that has been proper to us for centuries, and is now worldwide: "To stop thought outside and study it through what it is capable of doing is to misunderstand the internal and dynamic nature of thought, to refuse to feel thought in a movement of its internal destiny that no experiment can capture. / I call poetry today the understanding of this internal and dynamic destiny of thought." Or: "We are against this rationalization of existence that prevents us from thinking ourselves, in other words from feeling like men, and our idea of man implies an idea of the power [*force*] of thought. And of the dialectical understanding of the power of thought."

Similarly, Artaud demystified that idolatry of culture in which we wallow in an increasingly spectral and somnolent manner. The body within thought watched space move toward it "rock by rock, bush by bush, horizon by horizon"—it was able to enter into a veritable culture in space: "Culture in space means culture of a spirit which does not stop breathing and feeling that it is alive in space, which summons the bodies of space like the objects of its own thought, but which, as spirit, sets itself *in the midst* of space, in other words at its dead center." And it is this culture that art or literature, if they wish to be in any way real, will need to delineate.

Thinking, as we have seen, can be nothing else for Artaud than the act through which we want to be our thought, or in other words the hurried multitude of its signs, that which comprehends and exceeds them, everything we have not yet become within the order of a limited and individual thought. When Artaud speaks of a materialist conception of the spirit supposedly possessed by ancient cultures, it is in order to signify that the distinction between spirit and body (between spirit and letter) is precisely our sickness, and that we fail to be materialist insofar as our body, which is to say our concrete knowledge of our spirit, escapes us. But not to see beyond the body amounts to not seeing the body; for the body must be thought if it is to see itself. Consequently, we have little choice: either we allow ourselves to be thought by idealisms that ignore the body, or by materialisms that are merely inverted idealisms and see nothing but the body, i.e., fail to see it—or else we agree to think our thought and accept the communication it implies, in an experience that admits of no codification, that is "poetry" (whose only rule is the opening up of thought), language lived as such. For we constantly live in a figurative sense, while sense shapes us [*nous figure*], while we *are* language at every instant and on every level.

Artaud described the social, religious, and sectarian obstacles he encountered as spells [*envoûtements*], in order to have done with them, to live himself. The "spell" is what comes from both inside and out, what robs me of my own body, what limits my will to think. In a certain manner, spellbinding (magic) forces play on the unconsciousness in which our codes and grammars maintain us, to the degree that they condition and inform us without being thought. What could be more difficult than thinking the words one speaks, than making "poems become real"? "Grammar has been the affliction of all the so-called great ideas of civilization and culture, that man bears like a yoke that keeps him from advancing." The spirit of the letter prevents us from practicing thought to the letter. The path from the condition "before language" (this *before* being neither temporal nor spatial, but rather qualitative) must pass through the repetitive, submerged organism of digestive humanity and situate me in an organic birth in which man becomes a body-tree, a body-fact: "There is no inside, no spirit, outside, or consciousness, nothing but the body as you see it, a body that continues to be, even when the eye that sees it falls. / And this body is a fact / Me." The language of the body, the body that thought speaks, has to be learned. For one who wants to make a "sharp descent into the flesh," the struggle against spellbinding and servile grammar is a struggle against fear: "If one is to exist, there is a fear that must be overcome, and this means carrying fear, the entire sexual coffer of fear, into oneself, like the complete body of the soul, the whole soul from infinite time, without recourse to any god behind one. And without forgetting any part of oneself." Artaud specified how a sort of universal language unfolds at this point, a language whose projection into this or that [specific] language is necessarily incomprehensible, insofar as we intercept, at this exteriorized moment, only its reversed and parodic image: "All true language / is incomprehensible / like the chatter / of a beggar [*comme la claque / du claque-dent*]." But how could we learn this or that language, this or that ensemble of signs, if we did not know it already? The world I live is that which I speak, which I am capable of stating [*de dire*]—or, as Wittgenstein notes: "*The limits of my language* are the limits of my world." These limits are grammatical insofar as I want to remain within communication— but I know I will not actually reach communication unless I am also the one who denies those limits in a shattering and irreversible moment, and who by means of this affirmation reaches the driving force of meaning [*pulsion du sens*]. "One can invent one's language," Artaud writes, "and make that language speak with extra-grammatical meaning, but this meaning must be valid in itself, that is, it has to come from anguish—anguish that old servant of pain, that buried genital yoke that brings verses out of its sickness: being, and won't let you forget it." Communication's strongest point, the point of thought, is thus the very spot where communication risks failure, and thus it is from noncommunication that I wrest the possibility of a fundamental communication—in other words, despite everything, a "syntax," but a syntax in which "everything must / be set down / to a hair / in a fulminating order." Thus Artaud, who had known the "hidden corners of loss" in his own thought, can speak of this "black pocket" where non-sense, the sense forever to come, both offers and withdraws itself [*se tient, se retient*]—and it is then that thought no longer presents itself as still to be thought, but as thought itself. "Me poet I hear voices that are no longer from the world of ideas. Because where I am there is nothing left to think." This "cogito" seems surprising if we do not understand it as thought's access to what is no longer reflection, to what no longer calls for reflection. The myth of the *idea* is destroyed, and we must "enthrone in its place / the thundering manifestation / of this explosive necessity: / to dilate the body of my internal night / the internal nothingness / of my self / which is night / nothingness / unthought [*irréflexion*] / but which is explosive affirmation / that there is / something / to make room for: / my body."[4]

As a redoubled moment of thought, Artaud's writing maintained itself in this incomparable dimension. "Because from time to time life takes a leap, but that is never written in history, and I have never written except to fix and perpetuate the memory of these gashes, these scissions, these ruptures, these abrupt bottomless drops that . . ."

This sentence ends there—and the *that* loosed into silence indicates and reminds us that language can neither complete itself nor sleep, that a "subject" must live it each time, or in other words leave it in suspension, must write himself in and through it, if he likes, fully aware of the narrow, insurmountable distance by which he makes himself readable. The rest is not silence, but rather belongs to this night that is not the contrary of reason or of day, this night that,

according to Hölderlin, should grant us a speech which is "on-rushing"
and "sleepless,"

> Since to the mad and the dead she is sacred, yet herself remains firm,
> eternal, her spirit most free.[5]

1964

Notes

1. Tr. note: Citations from Artaud are drawn, with modifications, from: *Selected Writings*, Helen Weaver, tr. (New York: Farrar, Straus and Giroux, 1976); and *The Theater and Its Double*, Mary Richards, tr. (New York: Grove Press, 1958). Passages from texts not included in either of these volumes are mine.

2. Note that Artaud's "complete works" (if such an absurd expression may be used in this case) are presently being published by Editions Gallimard. We owe the fine quality and precision of this edition, its notes and indispensable appendices, to an anonymous editor whose careful work merits praise here.

3. Tr. note: See *La Littérature et le mal*, in G. Bataille, *Oeuvres complètes* (Paris: Gallimard, 1970–), 9:312.

4. " 'Reason' in language—oh, what a deceptive old woman! I am afraid we'll never get rid of God because we still have faith in grammar" (Nietzsche, *Twilight of the Idols*). Isn't the "death of God" above all a death of the *final word*, or words as idols that hold us prisoner to words? Thus we rediscover the necessity of a radically new position vis-à-vis language (of a practice beyond the word). Here in any case is how Artaud spoke in order to have done with the "instrument" he wanted to employ: ". . . this instrument will not depend on the letters or signs of the alphabet, which are still too close to a figurative and ocular and auditory convention, / Which has linked sense, linked thought, and which has linked sense-thought, has linked them in terms of a preventative ideation that had its formal tablets written on the walls of an inverse brain. / Since the human brain is only a double that releases and projects a sound for a sign, a sense for a sound, a sentiment for a sign of being, an idea for a movement. . . ."

5. Tr. note: *Brot und Wein*, stanza 2: "Weil den Irrenden sie geheiliget ist und den Toten / Selber aber besteht, ewig, in freiestem Geist." Translated by Michael Hamburger, in F. Hölderlin, *Poems and Fragments* (London: Routledge and Kegan Paul, 1966).

5

The Roof:
Essay in Systematic Reading

Nothing is closed to whoever will simply recognize the material conditions of thought.

WITH THE SELFSAME assured and reasonable gesture, the normal, the cultivated man simultaneously avoids facing death, writing, mysticism, nondomesticated animals, and obscenity. In a more general way, the serious, sensible man bases his life on the awareness of a discontinuity that protects his own existence in the midst of a society which is profane, yet sanctifies the notions of individual and object. The fracture inherent in separated identity, belief in liberty, self-possession, mastery of the inorganic, and in the fragmentation within the limits of the family and person, passes from one organism to another, from one thing to another. Consider, for example, the urban landscape that surrounds us now: an accumulation of superimposed and even rolling boxes that perpetuate corporal separation—a generalized staging of isolation. Ultimately, for our society, the cemetery raises this form of organization to its height—and nothing scandalizes us more than the opening or violation of tombs. Revolutionary movements know this so well that often one of their first gestures is to react

Originally intended for the number of *L'Arc* devoted to Georges Bataille, this text was omitted by the editors of that review on account of its *dimensions*. Or to be more specific, so that the word *dimension* is not taken to mean *length*: on account of its Marxist orientation, since a thought like Bataille's permits a recuperation from which this study wishes to separate itself in no uncertain terms.

against this parody of immortality consecrated to death: in Spain the people exposed the skeletons of the clergy, and in Peking the assembled remains of the Westerners, symbols of colonialism, were recently rebaptized as an "orchard." These acts cannot fail to clash with the settled, well-bred consciousness and heavy tranquillity into which Western man has chosen to withdraw. They constitute a radical profanation that challenges a supposedly irrefutable reality, transforming it into a spectacle, into fiction, into a fetish openly displayed and thus deprived of meaning.

The transition from the discontinuous (from the significant world comprised of individuals and things) to the continuous (manifested by death, violence, revolution) is part of the fundamental play of prohibition and transgression. In historical terms, animality, sacrifice, the deviations [*écarts*] within religion, what has been called "madness" or "eroticism" (although these words are already foreign to us), and finally, in a manner yet to be elucidated, the infinite usage of language ("literature"), have up to now perhaps designated the exemplary loci of this persistent and obscure transition. It is to Georges Bataille that we owe the recovery and systematic study of these movements' coherence: in this sense, *Eroticism* and *La Part maudite* (practical consequences of *L'Expérience intérieure*) sketch out a still-unfinished gesture of thought, the rapid, burning outline of its very economy. "In the widest terms [*Dans son ensemble*]," wrote Bataille, "I perceive a convulsion that brings the entire movement of beings into play";[1] we know ourselves summoned to be this convulsive movement [*convulsion d'ensemble*], although what this position allows us is not to master or see this movement, but rather to mark out its precise range and scope. We are undoubtedly in a dying world—we are that decadent and dying repetition; and thus death has much to tell us, here, today, in this aging, saturated, closed time.

Eroticism is a clear book. But it is also an insistent, repetitive text whose purport escapes us, apparently, because of its extreme simplicity. It is not merely a matter of superficially seeing an apology for "transgression" there. The comprehensive perspective [*vue d'ensemble*] proposed by Bataille, based on the prohibition/transgression relationship, must be clearly situated; these *two words* must be charged with exactly the same value, and it must be made as clear as possible that they possess no meaning save in relation to each other. Therefore the difficulty is this: since the word transgression tends to efface the word prohibition (in a society where the notion of prohibition is practically invisible), we must begin by reaffirming prohibition, and this on a level that Bataille has merely suggested, but which henceforth—to the degree that our culture undergoes a simultaneous weakening and torsion—becomes the surface on which the fate of awakened thought is played out. This level, in Bataille's writing, is that of the apparent discourse/silence opposition and of what must be understood by the ambiguous term "inner experience." One point, however, remains undeveloped here—and perhaps had to remain so—and it is toward this point that we must now proceed, or rather toward this " 'temple roof' from the top of which whoever opens his eyes wide, *without the shadow of fear*, will perceive the interrelation of all oppositional possibilities." The "roof" is not reducible to the ideal "point" Breton designated as the "point" of the spirit from which life and death . . . etc. cease to be perceived contradictorally," inasmuch as it is no longer a question of *spirit* or of *perception* but, in a more material way, of *space* and, above all, *relations*. The difference between these two formulations is crucial (it undoubtedly allows us to understand how Bataille and Breton assume irreconcilable positions vis-à-vis Hegel). Actually, the question is not simply—What can be seen from the "roof"? but—what is this "roof" itself? And in addition: How is it that no one, in principle, is even concerned with thinking that there is a "roof"?

Pseudo-Transgression

Our era, then, on the basis of a scientific self-assurance, believes itself to be the one that has *finally* lifted prohibition (prohibitions) and recognized desire. On the plane of banal, day-to-day activity, this pretension (that of the neo-capitalist society) becomes a demand for the satisfaction of needs at any cost, as well as, concomitant to an unprecedented glut of consumption, a demand for "leisure," for a "return to nature," or indeed for "drugs." What leisure, nature, and drugs have in common is that they place work *out of bounds* [*hors circuit*]: the ensemble of gestures constituting work is taken to be as insignificant and inevitable as the functions of nutrition and excretion, and the psyche becomes the "all-encompassing" milieu of an increasingly hallucinatory fantasy of information. In such a context (which, on the model of "religion, opium of the people," might be described as: "information-ization [*mise en information*], a way to make the people disappear"), there evolves an illusion that limits have been overcome, notably and above all those of sexuality. Sexuality is in effect represented as being henceforth "unmysterious"; exposed and over-exposed, sexuality thus becomes *natural*. However, Bataille writes: "Transgression is different from a 'return to nature': *it suspends* [*lève*] *the prohibition without suppressing it.*" [2] What is the significance of this operation whose gesture is irreducible to classical rationality? Of what misunderstanding is it the permanent and sure index? What is it that seeks recognition in and through it? Let us give one element of our answer straightaway: transgression, which, far from opposing prohibition, completes it; and law, which therefore implicitly demands violation of the law, are, within the social economy that produces "man," within the play [*jeu*] that results in his birth, development, expenditure, and death, the empty "compartments" of what we might call his symbolic organ, as invisible as it is intangible. This is the organ of repetition insofar as it conditions, like so many "moves" [*"coups"*] in the play that governs it, the possibility of passing from a state of belief and internal division to a thought that would know, with an irrational knowledge, that it *alone is responsible* [*en cause*], that in itself it conjoins the complicity and interaction of opposites, that it is, in sum, the basis of conscious selection. Of the two states brought about by this situation—prohibition without transgression or pseudo-transgression that remains blind to [*méconnaissant*] prohibition—the second is thus paradoxically the more disadvantageous. As if the absence of resistance made it impossible to anchor thought, abandoned it to a shapeless and contemptible gratuitousness, incapable of understanding itself in its own movement. In the first case there is either no experience or else it remains unconscious. In the second there is a fantasy of experience, prohibition has disappeared from the field of consciousness, and the resulting "liberation" is no more than the mask for a redoubled repression. Those who live unquestioningly beneath the hand of the law and those for whom the law is nothing are thus in perfect agreement: and it is not difficult to verify this contract linking repressive nullity and libertarian ideology every day. We shall see farther on how this proposition can assert itself brutally in the implicit marriage/homosexuality relation. Which leaves the singular case of prohibition/transgression (what Bataille means by *eroticism*, or in other words "the approval of life even into death") for which no logic seems to have been constituted.

This extraordinary logic is therefore simple and difficult to establish insofar as it challenges, first of all, the scientific knowledge and symbolic logic that organize it as *abstraction*. "By making sexual life innocent, science emphatically ceases to recognize it. It clarifies our consciousness, but at the cost of a blindness." "Most frequently, for science, prohibition is not justified; it is pathological, an indication of neurosis. Hence it is seen *from the outside:* even if we experience it personally, insofar as we consider it unhealthy, we regard it as an external mechanism intruding upon our consciousness. This manner of seeing does not suppress the experience, but it minimizes its meaning. And thus if they are described at all, prohibition and transgression are described as objects, by the historian—or the psychiatrist (the psychoanalyst)." The scientific attitude—the legal attitude—is thus immediately caught in the trap of its logical presupposition, regardless of the progress, the increasingly complex developments and results it obtains: the more it denies prohibition, the more it sees it as contingent, explicable, and formalizable, the more it reinforces prohibition's *manner of being*. "If not observed with fear, prohibition lacks the counterpoise of desire which is its profound meaning. The worst is that science, whose movement requires that prohibition be treated objectively, is based on prohibition and yet refuses it insofar as it is not rational." The culture established by these (our own) presuppositions will thus be a culture of so-called transgression that risks leading us into a sort of defensiveness, an impasse, a stagnation: transgression becomes entirely metaphorical, isolating a knowing subject, a known object, and a knowledge exiled from the ambiguity at the source of all knowledge, from the interior/exterior totality [*ensemble*] where the adventure of its limits is played out.

In order to clarify this difficulty, Bataille resorts to a paradoxical type of statement: he wants to bring us to a point where we no longer differentiate between inside and outside, yet he himself makes a radical distinction between "inside" and "outside." Through his violence, he separates himself as far as possible from any "interiority," and yet he speaks of an "inner experience." He admits the validity of philosophy and science, but the common space he assigns them must be irrevocably separated from philosophy and science. He is not opposed to knowledge (on the contrary), but does not hesitate to rely on a "non-knowledge" ["*non-savoir*"]. From the start, then, his extremely coherent formulation [*mise en forme*] runs a strategic risk of misunderstanding: accusations of "mysticism" and "obscurantism" will inevitably be directed against him. But Bataille addresses himself to reason, and it is reason that he wants to convince of its own active enclosure [*enveloppement mouvante*]. Here he plays the role of other to all discourse, of other to absolute knowledge; in a sense, he plays the "devil" (he wants to be Hegel's "devil"), and does so not to return to some sort of anti-dialectical subjectivism, but in order to summon dialectic onto the very terrain of its wager, at the depths of the dissimulated logic whose language has made it possible. What is at stake is to show clearly—at an equal distance from science and from philosophy, whose antinomy is suspended here—that "scientific" and "philosophical" postures, however justified and necessary, allow the essential to escape. *They must be affirmed,* if for no other reason than to eliminate idle naive attitudes, but the "equal distance" to be maintained from them consequently remains to be determined. This of course is what gives the possibility of playing on "the two sides," of grasping the contradiction of the prohibition/transgression slopes—which are such that we never see them from a distance, but are automatically on the one and/or the other. Though different from the apprehension of an object, this "at an equal distance" (this divided habitation of the equal sign) is nonetheless not a flight into ignorance. Bataille is neither a "man of science" nor a "philosopher," but he is above all not a "writer" or a "poet." What is he? Nothing that can be expressed by a substantive, nothing the society we live in can invest with a positive value without falsification. He is this "we others" summoned by Nietzsche, this "we others . . ." that precedes every qualification and may be followed by "philosopher," "madman," "adventurer," "saint," "criminal," "worker," "savant," "actor," "poet," etc. In this sense, we should recall these phrases: "I am the savant in the dark chair" (Rimbaud), "the science I am undertaking . . ." (Lautréamont)—phrases that tell us that discourse is henceforth to face its irreducible negation, a negation that itself is part of discourse and at work within discourse. Any possibility of a "final meaning" is thus brought into question (we shall examine the role of this *god*), and the overall movement of Bataille's thought functions to introduce us along with him into this absence of an end, to endlessly introduce us, like isolated words thrown into an endless sentence, into what can have no other significance than the consumption and expenditure of an insatiable energy. So that we see how, speaking from without science, he is in effect speaking for science and its future.[3]

Discourse

"Man" has defined himself through work and consciousness, in other words *only subsequent to* prohibition, and consequently he situates prohibition on the outside of laborious rationality: "We have to take the irrational character of prohibitions into account if we want to understand an indifference to logic that always adheres to them. In the irrational domain to which we have limited our inquiry, we must say: 'Sometimes an intangible prohibition is violated, but this does not mean it ceases to be intangible.' We can even go so far as the absurd proposition: 'The prohibition is there to be violated.'" Bataille adds: "This truth seems novel, even though it is based on immemorial experience. But it is quite the opposite of the world of discourse that science derives from." How should the word *discourse* be interpreted here? Undoubtedly we should understand that it corresponds to the noncontradictory linking of semantic elements [*l'enchainement significatif non-contradictoire*], the necessarily unique meaning on which man's identity as consciousness and work is founded. To put it another way, THE WORLD OF DISCOURSE IS PROHIBITION'S MODE OF BEING. This "world" makes language the instrument of a meaning, coordinates statements which have "truth" as their object, and for it prohibition is the signifier itself. What is told [*dit*] by discourse *is not* what discourse tells. Hence the reign of prohibition betrays itself in the accidents of discourse, and hence the "unconscious" (inevitably aroused by the elaboration of the real as conscious, of discourse as consciousness) can ignore contradiction and the "no." Freud's discovery of the "unconscious" has thus long been awaited by a culture and science to which the meaning of discourse can only be exterior. Meaning, therefore, is the object, and "discourse" becomes the effect of a belief in a language that would be able to speak about language just as language speaks about "things," without asking itself whether anything can *really* speak *about* anything else. Actually, we never speak *about* anything, but *with* (or at the same time as) something. To say "something" is to place oneself in the space where this "thing" and the saying [*dire*] that supposedly delimits it coexist without annulling one another. There is nothing in the thing of what is said about it / there is nothing, in what is said, that "belongs" to or replaces the thing. That, perhaps, is the "scandal" we can recognize only by means of a fundamental transgression. A transgression that would recognize the *necessity* of the prohibition to which it is linked—as *history*, insofar as this prohibition alone makes transgression possible by ensuring a hold on the ground where transgression takes place [*doit jouer*].

The "coexistence" we are speaking of is therefore, in fact, a war dialectic in which provisional dominance alternates between prohibition and transgression, according to whether the field of objects and things (the discontinuous) prevails, or whether there is an opening of the dimension that passes beyond [*du franchissement des*] objects and things (the continuous). Now this is precisely where the problematic of eroticism is situated, and first of all the understanding of the need for work and consciousness, science and prohibition: "Insofar as man has defined himself through work and consciousness, he not only had to moderate, but also to repudiate [*méconnaitre*] and sometimes curse his own sexual excess. In one sense this repudiation has led man astray, if not from the consciousness of objects, at least from consciousness of himself. But if he had not first become conscious by working, he would have no knowledge at all; there would still be nothing but animal darkness." Hence eroticism bears the mark of this "transition" from animal to man, and from "animal darkness" to the light of systematic reason there is therefore a leap—that of the sexuality of an animal whose particular gift is language: "Man is an animal that remains 'dumbfounded' ['*interdit*'] before death and sexual union." Discourse is thus the avoidance of fatal sexuality, and "man" is able to come to grips with himself only through the detour of the forbidden [*l'interdit*] (of science), to the degree that he transgresses the world of discourse at one point, and that he makes of this inevitable detour the means by which he confronts his limits. It is, in fact, as if the problem of dialectical materialism's *other side* were now being posed, the reverse face of the dialectical ribbon which would then be "the inner experience" such as it can be thought today without appearing to be a resistance to history.[4] Bataille indicates this in a passage concerning Lévi-Strauss: "We can only grasp being within history: in changes, transitions between one state and another, rather than in successive states considered in isolation. In speaking of nature, of culture, Lévi-Strauss has juxtaposed abstractions; whereas the transition from animal to man implies not only formal states, but also the movement by which they came to oppose one another." We can consider this *movement* as in continual process, although in fact "inner experience" must experience it in order to wrest from it each time afresh its forms. Consequently, a positive and active (scientific, philosophical, political) discourse is answered by an activity interior to discourse (where "literature" assumes a transformational role). The age of religion in all its aspects changes into an age of language that assumes humanity's dark and bloody past and becomes capable of surpassing it as it redoubles it: "Literature, in fact, follows religion and is its heir. The sacrifice is a novel, a tale with bloody illustrations, or rather, a rudimentary form of theatrical presentation, a drama reduced to its final episode, in which the animal or human victim acts alone, but acts out its very death [*joue seule, mais joue jusqu'à la mort*]."

The Sacrifice

Thus we must return to this fringe of our culture that Christianity, linked to industrial civilization (and its congenital "Protestantism"),[5] has constituted as denial and repression. "Piety," says Bataille, "forsook the will to reach the secrets of being through violence." And further: "The misunderstanding [*méconnaissance*] of transgression's sanctity is fundamental to Christianity." Our entire culture is hostage to this insipidity and this diffuse religiosity displaced onto money (Christianity is the least religious of religions), which govern the current morality that presents itself with a show of emancipation lacking any real hold on the gestures of the individual: the image and representation of violence coexist with the narrowness of the Christian rendered unconscious by his civilization, of the cynically moral *and* immoral individual, of the quasi-universal petit-bourgeois who now dominates our societies. Perhaps he mouths the words of violence: "eroticism" is one of the words whose effect is thus neutralized. But the sexual act/sacrifice relation can never, even for a moment, interrupt his pseudo-transgression; for this phantasmatic individual, the eroticism envisaged by Bataille is the intolerable itself. However, "if transgression is not fundamental, then sacrifice and the act of love have nothing in common." But what does "sacrifice" mean here? Bataille writes: "The spirit of transgression is that of the animal god who dies, this god whose death animates violence and is not limited by the prohibitions restraining humanity." It is necessary, then, to understand what this *animal god* signifies, this animal god we will henceforth contrast with him for whom there is a "problem of man" that for us derives from a generalized neurosis.

The "animal god" is that part of us which rejects the reductivity and hierarchization of discourse, the finite lexicon and linear thought overshadowed by a word that supposedly puts an end to words (God).[6] The deified animal, which underlines the "transition" from animal to man (but to a man who consequently has no god), recalls this deep stirring of carnal life that opens directly onto the ground of which it seems to be the multiple and purposeless body. Bataille writes: " 'Animality,' sexual exuberance, is that part of us that prevents us from

being reduced to things: 'Humanity,' on the other hand, in its specificity, from the point of view of work, tends to make us into things at
the expense of sexual exuberance." In the symbolic system, sacrifice
acts as an effective reminder of the fact that prohibition is not imposed
externally, that we divide ourselves through the detour of an in-
side/outside whose only unresolved metaphor remains for us the sexual
act in its connection with language and death. Always, if we want to
tear a thought away from the formal system that constrains us to think,
we must rediscover the power of a *nascent* [*naissant*] world ("prevital
and transbiological," in the words of Lacan, who specifies: "It is thus
that if man comes to think the symbolic order, it is because he is
already held there in his being"[7]), a world that possesses the constitutive function of myth. "The spirit of this nascent world," writes Bataille, "is initially unintelligible: it is the natural world mingled with
the divine; and yet it is easy to conceive of for anyone whose thought
can rise to this movement: *it is the human world which, having been
formed in the negation of animality, or of nature, denies itself, and in
this second negation exceeds itself* [*se dépasse*] *without returning to what
it first denied.*" This "natural world mingled with the divine" should
undoubtedly be soberly interpreted as the signifying (playing [*joueuse*])
envelope of the dialectical process, producing itself on the interior of
play and as a form of play. It is transgression, the space of language's
organic effervescence, the affirmation that takes on the force of negation. It is in sum what Bataille wants to introduce into the scheme
which has forgotten to think, and thus excluded, these major categories: expenditure, consumption, waste, death. Without them, the system of work, of consciousness, of production and science, is clearly
consecrated to non-sense. But it is only on the basis of this constellation of prohibitions (on the basis of the theory that takes them most
fully into consideration—historical and dialectical materialism) that
the former will in turn have a meaning. This "double-play," so difficult to grasp, is essential here: "A great deal of strength is required to
perceive the connection between the promise of life, which is eroticism's meaning, and the luxurious aspect of death. Mankind agrees to
ignore [*méconnaitre*] the fact that death is also the youth of the world.
Blindfolded, we refuse to see that only death guarantees the continual

upsurging without which life would decline." "Viewed globally, human life strives toward prodigality to the point of anguish, to anguish, *to the limit where anguish is no longer tolerable.* The rest is moralizing prattle. How could we not see it, lucid as we are? everything points to it! A feverish agitation within us calls on death to wreak its havoc at our expense." "Sexuality and death are only the most intense moments of a festival that nature celebrates with the inexhaustible multitude of beings, and both signify the limitless waste toward which nature advances as it opposes the desire to endure that is proper to every being." "Nature," for Bataille, is what "advances in a senseless [*insensée*] manner; whereas "the desire to produce at low cost is pathetically human"—"nature" is in no wise a capitalist. On the plane of discourse—which already situates the man/nature relationship and consequently represents the radical level where this economy will have to be thought—the "senseless" in fact announces the end of naturalistic ideology, the end of closed, separated, saving, economizing individuals, shattered and melted by the emergence of the proletariat and the reshaping of all the functions of the fragmented class world. In this sense, Bataille is our most telling witness to this disturbance of the Western World, of its grammatical metaphysics, or *in other words* of a system of discourse for which the hierarchization of utterances, the separation and opposition of concepts, the ignorance of their reciprocal relations, are a kind of *second nature.* Eroticism—the fact that it receives its theoretical statement only today, in the wake of Sade—takes on its full significance here: it is not only what emerges, in history, as the end of the theological, philosophical, and prescientific era—as what clearly *puts an end* to their logical presuppositions—but also the *rape* of the individual constituted by this period, of the organic and economic unity which was its support: "The principle of all erotic activity [*la mise en oeuvre érotique*] is a destruction of the structure of the closed being which, in its normal state, is a participant in this play. . . ." "What does eroticism signify, if not a violation of the participant's being?—A violation bordering on death?—on murder?" In sum, understood as the unveiled abundance and promise of language—as its power of expenditure and gratuity—eroticism functions as a single point where the penetration and destruction of discourse takes place: "The point is to bring as much continuity to the interior of a world based on discontinuity as that world can sustain." But now let us read what Marx says of dialectical materialism: ". . . because its positive comprehension of existing states likewise includes the comprehension of their negation, of their necessary downfall, and because it grasps every fully developed form in the flow of movement and thus in its transient aspect as well, it lets nothing dazzle it, and is, in its essence, critical and revolutionary."[8] This juxtaposition may seem surprising, but it is assuredly what Bataille is aiming at in *La Part maudite*, when he writes: "It is a matter of reaching a point where consciousness will cease to be consciousness of *some thing*. In other words, to become conscious of the decisive meaning of an instant when increase (the acquisition of *some thing*) will resolve itself into expenditure, is precisely *self-consciousness*, which is to say a consciousness that *no longer has an object*."[9] Does this amount to a return to a mystified and mystifying Hegelianism? On the contrary, it seems to us that in his audacious discovery of the "mystical" perspective and its coherence with sexuality, Bataille's admittedly untenable position questions dialectical materialism in a decisive manner, and in such a way as to rule out any return of this latter to a humanistic ideology (which would be a swing back into petit-bourgeois ideology, into the world-wide apotheosis of the so-called scientific, simple-minded, comfortable, docile, shallow, petit-bourgeoisie). "A point must be laid bare where dry lucidity coincides with the feeling of the sacred. This supposes a reduction of the sacred world to that element most purely opposed to the *thing*, or in other words to pure intimacy. And in fact this takes us back, as in the experience of the mystics, to an intellectual contemplation 'without form or mode' opposed to the seductive appearance of 'visions,' divinities and myths. This means . . . a decision in a fundamental debate."[10] The problem is thus to envisage an expenditure that would be this "ocean" where production and knowledge will overflow ("be this ocean, and there will be one," in Nietzsche's words) so as not to betray the very history of humanity in its entirety (and not merely that of Greco-Roman civilization in its pursuit of an illusory subject of absolute knowledge). By carrying our proposition to its farthest consequences, in other words to the categorical *yes* given to dialectical materialism and the science that flows from it, as well as to a demystification of sexuality thought in its irreducible dimension (our civilization's shortcut: there where the mystical and reason find the explanation for their division), we have an opportunity to understand what is announced by means of a detour through other cultures—in time and space, in language and history. We may guess how Bataille justifies taking on the dangerous right to say: "We have been given the power to face death directly, and to see there at last the opening onto the unintelligible and unknowable continuity which is the secret of eroticism, and of which eroticism bears the secret."[11]

The Flesh

This opening is achieved not abstractly, but through the body. Not through the abstract element generally designated by this word, but at the heart of the material mass whose effects, opacity, resistances, and deviations we believe we dominate. The body is what the idea of "man" does not manage to destroy; it is what cries out mutely before the self-assurance of reason and propriety; it is that tapestry in which our shape shifts and alters, the weaving of desire and of the dream, of deep organic life pursuing its work of death; it is the "continuous" from which we fashion a visible, insistent discontinuity for ourselves and for others. The body is that in us that is always "more" than us, that kills its own representation in us and kills us silently. Through discourse and science, we can know this body's conspicuous activities, its contingencies, modifications, uses, and speech; in sum, its formal activity. But only eroticism gives us access to its *flesh*, in other words not to a "substance" but to its own inscription, to the excess which is this ungraspable inscription's relation to itself. "The flesh is the born enemy of anyone haunted by Christian prohibition. But if, as I believe, there exists a vague and global prohibition opposing sexual freedom in ways that vary with time and place, then *the flesh* is the expression of a return of this threatening freedom." Or in other words, the flesh presents the upright and self-contained body with an "impersonal plethora," just as "poetic" language appears to scientific discourse as the ultimately "repulsive" activation [*mise en jeu*] of the subject of discourse. In "the flesh" we can no longer pretend to be anything other than one separate element, withdrawn from itself and above itself, which is undoubtedly what the symbolic act of sacrifice served to indicate: "What the external violence of sacrifice revealed was the inner violence of being, seen under the aspect of bloodshed and disembowelment. This blood, these life-filled organs, were not what anatomy sees: only an inner experience, not science, could reconstitute the feeling of the Ancients." An inner experience—let us understand: an experience of corporal writing (and it could be shown how, from *Juliette* to the *Chants de Maldoror*, to *The Theater and Its Double* and *L'Histoire de l'oeil*, all of modern literature is haunted by this real dimension, so much so that the body has become the fundamental referent for its violations of discourse). An experience accessible today only in and through language, in and through which sexuality must either constitute itself or give up what it is there to "teach." Our loss of contact with gesture, with food ("We no longer eat anything but prepared, inanimate meats, abstracted from the organic seething where they first appeared. Sacrifice related the fact of eating to the truth of life revealed through death"), indicates here the incommensurable distance separating us from the explosive nudity from which we "come." If we had a history of disgust and revulsions, we could perhaps come to know what possibilities our consciousness has failed to pursue, and it is Sade, more than any anthropologist, who set about to assemble that history through the sheer force of his freedom. In fact, if Bataille is right in noting that "there is no form of repulsion in which I do not discern an affinity with desire," how is it possible not to see that we ignore our desire to the same degree that our revulsions still victimize us without our suspecting it? How, in our will not to equate the extremes of attraction and repulsion, of pleasure and pain, can we not perceive the shape of what becomes a limit within which we think and carry out a circular and repetitious journey? The thought Bataille is questioning is well described by the expression "that goes without saying [*cela va sans dire*]." As a rule, it *goes without saying* that any human animal will turn aside without a word from certain situations, from certain acts, certain substances: "We believe that an evacuation disgusts us because of its stench. But would it stink if first of all it had not become the object of our disgusts?" . . ."the strange aberration which is disgust, that touches us at our weakest point, and whose contagion comes down to us *from the first men* through countless generations of scolded infants." Most often, we prefer to ignore or deny those "low" elements which our humanity shrinks from. We use a moral adjective to rid ourselves of those who accept them without restriction or remorse. We even go so far as to lose consciousness when insistence on this point becomes too intense. Bataille never ceased examining this "marriage" of high and low, in William Blake ("this man was never priggish"), in Michelet (interrupting his work to go and inhale the odor of urine), and Proust (and the "story of the rats," which virtuous biographies present as secondary or accidental). "I will never forget," writes Bataille, "what connects the violent and the marvelous to the will to open one's eyes, to face *what is happening, what is.*" "To open the body"—or "to make the body flower," as the early Mexican texts put it—thus consists in wanting "to equate oneself with *what is,*" not under the cover of this or that sly, unconscious perversion, a shameful accomplice to its opposite (the dignity/shame pair is pulverized forever), but in a redoubled tearing where thought intervenes as the trace of the tear itself. It is just as negative, in sum, not to feel anguish, nausea, and horror, as it is to be limited by these sentiments. "There is nothing sickly about these sentiments; but they are, in the life of man, what the chrysalis is to the mature animal. Man's *inner experience* is given in that instant when, breaking the chrysalis, he becomes aware that he tears himself, not something exterior that resists him. His overcoming [*dépassement*] of objective consciousness, which was bound by the wall of the chrysalis, is linked to this reversal." Now this tear cannot be thought (written) unless we deliberately associate *jouissance* and horror rather than believing we rise above horror through mastery, only if we know the price of "respect," if we acknowledge our physical participation, an acknowledgment that actually corresponds to an extreme "delicacy" (as Sade put it), diametrically opposed to the criminal gesture it denounces (the real executioner is inevitably he who fails to be a symbolic executioner, in other words his own ecstatic victim). "The essence of eroticism is the inextricable association of pleasure and prohibition. In human terms, prohibition never appears without the disclosure of pleasure, nor does pleasure ever appear without the feeling of prohibition." Eroticism is irreducible contradiction (symbolic furor/real delicacy), it is what must be hidden as the *mise en scène* of this absolute contradiction, what must be excluded from a social system that is based on the identity and conjuring away of opposites. Eroticism is the anti-matter of realism. Prohibition and transgression in fact are not "identical" (no more than *jouissance* and horror), but related through a contradictory redoubling: the prohibition is never "eliminated," never definitively transgressed, and it is here that a new logic must come into play. The erotic "crisis" presents us with a series of signs whose properties are incompatible: "The development of signs has this consequence: eroticism, which is fusion, which displaces our interest toward an overcoming of personal being and of all limits, is expressed nonetheless by an object. We are confronted by this paradox: an object signifying the negation of all objects' limits, an *erotic object*." And this object has a name: the *detour*, the textual detour, the written detour toward death.

Woman

Bataille insists on one particularly important point: "The prohibition against sexuality is general, universal; particular prohibitions are variable aspects of it." The universality of the incest taboo, for example, demonstrates the hidden universality of the prohibition against obscenity. If "incest is the first testimony to the fundamental connection between man and his negation of sensuality or of carnal animality," if this testimony is, in a sense, "spoken" by man (and introduces him to speech), then obscenity (bearing on the *excreta*, for example) is part of an ultimately silent level. "Fundamentally, man denies his animal needs. This is the point most of his prohibitions bear upon, and whose universality is so striking and seems to go so much without saying that it never raises a question: *Therefore there exists an aspect of the transition from animal to man so radically negative that it remains unspoken.*" Incest is the simple "eruption" of this silence into humanity's system of exchanges and symbolic economy; analysis of it will thus cast light on the implicit structures of this humanity, but it may also hide their "silent" modality from us. A "normative" presupposition obstructs most research here: we accept as norm, or as anomaly, that which is based on a mute avoidance. That the norm explains or punishes the anomaly while implicitly recognizing it, or that the anomaly consequently claims its rights by recognizing the norm, thus amounts to *the same thing*. The most striking proof is this: we now know that marriage does not occur as the action of "partners," but as a transaction between a "giver" (father, brother) of the woman and "a taker." Marriage—normative heterosexual activity, "the aspect of economic association geared toward reproduction"—is in fact (as becomes immediately evident once the analysis is carried a bit farther[12]) based on a rite serving to exorcise homosexuality. Its function is less to regulate man/woman relations than to prevent both incest and homosexuality (unknown in animals). Implicit although never expressed in Bataille's text, this illustrates how it is possible for what is avoided to become obsessional and thus gradually to "penetrate" consciousness; these are the effects of the *detour* through which we see that woman plays a decisive communicational role. Marriage and homosexuality are in effect homologous; in either case we can say that woman remains "prohibited." Which amounts to saying that, since a society without marriage—and thus without exorcised homosexuality and incest—is unthinkable, woman—since the signifier is prohibition itself—acts as the figure for prohibition. "Women," Bataille writes, "have accepted the restricted meaning of their fecundity and their work." And the feminine attitude is thus modeled after the social form of the prohibition's "manifest invisibility": *"To offer oneself is the fundamental feminine attitude*, but the initial movement—the offering—is followed by one that pretends to negate it." "It is through shame, feigned or not, that a woman accepts the prohibition that founds humanity through her." Woman therefore signifies the compromise that humanity establishes between prohibition and transgression, a compromise which, through "marriage," is transpierced by the possibility of erotic violence; not only does she assume the role of the (pure) mother and the (impure) animal, of respect and the violation of respect (of "sexual frenzy and childcare"), but she lends her consistency to a structure of exclusion within which a resistant milieu—a stage [*scène*]— may be constituted in terms of its potential for reversal. "What matters essentially is that there exist a milieu, however limited, where the erotic is unthinkable, and, conversely, moments of transgression when eroticism constitutes a reversal." Woman is thus depositary of the "social secret" insofar as, without thinking of them as radically incompatible, this category allows the coexistence of opposites that produce their effects in relation to each other. "There would be no eroticism without its converse, respect for prohibited values (There would be no full respect if the erotic gap [*écart*] was neither possible nor seductive)." The "spouse" becomes the mother a conscious or unconscious homosexual respects, and *in relation to whom* he lives the radical prohibition inscribed in woman as the matrix of her own body (as the figure of the signifier). But therefore woman also bears the opportunity for the only possible transgression, that which affirms the prohibition, which effects the signifier itself (and its incestuous figure): "Respect is undoubtedly only the detour of violence. On the one hand, respect organizes the milieu where violence is prohibited, and on the other, it provides violence with the possibility of an incongruous eruption into domains where it is no longer permitted." This "double" aspect of woman is dramatized not only in Bataille's novels, but also in this passage from *Eroticism*, which must be cited in full:

Only our experience of banal sexual activity, of its discrepancy from conventional social conduct, allows us to recognize an *inhuman* aspect in that activity. The plethora of the organs unleashes mechanisms foreign to normal human conduct. A rush of blood reverses the balanced life functions. Abruptly, a rage seizes one's being. Although the rage is familiar to us, we can easily imagine the surprise of someone who had no knowledge of it and who, by some device, had secretly witnessed the amorous transports of a woman whose dignity had impressed him. He would see a disease, analogous to that of mad dogs. As if some rabid bitch had taken the place of the personality who received him with such distinction . . . Even the word disease is not strong enough. For the moment, personality is *dead*. Its *death*, for the moment, gives full reign to the bitch, who profits from the silence of the other's *absence in death*. The bitch *comes* [*jouit*]—comes as she cries out—in response to this silence and this absence. The return of personality would freeze her, would bring an end to the sensual delight that has seized her.

Play

Such is the so-called "dualistic materialism" of Georges Bataille, which does not posit opposites destined for reconciliation in identity or unity, but from the very start *two* principles, a "two" not coming from "one" but preceding it. Denis Hollier notes that this dualism, "instead of positing two principles within the world, posits two worlds," and that "it is in the opening of this duality, which it defines as between-*two*, that dualist thinking situates itself and exerts its tension."[13] An untenable position, and one that could be described as deliberately "false," a position that locates itself at the limit of all "real" thought. This dualism irreducible to unity mimics the economy of language divided by the concept of the sign, but "divided" according to theological and ontological presuppositions. To devalorize this division while affirming an irreducible contradiction (as any "materialism" must) must entail, when generalized, the disappearance of the concept of the sign (signifier/signified) or what Bataille calls the "execution [*mise à mort*] of language." The only system of thought that resembles this method which is so alien to our own mode of reflection would be Chinese thought: the yin and the yang are in effect *immediately* two, and Tao has no conception of a unity (and even less of a God), being rather the "milieu" in which contradiction produces itself. The chain of dualities emphasized by Bataille—diastole/systole, compression/explosion, prohibition/transgression, etc., where each element *ignores* the other but exists only in opposition to it—is situated in this perspective, which remains "incomprehensible" for those who do not lend themselves to this "putting to death" of knowledge (linked to the separation of the sign) by nonknowledge (which announces eroticism's "development of signs")—there where "the unknown causes laughter." Bataille writes: "And thus what emerges from the death of thought is not precisely a science, but what I might call a study of sovereign moments . . . What characterizes such a study is the fact that it cannot be undertaken without first-hand experience." "Such an experience is necessarily prepared for, but it is not that simple to bring about an abyss, or rather the appearance of the abyss constitutes a rupture at once willed and undergone only involuntarily." Thus we see the concept of *play* affirmed and resolutely maintained: "My thought has but one object—play, in which my thought, the work of my thought, annihilates itself." This position is not intended to establish a "philosophy of play"—for play, at this moment, *is not a symbol* (does not refer to "a world")—but, as "major play," aims for "non-knowledge . . . the indefinable, what thought cannot conceive." [14] Here it might be better to speak of an *objeu* [object/play], as does Ponge, that is, of "a verbal activity with neither laudatory nor pejorative coefficients." If play is changed into a philosophy of play, we return to a "minor play" that can no longer be *the end* of serious activity; play becomes derivative, we fall back into a unity where the word "play" replaces the challenged unity. The only way to indicate major play outwardly will therefore be to maintain a complete materialism of the discourse of play, an enouncement in which the enounced are always bound to their context, as far as possible from any "truth," even the truth just stated. In this way language presents itself as the source of its own destruction, as the liberation, rather than the expression, of all possible "referents." The "silent wakefulness" of eroticism—which is consciousness of self as opposed to that of things, and "reveals itself in its accursed aspect"—is this *passage* by way of the expressive detour: "In order to attain intimacy (that which is profoundly within us), we can undoubtedly, we must, pass through the detour of the thing it is mistaken for [*pour laquelle elle se fait prendre*]." Language, being civilization, is actually based on prohibition; in principle it denies violence a voice, as the object of a negation that repudiates [*méconnait*] what it writes despite us and through us: "Without trembling—without cheating—human life cannot follow the movement that draws it toward death. I have shown it cheating—swerving aside—along the paths of which I spoke." "If we want to bring language out of the impasse in which this difficulty holds it, it is therefore necessary to say that violence, which belongs to all of humanity, has in principle remained voiceless, that humanity as a whole thus lies by omission and that language itself is based on this lie." A *fundamental proposition*. Fundamental, for it defines a new consciousness capable of scrutinizing the texts of official history and discovering what they exclude, what they censor, what their gestures serve to exorcise. Fundamental, because it reveals the collusion between "positive" discourse and what it implicitly excludes, which is thus reinforced and effectively redoubled. Fundamental, finally, in that it shows us the dialectical effect of the "human" that unfailingly arouses its corresponding "inhuman." It is this new attitude toward texts that Marx, Nietzsche, and Freud have opened up into a history that we are now obliged to enter. In this they have a radical predecessor: Sade. "Sade . . . writing, refusing to cheat," comments Bataille. "Through the detour of Sade's perversity, violence finally enters consciousness." Batille writes: *finally*. It is as if the paradoxical burden of the prohibition/transgression pair had *awaited* a bringing to consciousness, a consciousness which by the same token arrived quite "late." As if we could finally grasp how society and history are actually the indirect [*détournée*] (filtered) form taken by violence (force) in order to penetrate the consciousness fabricated by this society and history. As if writing were *the form of this detour*, so that only an act of writing, carried to an extreme, could reveal both the lie of history (its fiction) and its truth (which is never the truth sponsored by this lie). As if the true/false pair had ceded its place to a physics of the written gesture in which the written is traced by the transgressive body itself, disappearing into its writing and writing history as a betrayal of violence (i.e., violence both abandoned and seized by the throat). This is the perspective announced by the Freudian "scene of writing" analyzed by Jacques Derrida,[15] the perspective that allows Louis Althusser to indict the religious myth of reading and to show how Marx broke "with the Hegelian conception of the whole as a 'spiritual' totality, to be precise, as an *expressive* totality." It permits him to suggest that "only since Marx have we had to begin to suspect what, in theory at least, *reading* and hence writing *means*."[16] And it is this perspective, finally, that opens up the possibility of a real efficacity for Nietzschean writing, which Bataille never ceased to explore. What is suppressed here is the illusion of self-presence, of a "conciliatory" presence that can no longer appear to us as anything but the result of an unacknowledged [*méconnue*] desire. What appears here is emphasized in these phrases from Nietzsche: "One needs to lose respect for the whole, to crumble the universe," and "I like knowing nothing about the future." And Bataille: "Beyond the annihilation to come, which will put an end to the being I now am, who still awaits being, whose very meaning is less being than awaiting being (as if I were not the *presence* I am, but the future I await, and which nevertheless I am not), death will announce my return to the purulence of life. Thus I can anticipate—and live in expectation of—this multiplied purulence that anticipates and celebrates the triumph of nausea in my person." Research into the mystical has revealed this "kinship" between "the saint and the voluptuary," a kinship that eludes science (and psychoanalysts in particular, since "these states . . . do not enter their field of experience") and challenges traditional humanism. The Christianity that has always been the enemy of the mystical (Eckhart) and of science (Bruno), and above all of their coherent duality, has thus condemned science to a humanistic blindness and religion to a servile obscurantism.[17] But "an ultimate possibility of convergence"— which does not mean of unification—can be glimpsed: hostility to what Christianity represents must therefore be emphatic, and all the more emphatic if one is to understand what its social function has served to hide, and the mystical must be stripped of its neuropathic "visions," imaginings, and hallucinations. For Bataille as for Nietzsche, the mystical is the locus, not of a "state," but of a *direct* ("annihilating") transition to theoretical and practical awareness [*connaissance*]; it is the index of a position which is distinct from that of conventionally meaningful signification [*l'articulation signifiante*], of a stance which is other in relation to language (what Nietzsche indicates with: "coordination—instead of *cause* and *effect*," as well as "We belong to an inverted world, for now all content appears to us as purely formal— including our life"). This means that "two worlds" (the two slopes of the "roof") are affirmed as being irreducible the one to the other, in such a way that an increase in the rational entails a like increase in the intensity of its senseless ground [*fond*]. This "ground" is silent, deprived of all symptomology: "The deepest pains are those that cries do not betray, and the same holds for the inner experience of being's farthest possibilities which is the mystical: 'sensational' instants do not correspond to a developed experience." In fact, the experience in question is not one of the elements of discourse (to call it "the mystical" is to say far too much), it does not intervene in discourse as a "something" (to express), and it has no other character than to provoke a mutation of discourse, a cleavage and threshold in its apparent form. Nonetheless, the unmasking of mysticism (in the word's historical sense) and eroticism, and the critique of their foundations, are the most effective weapons against naturalistic ideology, insofar as it has emphasized the prohibition of death at the expense of genetic activity—which is thus seen as relatively unimportant. The direct and sliding confronting of death (the mystical) as the serious and tragic, associated with sexuality (eroticism), is consequently banished: to laugh at death is forbidden, but pleasure has become a laughing matter. This is why, says Bataille, "eroticism viewed seriously, tragically, represents an inversion [*renversement*]." But we quickly see how writing has now taken over this inversion, how it henceforth has the same status, the same function, and, ultimately, the same meaning as eroticism: excluded, contriving its own exclusion. We better understand how intolerable it is to any ideology that reduces language to an instrument (of a knowledge [*savoir*], a "real"). Tragic writing (tragic not in its "expressive" aspects, but in the ordered play to which it condemns whoever surrenders to it) finally carries on the work of transgression.

Excess

How can this writing be recognized? What distinguishes it from "literature" taken in the restricted sense (as production of an "*oeuvre*")? Why can it appear only beneath the mask of literature, and not as science or philosophy? Why, when it is perhaps *the* science and philosophy of its time, is it destined to wear this mask of literary gratuitousness? The phases of Bataille's writing and the strategic arrangement he adopted ("obscene" novels, journals, essays) show that he not only "wrote" but in fact elaborated a system of reading inside and around this writing; a system capable of making each text the outside or absent center of another text, thus making his own writing non-unifiable and separated from itself, like the "two worlds" of which it is the reverse face. To link one's writing to obscenity [*Ne se faire lire qu'à partir de l'obscenité*] (prohibition) is to indicate clearly that any other reading will be repressive. It is also to emphasize the *disastrous* war that results from our culture's definition of literature as "gratuitousness." "The specialist can never really deal with eroticism": this phrase is directed to the monovalent writing of scientific or philosophical discourse. But: "Philosophy is the sum of the possible, in the sense of a synthetic operation, or it is nothing" is directed to the nullity of the writer who believes himself beyond philosophy, work, and logical knowledge as a whole. The savant and philosopher will not fail (indeed, they have not failed) to declare Bataille a pseudosavant, a pseudophilosopher. Likewise, "oeuvre"-enthusiasts and "writers" will be incapable of grasping the amplitude of a body of work ultimately so un-"literary." But we can leave time to sort out these names (which is to say, these languages); what is certain is that the words Bataille traced across the literature, science, and philosophy of his time have yet to find their future.

"The *specialist* can never really deal with eroticism . . . For anyone who cannot avoid his own nature [*se dérober*], anyone whose life is open to exuberance, eroticism is the personal problem par excellence. At the same time, it is, par excellence, the universal problem." The personal (diaries, novels) and the universal (essays) form in effect two worlds which, like those of prohibition and transgression, bring each other into existence, ignore each other, and form a "roof" which in principle is inaccessible. On one side we have expenditure, the possibility of a written awakening, the instant violently torn open, the *I* that touches the body over against it and the opposition of its own body; on the other, historical inquiry, insistently lucid dialectical argumentation. The "senseless" thus becomes the moment when opposing terms pass into each other without ceasing to remain in opposition, the interval in which all things *have* the same meaning without anything any longer having *any*, where the power of the continuous seizes us, announcing what will be our death as it abandons us to nudity. But to write the senseless, *to make it write itself*, to produce it in its integrity, is at the same time to show that it does not exist, that in dismembering the world we play at our own murder, that we are also, in fact, the stretching, quartering, and fracturing that destroys us. Clearly then, what is ultimately at stake here is a WE: theory can be written only in terms of a community without classes where the only distinction will be the contradictory disposition for work and for transgression, the ability to employ a doubled language that, instead of believing it understands itself, will multiply, renew, reverse, and negate itself: the "novel" becomes a detour toward theory, itself submitted to the "silent awakening" whose form is writing.

"In agreeing to compete, I have personally felt it necessary to accept the difficulties of both options, that of transgression as well as that of work" . . . "It is difficult to imagine the life of a philosopher who would be continually, or at least quite often, beside himself [*hors de soi*]. *The act of holding ourselves open to a possibility bordering on madness (this is the case with any possibility connected to eroticism, to whatever is threatening, or more generally to the presence of death or holiness) continually subordinates the work of reflection to something other, where, precisely, reflection halts.*" What Bataille says to us is spoken from the very brink where the death drive, in its indiscernible eroticism, takes on meaning [*se fait signifiante*]—in other words simultaneously "exceeding the limit ["*sortie des limites*"] and "inconceivable." If death is "inner" for the being that dies, so that through death he "emerges" ["*sort*"] in the ungraspable form of his desire; if the being that dies dies in no *other place* than the signifier that animates him, then the desire for death (which irrigates the physics of the written gesture through and through) unmasks the substitution that sets us upon the "rails" we inevitably follow: "Not only do we renounce dying: we annex the object to the desire, which was actually for death, we annex it to our enduring life. We enrich our life instead of losing it." The continual artifice consists in repositing the limit, in displacing it, in once again distinguishing between container and content because powerless to transpose ourselves into a content becoming an overflowing container:

Let us suppose then that philosophy truly laughs at philosophy; this supposes discipline and the abandonment of discipline. At this moment the sum of possibles comes totally into play, and the sum is a synthesis, which is not simply an addition, since it arrives at this synthetic view in which human effort reveals a powerlessness, in which it relaxes in the feeling of its powerlessness without a regret. Without discipline it would have been impossible to reach this point, yet this discipline is never pushed to the end. This truth is experimental. *In every case, man's mind, his brain, is reduced to the state of an overflowing container, burst by its contents.*

The breaking, the tearing of the "chrysalis" thus forces the disappearance of the fantasy of domination, exploding the idealist dialectic as veil and revelation of an "absolute spirit": as the "approval of life even into death," eroticism traverses death in THE LUMINOUS FORCE OF OBSCENITY. A word, an object, planted alive within death like so much *yes* in the face of death, or rather a series of words or objects *falling* in a fatal orgasm—at which point, paradoxically, thought is freed for its concrete, political tasks: *"The point is to know whether desire is not more in keeping than specialization . . . with the essence of philosophy."* If indeed this is so, then we can begin to see the meaning of this other phrase of Bataille's (from *L'Impossible*): "As it died, logic gave birth to incredible [*folles*] riches."[18] These "riches" are what becomes available to thinking that both affirms and exceeds the boundaries of a *finite lexicon* (Nietzsche: "Logic itself is for me a sort of irrationality and chance"). Such writing (eroticism) is the movement through which it becomes impossible to take any one word as "superior" to others, as their aim or pole: any other discourse posits a god. Or we can say that a system of formal relations, a PROCESS, corresponds, according to a "dying" logic, to an EXCESS that continually puts that logic, any logic, to death. The process constitutes and produces an excess that consumes the process and founds it. If "the supreme philosophical questioning coincides . . . with the summit of eroticism" (this summit remaining *empty* and having no other function than to pour its effects back into a logic and a dialectic), then we must know that the moment of *summation* [*l'ensemble*] touches with that of *dispersal*: "And thus language, as it assembles the totality of what matters for us, at the same time disperses it." The "dissolution" of philosophy into the world of play (and here we have the dissolute philosophy of Sade) is therefore comparable to the "putting to death" of language—it *is* this dissolution of final meaning, a meaning that intervenes only in order to oppose itself to silence (to death): "Philosophy does not emerge [*sort*] from itself, it cannot emerge from language. It utilizes language in such a way that silence never follows it." A major irony: philosophy—or to simplify somewhat, and according to a confusion authorized by Bataille himself, let us say "shared thought"—believes it "emerges from language" while in fact it simply revolves around its refusal of death, signified by a "master word" (a "final word," a "last word"). For it is not a matter of "emerging" from language, but of delivering it over to *its* death: "To make transgression the foundation of philosophy (and this is the bearing of my thought) is to substitute a silent contemplation for language. *This is the contemplation of being at the summit of being.* Language has in no way disappeared. Would this summit be accessible if discourse had not revealed its approaches?" In effect then, what is at stake here is a redoubled affirmation of language (an approval of language even into the silence which is none other than its absent shape): "What would we be without language? It has made us what we are. It alone, at its limits, reveals the sovereign moment when it no longer rules." *This moment?* "In this moment of profound silence—in this moment of death. . . ."

The Roof

I would even say here that, for me, philosophy is also the execution of language. It is also a sacrifice. The operation I have spoken of, which effects the synthesis of all possibles, is the suppression of everything language introduces that replaces the experience of seething life—and of death—with a neutral domain, an indifferent domain.

I have attempted to speak a language equal to zero, a language that would be the equivalent of nothing, a language that returns to silence. I am not speaking of emptiness, which sometimes seems to me a pretext for adding a specialized chapter to discourse, but of the suppression of what language adds to the world. I feel that this suppression cannot be rigorously carried out. . . . From this point on, everything that does not lead us away from the world (in that sense in which, beyond the Church, or against the Church, a kind of holiness leads us away from the world) would betray my intention . . . This experience has its own discipline . . . first of all opposed to any form of verbose apology for eroticism.

I shall conceal myself [*me déroberai*] in such a way as to impose silence. If others take up this task, they will accomplish no more, and their speech, like mine, will be cut short by death.

These three propositions by Bataille (the last drawn from his *Nietzsche*) show well enough the range and nature of his project [*calcul*]. But what is this "silent contemplation," if not another mask of the writing whose name we have been seeking? What is this "speech cut short," if not the castration of the written trace? What does it mean "not to limit *what does not know what the limit is*," if not the very posture of one whose excess excedes excess? "My death, which will prove how impossible it was for me to limit myself to being without excess . . .": in copying out (or reading) these words, what do the signs *I* and *my* become? They take on a transparency here that opens up air breathed beneath the sky, in the city, on the earth where the "human" convulsion casts off the shape of a promised humanity from the aleatory whole [*jeu d'ensemble*] it does not want to see, a more and more rational and incomprehensible humanity (as incomprehensible and massive as the stormy sky I see through the leaves in front of me now). "So true is it that *creation* is inextricable from, irreducible to any other movement of the mind than the certitude, being exceeded, of exceeding." Just as eroticism consists in playing the other while knowing that one loses oneself in the reverse side of this play, "man," in the play of writing, is the figure of a *replay* [*rejeu*] that consists in transforming the play as he retraces signs, like ideograms, *on the inside of his hand*: "I do not reject the knowledge without which I would not write, but this hand that writes is *dying*, and through the certainty of death, it escapes the limits accepted in writing (accepted by the hand that writes, but refused by the one that dies)." Whoever writes and copies these lines will in turn leave a skeleton and a string of words behind him. The "two hands" in question can then, for a moment, in their swiftly effaced contradiction, become the emblem of this "roof" of writing, this roof that only *an other* may finally observe: "Whoever you are who read me: take *your* chance [*joue ta chance*]. As I do, patiently, just as in the instant I am writing, I play you."

1967

Notes

1. Tr. note: *L'Impossible*, in *Oeuvres complètes* (Paris: Gallimard, 1970–), 3:102.

2. Unless otherwise indicated, citations from Bataille are drawn from *L'Erotisme* [(Paris: Minuit, 1957). Eng. ed., *Eroticism*, Mary Dalwood, tr. (London: John Calder, 1962); translations from this edition have been extensively modified.]

3. "The savant speaks from without, as an anatomist of the brain . . . But I speak of religion from within, as a theologian does of theology. . . ." "[Occultist presuppositions] make those who accept them seem like a man who knows about arithmetic, but refuses to correct his mistakes in addition . . . I am not a man of science to the degree that I speak of inner experience, not objects; but the moment I speak of objects, I do so like men of science, with the appropriate rigor." "It is necessary to make a sharp distinction between studies that extend themselves *as little as possible* toward *experience*, and those that approach it boldly. We must admit that if the former had not been done in the first place, the latter would have remained condemned to a gratuitousness we know only too well. There is little doubt that a condition which seems adequate to us today has not existed for long." The *condition* Bataille refers to here is Mauss's formulation of the prohibition/transgression pair. The *experience*, on the other hand, functions to move beyond [*déborder*] scientific rigor. The science Bataille outlines is thus an *Economy*: its sectors might be designated by the words: "the mystical" / language / eroticism / politics. It goes without saying that a savant is necessarily cut off from the experience of "mysticism," and that only someone free from institutional allegiances can approach the subject without prejudice.

4. It can be observed here that Bataille took adequate precautions to render his words useless for spiritualism or idealism, and that any attempt at falsification along these lines is destined to fail: ". . . in [Marx's] provocative clarity, one may perceive a complete discretion and an aversion to religious forms in which the truth of man is subordinated to hidden ends. Marxism's fundamental proposition is to completely liberate the world of *things* (of the economy) from all elements exterior to *things* (to the economy): by pursuing the possibilities implicit in *things* to their furthest point, by unreservedly obeying their requirements, by substituting the "government of things" for the government of private interests, by carrying to its ultimate consequences the move-

ment that reduces man to a *thing*, Marx decidedly wanted to reduce things to man, and man to the free disposition of himself" (*La Part maudite*). [In *Oeuvres complètes*, 7:129.] It must be clearly noted that Bataille not only opposes the manner in which bourgeois democracies reconcile Hitler and Stalin, but unreservedly approves of the Communist revolution and finds no words severe enough for the reactions of the bourgeois individual faced with it: "In truth, a marvelous mental chaos proceeds from Bolshevism's action in the world, and from the passivity, the moral inexistence it has encountered" (*ibid.*). [P. 144.]

5. *Protestantism* refers here to everything that is still *Christian* in the so-called modern era, in other words to the economic predominance of the U.S.A. (in opposition to medieval Catholicism), or in short to the capitalist and imperialist period. In *La Part maudite* Bataille cites Weber and Tawney, for whom Calvin "was to the bourgeoisie of his day what Marx was to the proletariat of our own: he supplied organization and doctrine" [p. 118] (B. Franklin: "Remember that money is of the prolific, generating nature. Money can beget money. . . .") [See R. H. Tawney, *Religion and the Rise of Capitalism* (New York: Harcourt, Brace, 1952), esp. pp. 112–13]. Bataille writes: "Insofar as humanity is an accomplice to the bourgeoisie (in a word, *in its entirety*), it humbly consents to be nothing more (as humanity) than *things*" [*La Part maudite*, p. 132]. This sentence can be taken as a definition of the bourgeois conception of the world and of its inability to make the transition to dialectical materialism and the "intimacy" of absolute expenditure. Further: "Hatred of expenditure is the *raison d'être* and justification of the bourgeoisie: at the same time it is the principle of its astonishing hypocrisy. The bourgeois have used feudal society's prodigality as a fundamental grievance and, having once seized power, their penchant for dissimulation led them to believe that the poorer classes would accept their domination . . . Against them, the popular consciousness is reduced to a deep affirmation of the principle of expenditure, depicting bourgeois existence as man's shame, and as a sinister refusal" (*La Notion de dépense*, p. 46). [In *La Part maudite, précédé de la notion de dépense* (Paris: Minuit, 1967).] It would seem that this judgment *also* needs to be transposed onto what we are calling the "textual" level.

6. "We cannot with impunity add the word *God*, the word that overshadows [*dépasse*] all other words, to our language; from the instant we do so, this word exceeds itself [*se dépassant lui-même*], vertiginously destroying its limits. Nothing can contain what this word is. It is everywhere and unforeseeable: itself an *enormity*. Whoever has the slightest inkling of it immediately falls silent. Or else, searching for an escape, knowing that he destroys himself, he searches within himself for what, in annihilating him, can make him like God, like nothing." Clearly, this applies solely to Western culture, whose fundamental *movement* is thus defined.

7. Tr. note: See *"Le Séminaire sur 'La Lettre volée' "* in Lacan's *Ecrits* (Paris: Seuil, 1966), pp. 52–53.

8. Tr. note: "Afterword to the Second German Edition," in *Capital* (New York: International Publishers, 1967), 1:20.

9. Tr. note: *La Part maudite*, p. 178.

10. Tr. note: *Ibid.*, p. 178.

11. Nietzsche: "Atheism and a kind of second innocence are interrelated." The "new feeling of power: the mystical; and the clearest and boldest rationalism serving as a path to reach it."

12. See G. Devereux, *"Psychanalyse et parenté,"* in *L'Homme*, July–December 1965.

13. Denis Hollier, *"Le Matérialisme dualiste de Georges Bataille,"* Tel Quel 25.

14. Georges Bataille, *"Conférences sur le non-savoir,"* Tel Quel 10.

15. See Jacques Derrida, *"Freud et la scène de l'écriture,"* in *L'Ecriture et la différence* (Paris: Seuil, 1968) [Eng. ed., *Writing and Difference*, Alan Bass, tr. (Chicago: University of Chicago Press, 1978)], (especially in reference to the concepts of "delaying," "detour," and "supplement").

16. Louis Althusser, in L. Althusser and E. Balibar, *Lire le capital* [Eng. ed., *Reading Capital*, Ben Brewster, tr. (London: NLB, 1970), p. 16]. And this: "The real history of the development of knowledge appears to us today to be subject to laws quite different from this teleological hope for the religious triumph of reason. We are beginning to conceive this history as a history punctuated by radical discontinuities (e.g., when a new science detaches itself from the background of earlier ideological formulations), fundamental reorganizations which, if they respect the continuity of the existence of regions of knowledge (and even this is not always the case), nevertheless inaugurate with their rupture the reign of a new logic, which, far from being a mere development, the 'truth' or 'reversal' of the old one, *literally takes its place*" [p. 44].

17. This has not been the case everywhere. Thus, in China, the relations between Taoism and science; see Joseph Needham, *Science and Civilisation in China* (Cambridge: Cambridge University Press, 1954–   ), Vol. 2.

18. Tr. note: *L'Impossible*, in *Oeuvres complètes*, 3:222.

6
Lautréamont's Science

This permanent publication has no price.

THAT THE TEXT of Lautréamont, through a slow but now apparently irreversible process of infiltration [*effraction*], has finally achieved some degree of (still-limited) legibility, is certainly among the most decisive phenomena in a discrete history. At the beginning of the twentieth century, just after the discovery of the *Poems*, André Breton could say of this text: "I believe that, for modern man, literature tends to become a powerful machine advantageously replacing old ways of thinking." But for surrealism, Lautréamont remains a pretext to verbal inflation, an insistent yet inadequately studied reference, an expressive shadow, a myth permitting the perpetuation of a lyrical, moral, and psychological confusion; there can be little doubt that this metaphysical grandiloquence is aging badly, that it finds support only in fewer and fainter echos. Very little has been said of the global functioning of the *machine* itself, although certain of its effects have been described. Marcelin Pleynet has revealed the interpretive bankruptcy that, through a sort of rhetorical mimicry, finds itself trapped by a language that no longer admits of qualification.[1] To fashion declarative sentences on Lautréamont, to construct the personage who might be the author of this pseudonym, to bestow a "meaning" on the *Chants de Maldoror* and *Poems*, is to persist in a mode of reading that was radically transformed by the very appearance of a writing comparable to the invention of an unknown language that must first be learned before one can speak about it. A language that articulates itself as if

outside the language it displaces, a language capable, seemingly, without disturbing the language that receives it, of killing this latter even
as it raises it to a second degree of efficacity; a "hollow" language, so
to speak, one whose avowed goal is to have done with representation,
with the sign and with the concept without which our society seems
incapable of conceiving a linguistic reality. An unapproachable text,
then, destined to play the role of "hieroglyph," of revealed, and, more
anecdotally, of projective text—which in fact it has not failed to do.[2]

One essay is an exception to this rule of blindness: Maurice Blanchot's *Lautréamont et Sade.* At least the difficulty of reading is affirmed and risked there: "That immanence of a change in which words
are no longer words, nor the things they signify, nor this signification,
but something *other,* something forever other, is so powerful that to
read *Maldoror* is to anticipate and experience this change." Nevertheless, Blanchot's reading does not escape the pseudo-contradiction between *Maldoror* and the *Poems;* that is, while this reading approaches
the *Chants'* particular mode of figuration, it ultimately fails to pass
beyond their representational structures [*dispositif représentatif*] ("images," "themes," "motifs"). While aware that it will never attain its
goal, this reading nevertheless proceeds idealistically, pursuing a "genuine meaning," a "supreme, total signification." The mark of an es-
sentialist reading is that it always (whether it withdraws into "impersonality" or not) necessitates: 1) an author (an individual adventure);
2) a noncontradictory text; 3) a truth-effect. Thus Blanchot accepts the
current interpretation of the *Poems* as a "repudiation" comparable to
that of Rimbaud, whose experience (according to an indefensible assertion) would be in some senses "more methodical, more theoretical,
and more deliberate." Thus Ducasse would be returning to "clear,
classical vision." It would appear that Blanchot, like all of Lautréamont's readers, despite his fascination, has no idea what to make of
the *Poems.* He is more at home with Hölderlin's "passion for the day"
and return to childhood—through which he reinforces a mythological
exploitation of the "poetic" and "originary" that, by way of Heidegger,
has the disastrous result of masking what today demands literally to be
thought, of hiding it beneath a "being of language" ["*être du langage*"]. Lautréamont (one should perhaps systematically say *Ducasse,*

in order to underscore the mentality that obliges our library to file this phenomenon under fiction), the physical reality to which this name belongs, remains in any case unique. To equate this with a "poetic experience," for example, is tantamount to deciphering a nonphonetic text by taking sentences for pictures. In this manner, we abandon the possibility of a certain *science*—a possibility in which the word "science" assumes a noninstituted and noninstitutable position and value, inaccessible to any received tradition of teaching. But the time has no doubt come to separate ourselves from what is ultimately a customary form of knowledge recoiling before the disturbance brought about by the play of writing and its consequences. The time has come to envisage that science defined by Derrida as a "science of the possibility of science . . . science of the 'arbitrariness of the sign,' science of the unmotivated trace, science of writing before and in speech," which must lead us to the exploration of a nonlinear, multiple, and dissimulated space.[3]

One of the first results of a textual approach to the *Chants* and *Poems*—one which Pleynet has achieved with admirable clarity—is to draw attention to the question of the *name*. Ducasse poses this question *dialectically*, and in a manner which has previously gone unnoticed. Yet it is impossible to grasp the *Chants/Poems* as a whole if we do not emphasize this passage from pseudonym to name, from figurative to proper name, and their reciprocal effacement which refers us to the articulation of a fiction and of the thinking that underlies that fiction. The operation accomplished here cannot be reduced to a simple chronological—diachronic—schema: "repudiation," contradiction. In accepting this sort of interpretation, we never leave the realm of psychological phantasmagoria. And indeed, this phantasmagoria refers us directly back to the status of scriptural practice in our society and culture, where the name is never anything but an *hors-texte*, an extra-textual supplement intended to support an object which is referred to as a "book" and which would *contain* the representational or conceptual text. We read only what is written *in* a volume and *by* someone—not this volume itself, not the scansion that allows the appearance and disappearance of this "someone." This is the system

clearly subverted by Ducasse, by the overall *mise-en-scène* of his written manifestations: as much by his letters as by the superposition of
two publications he signs in their difference, as much by the effacement of all biographical traces—a fact which must not be interpreted
as mere historical happenstance—as by the reversal whose laws he was
the first to set forth. Thus, concerning the passage from *Lautréamont*
to *Ducasse*, from the *Chants* (situated in the perspective of transgression) to the *Poems* (elaborating a "deferred" ["*après-coup*"] thinking of
the transgressive law—a deferral we will need to think in spatial rather
than temporal categories), Pleynet is correct in stating: "The pseudonym has allowed the proper name to have a reference other than
that of its paternal heritage. *Ducasse is henceforth the son of his works*"
(emphasis added). This sentence must be taken quite literally—as designating a birth occurring in and by writing, in and by the calculated
practice of a gesture which still remains to be elucidated.[4] Pleynet
writes: "Insofar as Lautréamont, through the elaboration [*tracé*] of his
works, was solely his writing, this writing becomes biographical through
and through; biographical not in the space of its statements (in what
it says), but in the gestural parabola of its elaboration." *Biographical*,
however, needs to be understood in a negative sense here, since what
is at stake is the very annihilation of biographical discourse—of a name's
placement in linear history—all biography being a consequence of
(historical) discourse which asks precisely that it be treated like any
other discourse. Thus in the system we are attempting to extrapolate
from Ducasse's writing, an essential point is the integration of the
death of the biographical subject (the death of both the subject of the
enounced and the subject of the enunciation), so that we read what
should be called a *thanatography:* "I write this on my deathbed"/"I
know that my annihilation will be complete."[5] The persistence of a
certain conception of the *subject*, insofar as this conception is linked
to a trivial language effect [*effet de langue bavard*], is subjected to a
definitive critique by such a system: to distinguish between a subject
of the enounced and subject of the enunciation, after the linguistic
model, is to remain within the metaphysical realm of speech. Freudian theory's inability to come to grips with "literature," for example,
results precisely from this same limited orality.[6] In fact, what the lit-

eral practice of writing reveals is not an enounced/enunciation duality, but—by means of a disjunction, a specific decentering and dissymmetry—*the enounced of the enunciation of the enounced*, or an infinite perpetuation of the enounced; or again, since the verb "to enounce" remains too closely linked to the speaking stage, a generalized *disenunciation* continually demonstrating the absence of any subject whatsoever (and even more appropriately, any problematic of the imaginary or the phantasm, as well as truth).[7] Just as the text does not divide into manifest or latent, into appearance or essence, just as it therefore cannot be conceived as the divided expression of a unity (which can only be a speaking unity), likewise it is not that which is produced between author and reader, between addressor and addressee. This space and this volume that it is have not yet been studied (the volume, here, belonging to a space), this space which in practice functions as a negative language, or an "undulating and negative network"[8] whose legibility offers an effect of double production: that of the trace and that of its decipherment, its retracing—a process without beginning or end, traversing both knowledge and its speech, the body and its sex, the real and its metaphor, narration and its "conscious" limits, in short the entirety of a culture in any given moment. This text, which has been pronounced pathological or unintelligible (and we are beginning to understand why), may thus be described as the encompassing of one space by another which is its inverted tissue [*tissu de retournement*], as the replacement of binary and measurable thinking by a dualistic thought which can experience itself only through traversal [*parcours*], layering, discontinuity, and mutation.

Consequently we have a culture defined by a speaking code on the one hand, the apparatus intended to bring about its *mise-en-abîme* on the other. We might say, for example, that for Empedocles or Lucretius the problem is to confront the sacred and the myth in their solidarity; for Dante, god and the symbol; for Sade, reason and the sign; for Ducasse, meaning and structure—those final metamorphoses of theology. For us the problem is to recognize how the "apparatus" functions vis-à-vis each of its manifestations. We need to be attentive, then, to the manner in which the *Chants* and the *Poems* outflank [*prennent à revers*] rhetoric and narrative, morality and the syllogism,

humanism and romanticism; the manner in which the space thus discovered makes use of what today we call "unconscious" or "formal
logic." What Ducasse offers us is less an interpretation or reading of
his text and those he utilizes to the end of creating a sort of permanent
integration, than a continual *changing* of texts, turning the textual
process into a practice unfolded and regulated against a background of
active emptiness. This writing which occurs beneath and between
writing and language, which brings with it, controls, conceals, and
reveals their manifestations, this "sub-scription" (Pleynet), this "spacing" (Derrida), must therefore present itself to us in language, in the
form of borrowings, junctions, instabilities, and, according to a punctuation that situates the text's readable matter on the level of accen-
tuations, intervals and transformations.[9] What we must grasp in this
process of negative and conspicuous doubling, finally, is the manner
in which this writing—within a field which does not belong to it but
which it enters by a kind of mute violence—assumes a series of alibis,
of *stage names* [*prêtes-noms*] and figures, a "world" whose arbitrariness
is continually underscored. We will see, for example, how comparison, ellipsis, and more generally, the "maxim" constitute, within this
economy of infiltration [*effraction*], neurotic and strategic points where
negation operates according to a reversible logic. Pleynet writes: "Lau-
tréamontian pseudo-dualities . . . come into play only at the locus of
their negative articulation. All of the ambiguities . . . beginning with
the concepts of good and evil, are connected to the hinge of negation
(neither good, nor evil), seen from the twin foci of reversal and identification."

These preliminaries are necessary if we want to specify the degree
to which the *Chants* and *Poems* dissolve the concepts of the "unconscious" and "history," so that the operation effected by Ducasse might
well be subtitled "from the text of the unconscious to that of history,"
emphasizing that this textual "exit" outside any subject and "psyche"
permits us to achieve an unprecedented practice of history (in relation
to which what has heretofore been understood as "history" effectively
becomes prehistoric). In relation to the "unconscious," we are finally
able to say that that concept was necessarily produced by a reductive
definition of language and of its logic. Benveniste clarifies this prob-

lem when he asserts the infra- or supralinguistic status of these "signs that cannot be split up," these "extremely condensed signs" which, in "organized language," would correspond "more to larger units of discourse than to minimal units," and states that between these signs, with motivation playing a causal role, "a dynamic relation of intentionality is established."[10] If we recall that the sentence "contains signs but is not itself a sign" ("the sentence, an indefinite creation of limitless variety, is the very life of language in action"), we may say that the sentence is the uniform shape that the indefinite space of writing assumes as soon as it is manifested in language, just as the ellipse is the privileged geometrical and rhetorical figure of its passage. The "unconscious," which in the "dream" employs a hieroglyphic writing and moreover recalls "literary" writing, may therefore, within a phonetic, speech-oriented culture, be defined as *speech's desire for writing.* The absence of negation and contradiction, the correlative and analogical function, their grouping and displacement in a permanent gesture of effacement are in fact the very symptoms of writing as a real object—becoming an object of knowledge through a language, or in other words through a system of coordinates. But rather than an infra- or supralinguistic reality—terminology implying a scarcely justifiable gesture of exclusion—we should speak of the *translinguistic.*[11] Likewise, we will consider the space of writing as belonging to the *transfinite,* and we will suggest that it is on the basis of this transfinite that writing continually produces, manipulates, orders, and overflows all structure, and consequently all "meaning." Through an empty movement of "resurgence" [*"relance"*], writing thus destabilizes the language of the *voice* that inverts itself into it and discovers its limits and milieu there, a milieu whose activity is definable solely in terms of its negative effects. The action of writing is therefore that of a generalized bracketing of language. In relation to the text, within it, language becomes entirely citational. Writing cites itself as it divides; it cites its own history, its productions, its hidden continuity with all languages. In a certain sense, we might even say that the "text" knows all languages in their entirety (which does not mean it does not have to learn them) insofar as it acts as the "outside" of the absence within languages [*ce "hors-langue" du blanc des langues*]. The text reads "man in language" as if "man" were a reading-writing apparatus and the textual apparatus were capable of simultaneously redistributing all the effects of language and their inverted inscription, of rediscovering assertion in negation, of accepting the "part" for the "whole," of opening itself up to the infinite by means of a series of marks—or, in sum, according to the project put forward in the *Poems*, of accomplishing the transition from *phenomenon* to *laws*. This amounts to bestowing or taking back from mathematics a fundamental calculation which is restrained and masked by an oral definition of writing. To this also, the *Chants de Maldoror* and *Poems* give pointed testimony.

As to "history," insofar as the linear model is contested and integrated within a textual pluri-dimensionality, insofar as the recognition of written negation produces a periodization implying a spatialization of time, a continual exchange of languages and texts, then the historical experience, in relation to what has been lived as such by the epoch of individual speech, extends itself considerably and alters its dimensions, becoming at once massive, monumental, and of a heretofore inconceivable complexity and differentiation. Writing which, seen from the perspective of speech, was reduced and rejected as an "evil," may now be presented as history itself: the "sequence of ages," the "future book," the "permanent publication," the "indestructible thread of impersonal poetry." We will see *why* the *Poems* can *comprise* this sentence: "In its own, *personal* name [*En son nom* personnel] and in spite of it, necessarily, I have come to disown, with implacable will and iron tenacity, the hideous past of whining humanity" [emphasis added].

It would seem that the reader is the principle "character" in the *Chants de Maldoror* (a title Pleynet has taught us to read as "mal d'aurore" ["sick of the dawn," or "dawn-sickness"]).[12] But we must specify that the introduction of the reading function into the text does not imply a relation between the text and an external reader, but on the contrary a means of emphasizing the perpetual movement that produces the text and its provisional actors [*ses figurants*]—the scriptor and reader. The *Chants* are first of all a *psychography*, in the sense that Empedocles, for example, can be said to have employed a psycho-teaching [*psychogogie*]; in the sense that this process entails a *katabasis* which, by means of a meticulously regulated dramaturgy, and while maintaining the narrative line, would explore the necessary constraint and arbitrariness of this narrative and line. The text will *seek out* the organism that remains unconscious of the text (i.e., speaking man) and demand that he embolden himself, becoming "for the time being, as fierce as what he is reading." [13] an exhortation addressed to the act of inscription itself, which is thus from the start dialectically connected with its other, an other that precedes it in a relation of reciprocal violence and opens the path for it by permitting itself to be written from the perspective of its own end. The schema of production is thus:

Indeterminate (multidimensional) text (writing) → reader → scriptor → written (linear) text (language)

a schema we must reverse in order to make contact with, to orient ourselves within, the self-referential textual process. We have here a question of "life" or "death"; it is no accident if this process takes the shape and function of a cure capable of subsequently reflecting on its own conditions, the conditions necessary for the establishment of a new law, a new logic, and the dialectic of prohibition/transgression. In any case, the text's first concrete word is *chemin* [path], derived from the Sanskrit *pánthāḥ*, about which Benveniste remarks: "The *pánthāḥ* . . . is not simply the road as a space to cover from one point to another. It implies difficulty, uncertainty, and danger, it has unforeseen detours, it can vary depending on who is traversing it, and moreover, it is not only terrestrial—birds have their road, rivers also. The *pánthāḥ* is thus neither plotted in advance nor regularly trod. It is rather a "crossing" attempted over an unknown and often hostile region . . . , or the route that birds invent in space; in short, a way into a region forbidden to normal passage, a means of going through a perilous or rough expanse." We need hardly insist on the sexual aspect of this opening [*frayage*] [14] that must penetrate the space of a universal scene of transgression (whence the brutal entry of the "maternal face"—the figure of the matrix-language—which is less to be "evaded" than reattacked through the agency of the paternal name)—

an ensemble of "abnormal" lines, a prohibited path that the philosophical birds (the "cranes") dare not brave in the sky ("you don't see
the third side formed in space by these curious birds of passage"),
although their advance (cf. the "starlings," farther on) defines that
which agitates and disturbs the linearity of language: "May it please
heaven that the reader, emboldened and having for the time being
become as fierce as what he is reading, should, without being led
astray, find his rugged and treacherous path across the desolate swamps
of these sombre and poison-filled pages; for, unless he brings to his
reading a rigorous logic and a tautness of mind equal at least to his
wariness, the deadly emanations of this book will dissolve his soul as
water does sugar." There you have the text's initial statement concerning "pages" as yet unwritten, and the reader-scriptor of these still un-
delimited, unexplored [*non encore . . . frayées*], and nocturnal pages—
pages using evil to counter evil, inventing a counter-poison against the
"deadly emanations." Drawing together a problematic of writing, of
sex, and of their interrelationships, opening [*se frayant*] a passage
through the repression of language, line, and "meaning" (the "good"),
the text adopts a "heroic" operator which is both a pictographic name
designating the work in progress (Maldoror) and an intersection of logical antinomies (Maldoror as the man with lips of sulphur and jasper,
the escaped convict, the civilized savage, etc.).

This head-on attack on all that is situated on the line of right-
thinking, on the horizon-line over which the textual storm arises, on
the reading that refuses to be a writing (the speaking logic of representation) is explicit from the start: "I will state *quickly* that Maldoror was
good during his first years when he lived happily. There you have it.
Then he noticed that he had been born evil: an extraordinary destiny!"
("He dares to repeat it with his trembling pen!"). And elsewhere, in
the *Chants:* "This mystery will not be revealed to you (it will be revealed to you) until later, when you and your anguish open philosophical discussions by your deathbed . . . and perhaps even at the
end of this strophe." It could hardly be more clearly stated that the
line is no longer accepted as regulatory principle. In the *ellipse* whose
sources are the scriptor and reader and which is now being inscribed
in the line, another agency governs the text—a "cruelty" whose devia-

tions tend toward the "infinite," denying that which the line com-
mands: a temporality, a conventional succession that obeys the representational frame programmed by a reasoning that accepts the
dimensions of sham realism (which is why the "glowworm" is also
"big as a house," and god's lost hair will end up a prolix pogo stick).
The cruel text unmasks "man," who agrees to be what he has been
told he is—who does not write: "I am the son of man and woman, *or
so they tell me*" (emphasis added). Thus, as part of this disturbance
and breaking of linearity, the permutation of pronouns (showing how
writing employs all of language's postures with equal facility) and tense
changes within the sentence effect a "disorientation" (the "point of
view" becomes a space), whereas contradictions ("how good he is, don't
you think, since he has no taste") and analogical shifts (intended to
stretch the lexicon to the limit in order to reveal its closure vis-à-vis
an unlimited *reverse side*) insert the text into a multiplicity without
confusion, a permanent nonstoppage (the dogs' barking is related to
the elephants' trumpeting, the hungry child's cry, the injured cat's
wail, the howl of a woman about to give birth, the sob of the plague-
ridden patient, the young girl singing; a locus is set *against* the stars
and cardinal points, the moon, the mountains, the cold air, the silence of the night, screech owls, frogs, the thief, snakes, *barkings*,
toads, spiders, cliffs, ships' lights, waves, man). Metaphoric condensation and metonymic displacement (classic axes of coordination) are
immediately at the height of their functioning and reversibility, their
saturation point, indicating the passage to another system capable of
indefinite metamorphoses and interconnections interrupted by punctuation alone. Each expression thus takes on the value of a *character*
which is inscribed, effaced, and reclassified in a milieu that seems
exempt from contradictions.

This context so resistant to any linear knowledge may be called,
among other things, the ocean. But let's agree to call it *text:* "In order
to contemplate you, the sights of the telescope must be turned in a
continuous movement towards the four points of the horizon, just as
a mathematician is obliged when doing an algebraic equation to examine individually all the different possibilities before arriving at an
answer." The "oceanic" text (without signs, and whose "moral gran-

deur" is the "image of infinity") is what accounts for the "human heart" better than any speaking ideology of "man" ("man says yes and thinks no"/ "Psychology still has a long way to go"). This then is the "hypnotic and fierce" text, the text becoming "ocean" in the linguistic line, and driving its sentences, its waves, with the "consciousness" of what it is: "At short intervals, they follow one another in parallel lines. No sooner does one subside than another comes to meet it. . . ." The movement of production and destruction, inscription and efface- ment, revelation and withdrawal—this movement that orders whoever would enter and disappear there *completely*: "Wash your hands, return to the road that leads to sleep"—has therefore neither beginning nor end, save those based on "the appearances of phenomena" ("If it is sometimes logical to refer to the appearances of phenomena, this first chant finishes here"). The text that establishes and upsets arbitrariness will designate itself, in this arbitrariness, by the necessary arbitrariness of its choice of a beginning and ending. When it *recommences*, what it was (on the previous page) will be as distant and removed as a for- gotten word [*parole*]; it will begin in an ever more radical manner, will "drive" [*"s'acheminer"*] toward an increasingly definitive end that will leave no more than a residue, a collection of traces "to be read" but entirely suppressed in relation to itself, having exhausted every- thing it has posited concerning itself—here, in his language, begin- ning with its first word.

The textual infinity to be sung (but which "does not allow itself to be read") renders "incandescent" the pages where it manifests itself (language playing the role of resistance): it penetrates "dark recesses and secret fibers of consciousness" that cannot resist it because they are constituted by it, it *disidentifies* the speaking subject by means of its contradictory and non-divine identity, it makes a science of this identity ("This much at least has been learned: that since that time, toad-faced man no longer recognizes himself") by developing "the subtle networks of its relentless perspicacity." It is also the "diamond sword" that strips both "man" and his "philanthropic tirades" naked: "these are accumulated like grains of sand in his books, the comic qualities of which I am sometimes, whenever my reason abandons me, ready to find so droll—but tiresome. He had foreseen it. It is not enough to sculpt statues of goodness on the spines of the parchments stored in libraries." Beneath the mask of *"mal d'aurore,"* its "least blows are fatal." Still the text must do battle with a *counter-writing*, the sanctification of language, "man" engendering himself through a "god" (a nontextual usurper presenting himself as omnipotent, eternal, paternal). This agency of counter-writing attempts to write the text's actor corporally; it is the "long sulphurous scar," the "huge gash occasioned by a punishment which for me is already lost in bygone nights," the organic programming (social, cultural, prehistoric) intended to circumvent the effects of scriptural writing "by distilling the drool from my *square mouth*" (emphasis added). "The joints [*articulations*] remain paralyzed, as soon as I begin my work. Yet I need to write . . . It is impossible! I repeat that I need to write down my thoughts: as would anyone, I have the right to submit myself to this natural law." The scriptural act is a *risk* that activates the world of phenomena—lightning, storm, rain, thunder—as its dialectical response, the possibility of a vengeful, castrating chaos coming to mutilate anyone who pretends to enter it "as would anyone," anyone who wants to be simply "anyone," the anyone of his will being able in turn to legislate with the text and say: "But finally, that's how it is." The material act of writing (on a surface, with an instrument, in language [*la langue*]), is itself no more than a figure that utilizes, for example, "the triple dart of platinum that nature gave me *for a tongue [comme une langue]*" (emphasis added). Language [*la langue*] (and its effect, the speaking subject) needs to be taken over by the "hollow carcass" of a *creator* supposedly external to its system, one who assumes that the origin or the infinite is extratextual, marginal in function, immobile—so that it becomes necessary "to turn him around like a spinning top with my steel-cord whip" (i.e., writing). Language must be ironized "with a firm, cold hand," so that the *dead weight*, the human body, can be expelled from it: "to whirl you around me like a sling, concentrate all my strength as I describe the final circle, and hurl you against the wall." Truly, it is time to "bring into play more forceful levers, weave *more skillful webs [des trames plus savantes]*" [emphasis added], to "know how to embrace more amply the horizon of present time."

The *Chants* refer positively—and not by chance—to logic, the ocean, the hermaphrodite (sex), and mathematics; negatively, to man, philosophy, god, and speech. "They say that I was born between the arms of deafness! In the first years of my childhood, I could not hear what was said to me. When, with the greatest difficulty, they taught me to speak, it was only after I had read on a sheet of paper what someone had written that I could in turn communicate my thoughts." "For a long time I have spoken to no one. Oh you, whoever you may be, when you are next to me, let no sound escape the cords of your glottis; do not with your motionless larynx strive to outdo the nightingale; and, as for yourself, on no account attempt to make your soul known to me by means of language." The exploiter of human speech, the ally of "filth," symptom of the impossibility of dismissing the body's otherness, of *caricature,* is the *louse* (the priest, the philosopher) "which men feed at their own expense." In the same manner, "god" is the agency that "eats" that which created him as if it were his own creation. One has only to "lift up one's eyes" to witness the bloody scene that forces out a cry, restoring voice and hearing, compelling one to speak (to sing against speech in writing). This transphenomenal, translinguistic (but in no wise transcendental) movement is made possible by *mathematics,* whose source, "older than the sun" (*Poems:* "The science I am undertaking is a science distinct from poetry. I am not singing this latter. I am trying to discover its source"), is desired instinctively, "from the cradle." "There was a vagueness in my spirit, something thick as smoke; but I managed to mount religiously the steps which led to your altar, and you drove away that dark veil, as the wind drives the petrel. You replaced it with excessive coldness, consummate prudence, and implacable logic." Thus the text may become an "impassive spectator"—allowing its "configurative lines" to vanish in order to nourish itself on "symbolic figures traced upon fiery paper, like so many mysterious signs, *living on a possible breath*" ["*vivant d'une haleine latente*"] (emphasis added), signs that are themselves a "glittering revelation of eternal axioms and hieroglyphs, which existed before the universe and will survive it." Mathematical writing—or rather that which accomplishes, through and despite language, a numerological thinking—is the sole writing capable of realizing the textual ocean's contradictory identity:[15] "Your modest pyramids will last longer than the pyramids of Egypt, those anthills raised by stupidity and slavery. And the end of the centuries will find upright on the ruins of time your cabalistic ciphers, laconic equations, and *sculptural lines*" (emphasis added). In the written struggle against linear man (and the "creator" constructed by his "cowardice"), mathematics are a "terrible auxiliary" through their logic and "syllogisms, whose complex labyrinth only makes them more intelligible." These will make it possible to inflict upon man "a wound from which he will never recover."

This wound consists in the destruction of the speaking subject's superstition, his fear, and his religion, by concretely demonstrating to him that these are nothing but the effects of his reduction to and acceptance of the representative line. Already, the text proves capable of taking account of its own genetic movement, the "big lips of the shadowy vagina from which immense dark spermatoids flow unceasingly like a river" (and later: "The time has come to tighten the reins of my inspiration and to stop for a moment along the way, as when one looks at a woman's vagina"); already, it knows how to master the text fallen into the deifying language that appropriates [*consigne*][16] the annals of impersonality by means of "some infamous intrigue": the project of infinitization implies a *re-establishment* of text (prior to its effacement) which no longer requires that the text be thought by an individual ("human") head: "The crocodile will not change a word of the vomitings emerging from beneath his skull." The guillotine itself is powerless against the seat of this thinking, which defends the scriptural organism by providing it with weapons to struggle against *consciousness* (another effect, like the "unconscious," of the representative, unifying line) and its "pride." And, consequently, to undertake a more objective, more textual examination of this "vile planet," this "stony chamberpot where the constipated anus of the human cockatoo strains."

The "imaginary beings," whose names are drawn from a "brain" and emerge on the page through the song of writing, shine "with a light of their own creation." "They die on birth like the sparks whose swift extinction on the burning paper the eyes can hardly follow." As it consumes language's representations, the text's work and invasion must produce the effect of spontaneous generation, of something new appearing on the horizon, of an apparitional, floating volume that deposits its traces of erasure on the linear screen before returning into chaos and creating other ephemeral "substances" which unmask and violate the space of religion as they sustain the force that moves through the ensemble, revealing the movement and complexity of an infinity in which the part continually, and legitimately, assumes the value of the whole: "A hungering love, which would devour itself if it did not seek sustenance in celestial fictions: creating, in the long run, a pyramid of seraphim more numerous than the insects which swarm in a drop of water, it will weave them into an ellipse which it will whirl around itself." As an effect of the extension of traces, the "whirlwind of unconscious powers" thus emerges from a body mutilated by counter-writing—a body which has "received life as a wound" but "has forbidden suicide to heal the scar"; a body subjected to a regular loss of thought and blood, a body *opened up* to incessant multidimensionality. As part of the same movement, texts and linguistic fragments that appear in the transfinite field of reading are immediately utilized, destabilized, rewritten, and literally violated by this continual process of contestation [*le procés en cours*]: realist novel, mythological sources, fantastic tales, naturalistic encyclopedia—in each case it is a question of noting the penetration of one (innocent, expressive) textual level by another (productive, raised to the second degree, criminal); a reversing, negative, nullifying process that doubles and destroys representation, that almost sexually reduces the tissue of representation to its graphic circulation (as in the episode on the madwoman's daughter and the bulldog). As a result of this excess, the hierarchical order—the order of meaning—is *comprehended* as an effect of sleep and drunkenness: "Did you know that the Creator . . . was inebriating himself?" Certainly no sentence underscores this orderly encompassing better than the following: "Everything was working out its destiny: trees, planets, dogfish." Within this process, "god" (meaning) appears as a drunkard, stripped of his mastery and delivered to the "shark of individual abjection" (as in the brothel episode). In his place, it becomes possible to say: "Oh! you will never know how difficult it can be to keep a hold on the reins of the universe! Sometimes the blood rushes to your head when you are seriously trying to draw one last comet from nothingness, and with it a new race of spirits." In its efforts to hide behind the logical line of truth, moreover, the hierar-chical—conceptual—pretension is continually obliged to deny its con-crete participation in crime and sex: but in this negating operation (a kind of lesser version [*temps faible*] of textual negation), it necessarily loses a hair (a sign) which falls within the jurisdiction of the text, for which all the hairs (all signs) are already counted. Thus the dialogue between the hair and its "master," witnessed through the "grating" of chant III, on the delimited stage of writing (where dimensions are no longer controlled, where an object is measured by the intensity of the word that carries it)—where the "primordial inscription" (the inscrip-tion of prohibition) is effaced and reinscribed on the wall (the page) with a knife.

   "It is [*C'est*] a man or a stone or a tree that is going to begin the fourth chant." It is a tree or a stone or a man that must complete its reading. It is, in any case, solely the proposition *"c'est"* which is thus designated. Just as it disarticulates and shatters the closed system of language, the infinite text traverses and thinks the body within a whole where thinking can no longer think itself, in a contradictory milieu where its multiplied points of view must assume every grammatical position and every "natural" condition. Language [*le langage*] be-comes a state of continual beginning *announcing itself everywhere* [*s'énonçant de partout*] whose nonauditory effects will have immediate repercussions on *comparison*, which is the hinge and pivot of particu-lar languages [*de la langue*]. Thus the wasps in the temple of Den-derah: "I compare the buzzing of their metallic wings to the incessant crashing of ice floes flung against one another when the ice breaks up in polar seas." Such a subversion and extension of the text is possible only if a deviation [*écart*], an irreducible difference, a non self-identity manifests itself in the function whose role is to "sing" at the surface, to say "I" for "him": "I alone against mankind." "He sings for himself and not for his fellows." This function "voluntarily" perceives itself among its "equals" to the precise extent that it no longer resembles itself and occupies the other locus [*foyer*] of "man": ". . . it isn't long that I have not resembled myself! Man and I, immured within the limits of our intelligence. . . ." Thus, in the tradition of Latin rhetoric (see, for example, in that other great work of demystification, *De Rerum Natura*, the discussion of "towers," illusions, and apology for the senses in Book IV, ll. 353–468), we find the sequence columns-baobobs-pins-towers opened up to identity by means of difference: ". . . that comparison of these architectural forms be *forbidden* . . . or geometrical forms . . . or both . . . or neither . . . or rather high and massive forms. I have just discovered, I will not pretend to deny it, the epithets appropriate to the nouns column and baobob . . ." (emphasis added). Here—on the line, in the "frame of this sheet of paper"—the arbitrariness of the subject-predicate relation proper to the language being used, the potential insubordination of the "real" to this narrow grid, the possibility of an altogether different functioning, are demonstrated in the very act of reading—and this (as in the case of Lucretius) with a manifestly didactic intent drawing a parallel between textual articulation and the understanding of an "outside." God-as-meaning, who "does not exceed the great general laws of the grotesque," effectively functions as the figure of linguistic prohibition, whereas writing—which is "metaphoricity itself" (Derrida)—transgresses the hierarchization of discourse and the world it implies by the activation [*mise en oeuvre*] of a specific deviation that might be called transference (to distinguish between this and any "reference"): "And yet, even if a higher power were to command us, in the clearest possible terms, to cast this judicious comparison, which everyone has been able to relish with impunity, into the abyss of chaos, even then, and especially then, let us not lose sight of this principal axiom, that the habits acquired over years through books and contact with one's fellows, and the innate character of each individual, which develops in rapid efflorescence, all these would impose on the human mind the ineffaceable stigma of relapse into the criminal use (criminal, that is, if we momentarily and spontaneously take the point of view of the superior power) of a rhetorical figure which several despise, but many adore. If the reader . . ." etc. It is thus that "the greatest effects are often produced by the smallest causes." It is thus that "reasoning will sometimes clash head on with the jester's bells of folly and the serious appearance of what is, after all, merely grotesque"—because this reasoning bases itself solely on the "laws of optics." Nevertheless, there is nothing gratuitous or, even less, *laughable* (senseless, in the sense that sense understands it) in such an undertaking. The philosopher may burst out laughing, but the transfinite text's actor does not. Laughter itself is the index of a logical weakness: one only laughs by virtue of a syllogistic thinking, a speech incapable of grasping the logic of certain "omissions" which, by contrast, cannot shock or surprise "those who have studied in depth the real and inexplicable contradictions which abide in the lobes of the human brain." Man laughs "like a cock" *because he does not know how to read,* and in this sense he is indeed more ridiculous than the parrot he thinks imitates him: "The cock does not change his nature, not because he is unable to do so, but because he is too proud. Teach them to read and they refuse. No parrot would go into such raptures at its own ignorant and inexcusable weakness." Nevertheless, "there is a simpler means of reaching agreement; this would consist, I translate it in but a few words which are worth more than a thousand, in not arguing [*discuter*]: it is far more difficult to put into practice than most would think. Argue is the grammatical word." In this manner poetry will finally be able to become "modest," ceasing to misconstrue [*méconnaître*] the "principles of its existence" (*Poems:* "The poetic whines of this century are nothing but sophisms"/"The first principles must be beyond dispute"), or in other words its fundamental scription, its sub-scription linked to respiration, to the production/consumption of the infinite text. "Just as oxygen is recognized by the property which it unassumingly possesses of relighting a flickering match, so will the accomplishment of my duty be recognized by the haste I show in returning to the matter at hand."

At the same time, the duality released by writing, and interpolated within it, manifests itself through a series of anamneses, of metamorphoses in which it becomes increasingly evident that all traces of the "subject" have long since disappeared, dissolved in the scriptural movement. Progressively embodied in the written non-body, the speaking body undergoes an animalization, a mineralization and vegitalization that allow it to reemerge in a divided position (accentuating the "reader") where its experience of the mirror permits a final leap beyond the representation of the sign and of "reason" (of the world of fictive details): "Let us search out this undiscoverable body which my eyes nonetheless perceive . . . The phantom mocks me, it helps me look for its own body. If I gesture [*fait signe*] to it to stay where it is, it makes the same sign back . . . the secret has been discovered . . . *Everything has been explained, the great as well as the little details; these last are too unimportant to bring to mind . . .*" [emphasis added]. The "temporary loss of memory," like the "misconstruing" of the subject's own image, is again regulated by the "inflexible laws of optics" (textual optics); recognition of these laws will allow a passage through sleep and the dream (the psychical apparatus) toward the attainment of a forgotten limitlessness: "Since I pretend not to know that my look can bring death even to the planets revolving in space, he who claims I lack the faculty of memory is not mistaken. *What I must now do is smash this mirror to pieces*" (emphasis added). The text, which set out in search of "man" in his perceptual, phenomenological, conscious, unconscious, and conceptual alienation, in his "lethargic catalepsies," will reengender him in a swelling tide, an "irreducible mixture of dead matter and living flesh." A passage through the "hog": "Not the slightest trace of divinity remained. I knew how to raise my soul to the excessive height of that unspeakable delight." Such a metamorphosis will bring about a corresponding change in "real" order, so that the interior/exterior pair will manifest its inanity with regard to the text: "It is not impossible to witness an abnormal deviation in the hidden or visible functioning of the laws of nature." To do so, a "pressure of the will" need only go beyond "the limit which good sense prescribes for the imagination" according to an "ephemeral pact." The whole unfolds in a contradictory movement, a double sliding of reading/writing as they leave the "sheet of paper" and move in opposite directions from each other, combining an extreme rapidity with an extreme slowness: "I warn him who reads me to beware of forming a vague and *a priori* false idea of the beauties of literature I shed in the excessively rapid unfolding of my sentences. Alas! I should like to develop my arguments and comparisons slowly and magnificently (but

who is master of his own time?), so that everyone might better understand. . . ." In truth, the reader should not approach the narration
with "the harmful impediment of a stupid credulity" (a representative
credulity), but rather abandon himself to the scriptural gesture that
would allow him to achieve the text's "rapidity," its scansion, articulations, and deployment outside the involution [*repliement*] of sentences. He will then—through criminal sequences of comparisons and
metaphors (encouraging "human aspirations towards the infinite")—
hear language [*la langue*] speak itself within the network of its auto-
production: "Using my own tongue [*ma propre langue*] to utter my
thoughts, I notice that my lips are moving and that it is I who am
speaking." A discovery which occurs only at the expense of all biological ("familial") filiation and at the price of a "bleeding thing," a murderous gesture whose violence haunts the *Chants*. Whence the irony
and seriousness of this abrupt statement: "I, too, am learned."

The ocean, mathematics, the whirlwind: such are the names by
which the infinite text permits itself to be known, as opposed to the
"singular ideas" of a limited (linear, linguistic) reading. "What an
abundant source of errors and confusions all partial truths are!" Textual, dialectical tactics correspond, not to those of the civilized voice,
but to those of "instinct"; these tactics are plural, but "regular and
uniform." Let us read, for example, the words *sentences* or *word* beneath the word *birds*, the word *text* beneath the word *squad* [*peloton*]:
"Their instinct leads them to keep on approaching the centre of the
squad, while the rapidity of their flight takes them incessantly beyond
it; so that this multitude of birds, thus joined in their common movement toward the same magnetic point, incessantly coming and going,
circling and crisscrossing in all directions, forms a kind of highly agitated whirlwind, the entire mass of which, though not moving in any
definite direction, seems to have a general tendency to turn in upon
itself [*un mouvement général d'évolution sur elle-même*], this tendency
resulting from the individual circling movements of each one of its
parts, in which the centre, endlessly tending to expand but continually
crowded in and repulsed by the opposing effort of the surrounding
lines which weigh down on it, is ever tighter, more compact, than any

one of these lines, which themselves become more and more so, the nearer they come to the centre." These *lines* are precisely, in the mobile and progressive ellipse of the chants, those that draw nearest to their "center," to their changing and generative void. This is what happens every time the text begins pointedly to "speak" of itself and abandons the convenient fiction of its "surrounding lines"—which are just as necessary to the work of the whole and its development as the borrowings or implicit citations that sustain the whole in its self-permutations, that is to say in its self-effacement as an ensemble composed from parts. This involves an "eminently philosophic conception which ceases to be rational as soon as it is no longer comprehended as it was conceived, that is, expansively." There is little need, then, "to multiply the divisions." The song must function as a *graft* rather than as meaning, *oeuvre*, or spectacle. The "sickness" to which dawn-sickness [*mal d'aurore*] subjects fiction is intended to free the reading function (and every reader trapped in language and the line of "education") from sickness: a cure taught by "cadaverous reason" by means of a practical assimilation (the text teaches itself and produces its effect less by comprehension than by contagion): ". . . habit is a necessity. And since instinctive revulsion felt at the first pages has noticeably weakened in intensity, in inverse ratio to the attentiveness of your reading, like a lanced boil, you may hope, even though your head is still sick, that you will shortly recover completely." A sentence that Ducasse is clearly addressing to himself as he pursues his reading of the multidimensional text under the name of Lautréamont and of Maldoror; a sentence the "reader" must understand according to a rule of writing that permits him to consent, through the "chant," to his reading of the infinite text (an operation which, as it *also* unfolds physically in space, demands, once again, the sacrifice of all possible "kinship": cf. the chain Mother / sister (woman) (hung) / pus / cyst / ovary / chancre / foreskin / slug): "If you follow my prescription, my poetry will welcome you with open arms, as when a louse with its kisses severs the root of a hair." The text's process of self-recognition, which arouses a "passion for riddles" in the scriptor-reader it shapes and elicits, is particularly marked in chant 5, in the scarab episode (first symptom of immortality): "I had followed in his footsteps [*J'avais emboîté mon pas sur ses traces*] though I was still far from the scene of the action . . . But what then was the corporeal substance towards which I was advancing?" This is the point at which the "as handsome as" series is introduced ("as handsome as a hasty burial"), acting as the turning mechanisms [*dispositifs tournants*], the pivots in the scene of writing's metamorphoses. What is "handsome" is not actually the "thing" (corresponding to speech), but rather the written sequence which itself is always an *as* (so that one should always write: as handsome as that which is writing itself). Here, writing opens up a multiple perspective as it draws together, on the line, the traces which, as temporary representations, constitute the sum of the lines that are no longer or not yet *there*. The index of this passage of the trace into itself, or in other words of the redoubling that effaces it by making it penetrate the matter it delimits, separates from, and supports, is the *I* that says "I" to counter-writing's *counter-I*. The *I* "sees" what the *counter-I reads*. It is a question therefore of simultaneity, of a plurality that *sets off* linear unity and functions only as contradictory, dialectical energy (i.e., as a destruction of the *line*, of *sickness*, of the *remainder*; and it is the *remainder* that narrates [*raconte*] the operation). Thus from *I* to *counter-I* there is a complete permutation in which the *I* learns what its written other reveals to it (unmasks for it). "And me believing it was excremental matter. Come on! What a fool I am."

This sort of permutational science implies not only breaks or "intermittences" ("the intermittent annihilation of human faculties"), but also a declaration of permanent non-somnolence: "Since the *unutterable* day of my birth . . . it was my own wish; let no one else be blamed" (emphasis added). "He who sleeps is less than an animal castrated the night before"/"Nevertheless, I do sometimes happen to dream, but without for a moment losing the unshakeable consciousness of my personality and the faculty of movement." Just as it excludes any "subjective" problematic (the "dream" as significant value), writing's continual transference questions the possibility of any "referent"—the "Great Exterior Object (who is not familiar with his name?)" posited as such by an idealistic conception of the sign, of meaning and of the phenomenon, by a causality that becomes the text's "dreadful spy," its self-styled decipherer, its self-styled other, the big other, its

nonsigned counter-writing scar, its parasite, its *louse*: "If I exist, I am
not an other. I do not acknowledge this ambiguous plurality in myself.
I wish to reside alone in my inner deliberations. Autonomy . . . or
else let me be changed into a hippopotamus. Bury yourself beneath
the earth, anonymous stigmata . . . My subjectivity and the Creator,
this is too much for one brain." The "other" is neither more nor less
than an effect of *discourse*, but writing has just done away with discourse (which "wanted to take up the reins of government, but doesn't
know how to reign!"). This is what the scriptural circle, the "eccentric
python," can say to the textual actor: "What monstrous aberration of
the imagination prevents you from recognizing me?" By destroying
false recognition in the form of denial [*méconnaissance*]—the hint of
a resemblance—writing sets up an implacable difference, or rather that
"great similarity-and-difference" in which all things resemble one another in one sense but differ in another;[17] a difference, therefore, in
which every particular, in the absence of any term of comparison,
takes on the value of the whole. "This same vulgar quality calls down
upon every object or spectacle it touches a deep feeling of unjust indifference. As if we ought to wonder less at the things we see every
day!" An incessant awakening, a dislocation of hierarchical discourse,
a concentration capable of periodically relating all things ("as handsome as"), is precisely the scriptural labor: "It is, *generally speaking*, a
singular thing, this *attractive* tendency which leads us to seek out,
and then to express, the *resemblances* and the *differences* which are
hidden in the most natural properties of antagonistic objects which
sometimes seem the least apt to lend themselves to sympathetically
curious combinations of this kind, which, I swear, graciously give to
the style of the writer who treats himself to this personal satisfaction
the ridiculous and unforgettable aspect of an eternally serious owl. Let
us therefore follow the current which is carrying us along . . ." (emphasis added).

   The sexual effects of this group of operations are particularly remarkable. For, just as the "body" is linked to a thought of speech, of
representation, and of mimetic propriety [*propriété ressemblante*], the
thought of the infinite text and of writing, which thinks and breaks

the body, recognizes only *sex* as the mark of its negative work, its thanatography: "My private parts perpetually offer the lugubrious spectacle of turgescence." Rejected by the *Poems*, homosexuality is a constant presence in the *Chants* and is explained there: "Oh incomprehensible pederasts . . ." "I need beings who are like me." This presentation [*mise en évidence*] and this "impartial" apology are—as always in the *Chants*—simultaneously a denunciation; the desire for what is similar consists in wanting to touch someone who would be reading what is written from the exterior, the same in the other: "The opacity of this piece of paper, remarkable in more ways than one, is a most considerable obstacle to our complete union." Homosexuality (autosexuality) is trapped in non-difference; but as such it is *generalized* (functioning as well in the "heterosexual" unconscious as in its pseudo-difference) in a civilization valorizing the unity of the speaking subject, and forms a barely disguised and revealing facet of this civilization. This is why Maldoror must be its complete, cosmogonic fulfillment (the universe likened to an "immense celestial anus"), thereby becoming the written phallus whose "sacred sperm" and "inexplicable enchanted talisman," by an inverted transposition, arouses the passions of the animals that issued from it: "I secretly hide in the most inaccessible places to inflame their ardour"/ "The scene of the battle is now but a vast field of carnage." Homosexuality (the obsession with the phallus as supreme signifier) is thus the force behind the scenes of and the accomplice to [*la coulisse agissante et complice*] the entire Platonic, Christian, anti-scriptural civilization—that of *knowledge*, of *truth*, of *man*, of the *father*, and of the *Creator*. It is, in sum, the open secret of the human race, that which it represses with "stupid" legislation but which never ceases to manipulate it. Far from being a transgression of law, homosexuality is in fact its complementary realization, that which the law never ceases to desire. "My intelligence always soars towards this venerable question, and you yourself are witness that it is no longer possible for me to remain within the bounds of the modest subject which I had planned to deal with at the outset. A final word . . . It was a winter night. While the cold wind whistled through the firs, the Creator opened his doors under cover of darkness and showed a pederast in." The text's "observer" cannot fail (as in the

hair and the brothel episodes) to note this fundamental dimension of
the system of the sign. After which: "Silence! a funeral procession
passes near you." The chant is now situated "beyond the tomb"
["*d'outre-tombe*"]. Enter, born by the "priest of religions," "a golden
emblem representing the genitals of man and woman, as if to indicate
that these carnal members are, most of the time, *all metaphor aside,*
very dangerous instruments in the hands of those who use them, when
they blindly manipulate them for whatever ends, instead of bringing
about a timely reaction against the well-known passion which *causes*
almost all our ills" (emphasis added). At this point the text is insisting
on its non-knowledge [*non-savoir*] of death,[18] which, in any case, cannot be communicated in the "picturesque language" of men, a language which is no more than a limited (structured) effect of textual
infinity: "Do not be so presumptuous, permit me to give you this
disinterested piece of advice, as to believe that you alone possess the
precious capacity of conveying the thoughts of your feelings." The
human being disappears like a fly or dragonfly, and a mortal risk runs
from one sentence to the next, from the beginning of a sentence to its
end. And yet the time will come when "we will understand better than
before how to interpret the separation of body and soul. Whoever believes that he is truly living on this earth is lulling himself with an
illusion whose evaporation it would behoove us to accelerate." This
acceleration will control the *Chants* from this point on, after the spider
episode ("We are no longer in the narrative . . . Alas! We have now
come to reality . . ."), which assembles the text's fictional figures,
exposes its mythic matrix, underlines its function as an "immense suc-
tion," and leads to its reversals of generation and of wakefulness, to
the space that will include, efface, and X-ray it in its "explicable hy-
perboles," at its "dawn," its "change of scene," its "shattered heart."

At this point, the scriptural function is going to demonstrate its
ability to control both the body and the outside in which this body
appears; directly announcing the retroactive and comprehensive effect
of the *Poems*, writing itself directly in the three dimensions of a volume linked to the future (and become already what it is: the "preface
to a future book," a book projected into the future as an unending

preface, an indefinitely postponed non-book preceding all books, a definitive exit from the book, that prison of the speaking epoch). The three abstract "characters" liquidated by the *Chants'* combat on the line—"man, the Creator, and myself"—will henceforth be inscribed in the "real" through fiction and cease to be "anathemas," "fictive personalities," "nightmares too far removed from ordinary existence." A general redistribution of writing is underway: "Vitality will surge magnificently into the stream of their circulatory system, and you will see how startled you will be to encounter, where at first you thought you saw only vague entities belonging to the realm of pure speculation, on the one hand the corporeal organism with its nerves and mucous membranes and, on the other, the spiritual principle which governs the physiological functions of the flesh. It is beings powerfully endowed with life who . . . will prosaically pose (but I am sure the effect will be very poetic) before your eyes, only a few paces away from you, so that the sun's rays, falling first upon the roof-tiles and chimney-pots, will then come to reflect visibly from their earthly and material hair." "Note that this very fact will make my poetry finer. You will touch with your own hands the ascending branches of the aorta and the adrenal glands; and then the feelings! The first five chants have not been useless; *they were the frontispiece to my work, the foundation of the construction, the preliminary explanation of my future poetic*" (emphasis added). The "synthetic" section (which outlined the destruction of the sign, of representation, of "man and He who created him") is thus completed and closed. Now the "analytical" section may begin, in which it will become clear that the text henceforth situates itself on the same side as space; no longer *in* space but rather *with* it, linked to it according to the same relation that allows the reader and scriptor, in a certain sense, to leave their reciprocal bodies in order to take part in the same permutative operation: "that which I affirm with complete awareness of the situation." Such a transformation, such a transition to the limit of writing—in a space which is translinguistic, open (inhospitable to structure, unavailable to the senses), acausal, still in the future and "outside"—will need time to be accepted and understood. "It is only later, when a few of my novels have appeared, that you will better understand the preface of the renegade with the soot-blackened face." From this point on the text is "outside language" (outside the law), and in consequence: "Before I begin exposing the substance of my discourse, I find it absurd that it should be necessary . . . for me to place beside me an open inkstand and a few sheets of unrumpled paper." This result was obtained through the deliberate production of an *astonishment* (before the line and language, and their *flat* coordinates). Nevertheless, a "clear and precise generalization" remains to be achieved—which is what chant 6 will ironically stage as the beginning of a series of "*instructive* poems" [my emphasis] and "unremittingly useful dramatic episodes." The point here is less that the textual activity should gratuitously break the "rules of logic" or "commit a vicious circle," than that its effects should be achieved in the midst of human societies, in history, "beginning with remote times set beyond history." "The dazzling past promises a brilliant future: it shall be realized. To gather my sentences together [*Pour la ratissage de mes phrases*], I shall perforce use the natural method, going back to the savages for instruction . . . There is nothing ridiculous on this planet. An outrageous planet, but a sublime one. Adopting a style which some will find naive (when it is so profound), I shall use it to interpret ideas which, unfortunately, may not appear awe-inspiring! . . . But note this, poetry is everywhere the stupid, mocking smile of duck-faced man is not. . . ." For the writing that thus becomes contemporary with itself, unfolding all representation from its generative tracing [*tracé producteur*] ("But in this place which my pen has just rendered mysterious"), every "novel" and every "realism" is hereafter denounced as an obscurantist and arbitrary line, while the multiple, anticipatory textual operation becomes a science of the aleatory: positioning and correlation of relays especially distant from one another whose intervals are filled by means of narrative development (cf. the series: fish's tail / beam / rhinoceros). Realist decor (the bourgeois and conventional) is linked directly to "sentences which have been sieved and decomposed by the obligatory metaphors." A radical anonymity, "a spiritually mysterious affair," is already taking place on the exterior: "I shall follow your example and refrain from signing this: we live in a time which is too eccentric for us to be in the least surprised by what might happen." By means of a clearly indicated knowledge-effect ("I realized that I had only one eye, in the middle of my forehead"), the neurotic world of unified speech is definitively enclosed: ". . . Unmoved spectator of the acquired or natural monstrosities which adorn the aponeuroses and the intellectual of him who speaks, I cast a long look of satisfaction on the duality of which I am composed . . . and I find myself handsome." The "as handsome as" series, which follows directly, concerns not only the sexual organs, but also, and for good reason, the arbitrariness of the conventions of musical language: ". . . or rather (as handsome as) the truth which follows: 'the system of scales, of odes and of their harmonic succession is not dependent upon natural invariable laws, but is rather the consequence of aesthetic principles which have changed with the progressive development of mankind and which will continue to change.' " Breaking with all representational pretensions (and therefore with the sign and its mirror function, the subject and its substitutional role), the text may thus affirm: "you need not in the least hesitate to believe what I say." A constitutive duality [*dualité composante*], the transfinite text and scriptural operation put an end to the fiction of a creative unity: ". . . several phenomena directly derived from a deeper knowledge of the nature of things speak in favor of the contrary view and formally contradict the viability of the unity of power. For we are both contemplating one another's eyelashes, you see. . . ." The text is the product of the two it produces.[19]

In order to "end," to visibly interrupt one of its arbitrary relations with language—not spoken language, then, but language cited, sung, destabilized, diverted [*défrayée*], transferred, "transfused" from one "brain" to another and finally situated in its revolutionary space [*mise dans son espace de révolution*]—the text must demonstrate the inexhaustible character of its fabric, an infinitization capable of decomposition, developments, minutiae, and detours which are, precisely, "endless." The appearance of the "crowned fool," the sequence of the "three Daisys," intervene as a systematic practice of nonsignificance, of scriptural acausality that finds nothing mad or insignificant in a correlational process that constitutes its own logic ("I cannot say everything at once: every stage trick will appear in due time, as soon as the thread [*trame*] of this work of fiction sees fit"). Narrative, metaphor,

and the "poetico-real" are definitively put to death: "The denouement
is about to unfold; and in narratives of this sort, where a passion,
whatever its nature, is given, there can be no obstacle as it *forges its
passage* [*pour se frayer un passage*], there is no reason for diluting in
a cup the shellac of four hundred banal pages. What can be said in
half-a-dozen strophes must be said, and then, silence" (emphasis
added). Writing's work of *dissection*, devoted not to "making itself
understood," but to "developing its thought" (a development that *me-
chanically constructs the brain* of the fiction—of the "somniferous
tale"—that brutalizes and hypnotizes the hierarchical reading of
meaning), overthrows "even absolute truths." The space where it unfolds, always before the word on account of its *mark*, beyond the sentence on account of its *volume* (or rather its infinite space), demonstrates its potential for "insane" ["insensées"] relations, its ability to
cross any lexical point with any other, but in an ordered and equa-
tional manner (great crab to albatross / beam / Almighty / rhinoceros
/ rope / fourteen daggers / cock / candelabrum). Thus, with the aid of
a "glacial silence," the text produces all its effects simultaneously,
eliminating any possibility of semantic accumulation [*accumulation
signifiante*] (of exterior, final meaning) or of unbroken development
in the form of a "conclusion." Now is the moment for the text to
demonstrate its exit from the line in a detailed manner, to indicate its
"immortal" entry into space. The figure being put to death, "head
downwards," "carries off into the air with him that which was not a
fixed point." The executioner has "piled a large part of the rope at his
feet in the shape of superposed ellipses." As for the textual movement
(controlling the whole of the *Chants*), it is "accelerated by uniform
rotation in a plane parallel to the column's axis." "The sling whistles
through space; the body . . . [is] always kept away from the centre by
centrifugal force, always maintaining an equidistant and moving position in an aerial circumference, independent of matter." And thus
"the original plane [*plan primitif*] of the rope's revolution" is changed:
"Thereafter he turns majestically on a horizontal plane, having passed
successively and by imperceptible degrees through several oblique planes
. . . *The renegade's arm and the murderous instrument merge in linear unity, like the atomistic elements of a ray of light penetrating a*

camera obscura" (emphasis added). Stretched to its extreme, redoubled in force by the textual arm that has just luminously shattered the *camera obscura* of language, the line is abruptly halted and released, driven by an "impulsive force which I suppose to be *infinite*" (emphasis added), projecting the body attached to it onto the external "spherical and convex surface" of the site where the so-called immortal names, the "great soft-heads" of speaking civilization, are buried. It is *there*, and on account of this "distance," that the end of the nineteenth century may find its "poet." It is *there* that his skeleton and its flowers of immortality may be found. "Go and see for yourself, if you do not believe me."

Abandon all despair, ye who enter here.

The *Poems* are immediately inscribed in the space and the outside thus discovered by the *Chants*, less "after" than *beneath* them, among them, and in their intervals, constituting the locus—no longer in the form of a line, but rather a [musical] *stave* (as if the *Chants* would henceforth form the "words" ["*paroles*"] of a multiply musical scription, or the woof underlying a warp which could become visible [*la trame d'une chaîne pouvant s'exposer*] after that warp's destruction)—in which the disruptive movement leading to the transfinite text will henceforth produce the formulas rather than the narrative of its genesis. Formulas, "maxims" written in a fragmentary and directly historical manner, one might say, insofar as they will present themselves spatially with the three-dimensional real, bringing language into play as memory (a dead cultural accumulation, a dead citational language), replacing the struggle against line and law (against representational meaning) with an empty *order* in which law and transgression are simultaneously affirmed and denied. The gesture accomplished in fiction under the cloak of language now leads scriptural space to a point of reversion where it will be able to disclose itself, fold back upon itself, comprehend itself, where it effects its own spacing [*s'espacer*], limitlessness, and impersonality (the figural name will have killed the personal, the proper name can sign the impersonal). *Once*

language has been thrown out [jetée] into space and effaced there,
along with the corpse of the subject it produces, it is no longer representation that will be destroyed but the concept; this destruction will
be accomplished by means of a periodical *apparatus*, a *"permanent
publication"* whose primary function is a power of replacement and
correction intended to institute an "exclusive good." The encompassing of the good/evil duality that depends on the line is obtained by the
inclusion of all contradiction ("Everything is evil" / "Everything is
good"), by the practice of a deviation and dissymmetry that will include
all of the evil referred to as "good" by sickness. In speaking communication "the roles of the poet and of mankind have been arbitrarily
reversed"; the "author" presents himself as being "sick" and adopts the
"reader" as his "nurse." But within the scriptural space (infinite text—
reader—scriptor—written text), on the contrary, "it is the poet that
consoles mankind." The uselessness of *discussion* and consequently of
"incredulity," superfluous once the reader's credulity has been "cured,"
allow us to pass from "tempest" and "tornado" to the "majestic and
fertile river." The apparatus has now mastered all of language's effects,
as well as their ambiguous status as "ideas" and "dreams" *[leur mise
ambiguë en "idées", en "rêves"]*: "One only dreams when one is asleep.
It is words such as dream, life's futility, earthly journey, *the preposi-
tion perhaps*, the disordered tripod, which have infused this dark lan-
gorous poetry like corruption into your souls. *It is but one step [un
pas] from words to ideas"* (emphasis added). This *pas* is also a *ne pas*,
a pseudo-negation (a denegation: "the spirit of negation") at work in
the space of speech—but not in the scriptural assertion, which is *entirely affirmative and entirely negative*. ("It is granted only to a few to
approach the extremes, either in the one direction or in the other.")
The yes-no that "goes from words to ideas" (that carries out the development of the sign and the concept) must be radically distinguished
from the yes without no and the no without yes, from the yes no of
textual writing and its process, a process in which words (ideas) are
never at less than one remove from transcription. The psychologizing
system of ambiguity must therefore be destroyed from top to bottom:
"It is finally time to react against everything that shocks and oppresses
us so regally." That is: "grimaces, neuroses, the bloody channels

through which logic is forced to retreat . . . platitudes . . . child-births worse than murders . . . reason howled down with impunity . . . (everything which is) *speaking seal* . . . cross-eyed, pederastic, bearded lady . . . that which does not think [*réfléchit*] like a child . . . vague perspectives which crush you between their imperceptible cogs." When you don't go "see for yourself" (when you are nothing but a representational reader, a representative of knowledge), "your mind is perpetually unhinged" by the system of the sign (the system of de-scription and phonetism). "The novel is a false genre because it describes the passions for their own sake: the moral conclusion is missing." "He who refrains (from describing) . . . but remains *capable* of admiring and understanding those with the gift (of describing so as to conclude) surpasses (he who describes)." In this twice-removed and demystifying practical perspective, the "good student"—"instruction . . . [is the] practical expression of duty"—is "superior" (because less contaminated) to any producer of fiction; "a good appreciation of the works . . . is preferable to the works themselves." In effect, the ravages of the linear, speaking system are incessant ("We must be relentlessly on our guard against purulent insomnias"), and these ravages are no less historical for being revealed by the "novel," since the novel and history both participate in the reduction of history to a spectacular surface where error becomes "the sorrowful legend." It follows that both "real" names and those of mythological fiction belong to the "noisy pack of paper devils" (Napoleon, Byron, Charlotte Corday, Manfred, Mephistopheles, Don Juan, Faust, Caligula, Cain, the gods of ancient Egypt)—and the text declares itself to be that which was summoned to efface them, their "preordained tamer." We must then first dismiss the pseudotext that constantly infringes, the scenic program projected by "degraded writers, dangerous buffoons . . . fabricators of forbidden enigmas by the dozen, of which I previously could not perceive, as I can today, the trivial solution *at first glance*" (emphasis added). Linear man is the Cartesian hoax of doubt, given to "bizarre and odious whinings," to "intolerable torpor"—a "*littérateur*" whose theoretical and practical "wickedness" (the fabrication of "enigmas") "has privileged the human backside in all its reasoning," or in other words the *discussion* that never regards itself as written. The "author," like his accomplice, "the reader who under-stands [*sous-entend*]," "gives himself away, relying on the good to justify his description of evil." That is, by ignoring scription he falls into denial [*dénégation*]: he "speaks." This speech argues, describes, questions, and denies; living parasitically on its writing, it can only lead to the expressive grimace, to the *tic. Littérateurs,* softheads, everyone—proper names incapable of *disfiguring* their name, incapable of obtaining the generic name of writing by turning back upon their own names placed in written space—these finally have no right to any but a fictive *surname* (trapped in the transfinite text which they were unable to recognize, and which unfailingly changes them into tics, reflections of oral ideology), for example, Jean-Jacques Rousseau, "the Surly Socialist." "Shameless explorers of melancholy, magnificent in their own eyes," they believed that by displacing themselves under the sign's law they had found "unknown *things* in their souls and bodies" (emphasis added). They believed, as a result of their own reduction of language and their position in relation to that reduction, that they had a "soul" and a "body." As a result of this descriptive and expressive misreading [*contresens*], "a nightmare is holding the pen," a nightmare that "creates sadness in his books" instead of formally transmitting "the experience that separates itself from sorrow," instead of "uprooting evil" (scription). We see that the transfinite operation, on the other hand, the scriptural movement of infinite beginning and permutation, *passes* through death but does not take death as its horizon or end (goal): "One must be able to tear out literary beauties even in the bosom of death; but these beauties are not part of death. Death here is only the *incidental cause.* It is not the means, but the end, which is not death" (emphasis added). Here once again, we find nothing gratuitous or automatic, nothing disordered or conventionally "rebellious," nothing pseudo-transgressive in this ordered, nonsurreal space for which no antinomy is appropriate, above all that of "old" and "new": "Those who wish to create anarchy in literature on the pretext of achieving the new are making a serious error." We might say, rather, that the revolutionary text is "as old as the foundations of the earth," or in other words: always new, freed from negation, being negation itself in its process of production and effacement without beginning or end, automatic, cosmic, immortal, deviant.

The apparatus of the *Poems* must make this deviation manifest. But since the text's knowledge cannot express (limit) itself, what it knows will appear in the deformations provoked by its passage into reading, in the manner in which, leaving nothing to chance, it utilizes the samples it appropriates from knowledge [*les prélèvements qu'il opère dans le savoir*] to institute a permanent act of citation, replacement, and correction. This *correction* is the manifestation of the deviation. "If these sophisms were corrected by their corresponding truths, only the corrections would be true; whereas the piece which had been thus revised would no longer deserve to be called false. The rest would be beyond truth, retaining a trace of the false, and would thus be considered null and void." Here we see the spatial and dialectical modification to which the *Poems* subject the mechanistic true/false division. Correction, which is not a truth, but a practice, is true (it is the textual act); the "corrected" piece is non-false (a truth among others); as to the piece to be corrected, it is "beyond truth," null and void (non-written). In other words, the piece to be corrected awaits its future, a future submitted to the "future book" which is no longer a book but rather an instantaneous correction process for all books, whose published text will be permanent and without price, historical, this rectification itself, this spatialization. Consequently: "Personal poetry has had its day of relative sleights of hand and its contingent contortions. Let us gather up again the indestructible thread of impersonal poetry. . . ." Historically, this *thread* is what the personal line, which was only its voice and shadow, will have usurped. And if science itself is affected by it, this is because even as it analytically delimits, structures, and signifies an object, it leaves "personal poetry" intact and in its place. Science does not necessarily compromise the fiction of a subject, it does not produce the *language* of its radical destruction. "Impersonal poetry" must therefore encompass science and become the science of this science, its textual, nonquantifiable *"hors-texte"* (not an *"oeuvre"* but the *functioning* of the corrective apparatus): "po-

etry is geometry par excellence" (movement, space, number). It activates a form of *complete* reasoning, a technique of annullment capable
of curing the "recurring dreams" produced by read, learned, and in-
jected linear texts, by the programming of the semantic illness [*mala-
die signifiante*], of "non-understood questions" that derive from the
acts of mythical languages. For that reason one must "be carefully
silent," "arrive each day," not believe that, rather than proceeding
from the transferential activity of writing, correction might come by
way of a simply referential influence ("All the water in the sea would
not be enough to wash away one intellectual bloodstain"). The apparatus never refers back to a meaning, a knowledge, a truth, an absolute
reality—but to a practice which is dialectical, formal and dynamic,
constant: "Poetry must have for its object practical truth" / "Criticism
must attack the form but never the content of your ideas, your sentences. Act accordingly."

   Having undertaken this practice, man is no longer the "hoax of
doubt" (a subject arguing and disappearing on the line), but immediately becomes "immortal," a "genius." The apparatus begins its work
of "correction," intended to liquidate bookish religion ("nothing is
said"), the cancer of a henceforth useless library (Dante, Vauve-
nargues, La Rochefoucauld, La Bruyère, Pascal), especially in its
"moral" stupidity. Like the *Chants*, and thanks to them, all texts become readable—to be reworked—in the matrix of the *Poems*. "The
heart is the source of all great thoughts" / "Reason is the source of all
great thoughts." This encompassing activity will replace the speaking
epoch's contradictory *ambiguity* [20] with a redoubling, a repetition intended to designate the milieu where separation without communication of affirmation and negation takes place: no longer the law of a
confused and double unity (passing from one to the other without
knowing how to say neither yes nor no), but the laws of a dual permutational *order* (in which all is yes / all is no). "I shall write my
thoughts in an orderly manner, according to a plan unmarred by confusion. If they are correct, the first to come will be the consequence
of the others. This is the true order. It indicates my aim by its calli-
graphic disorder [*Il marque mon objet par le désordre calligraphique*]."

Scriptural space is thus shaped by the effects of *retroaction* and *marking* (the subject is in the object it marks; writing is *in the other* and thereby produces its deviation; what comes first is the *consequence* of what follows in the periodization, and thus is determined as a function of the whole).

This space thus eliminates all possibility of origin, of causality, of hierarchy, of fetishization ("religions are the product of doubt"), of the "hymn"—and does so through an effort related to affirmation and negation. But this reversal is not a reversal pure and simple. Actually, even a "pedant" [*pion*] could understand the "poets of this century" if "he would replace their affirmations with negations. Reciprocally." But this reciprocity would remain the practice of a "pedant" nevertheless. "If it is ridiculous to attack first principles, it is even more ridiculous to defend them against such attacks. I will not defend them." The *Poems* are not the *defense* of "exclusive right," of "necessary truths" or "first principles"; only the least evil called *good* "defends" itself in this manner, with the commonplace that the affirmative is elaborated by the negative and the negative by the affirmative, that denial resists the disengagement of the deviation and its change of logical levels. What is at work in scriptural "non-defense" is the activating of a space *that knows no contrary*, being itself contradiction in action and the awareness—the science—of that contradiction: uncontradiction, *contrascription*. It is not a matter of simply replacing affirmation by negation, but of finding the locus (historical, concrete) of the "I replace," the very gesture of this "I replace" and not its formulation. "When I write down my thought, it does not escape me. This action reminds me of my strength, which I constantly forget. I teach myself in proportion to my enslaved thoughts [*à proportion de ma pensée enchaînée*]. I strive only to know the contradiction between my mind and nothingness." The modification of Pascal's "in writing down" and the introduction of the word "*enchaînée*" (in place of "*oubliée*," "forgotten") specifies the dis-alienation at work in textual writing.[21] Enslaved and economized in the line, thinking loses its power of expenditure, believes itself weak and begins to take itself for nothingness (for the negation that bears it). This is an escape route to which the "when I write" replies by recalling that thought is never anything but its writing. Thus the "heart of man" becomes a "book that I have learned to value." The affirmation of "man" coincides here with its most powerful negation—the man of discourse is definitively demystified: "The fly is not thinking clearly now. A man is buzzing at its ears" / "One can be just, if one is not human" / "Not imperfect, not unfallen, man is no longer the greatest mystery." Textual man, on the other hand, becomes "a subject devoid of error" / "the conqueror of chimeras, the novelty of tomorrow, the regularity which makes chaos groan, the subject of conciliation" (and not of contradiction, as is every subject of discourse, reduced and divided between enounced and enunciation). For Pascal, for example (and the emphasis of the *Chants* and *Poems* on Descartes and Pascal is, in this, historically justified), the incomprehensible is based on contradiction. But for a dialectical theory and practice of the transfinite text (the text without a subject)—of which the written text, we should recall, is only a trace to be continually rewritten—"there is nothing incomprehensible." "Thought is no less clear than crystal." At this point the text may "state [*énoncer*] the *relations* that exist between principles and the secondary truths of life. Everything stays in its place" (emphasis added). The text becomes the science of the enounced of relationships, the science of the enounced of the enunciation of the enounced of relationships, and by the same token the science of the place of "things" (of their dynamic spatialization, of their variable and indefinitely displaceable theater, without actor or spectator). It "discovers the laws by which political theory exists," the "psychology of humanity." It is the only definitive suppression of "cults" ("It is ridiculous to address one's *speech* to Elohim . . . *Prayer* is a false act") (emphasis added). It has, at last, crossed the horizon of its own birth: "I know no other grace than that of being born: An impartial mind finds this adequate." It denounces all sentimentalization: "Love is not to be confused with poetry." It establishes *work* as a dialectical force capable of a production ("Work destroys the abuse of feelings") free of all subordination to truth save that which is "manifest" ["*montrée*"] or practical: "I know of no obstacle surpassing the strength of the human mind, except truth." There is an absolute rupture with phenomenological fragility: "The phenomenon passes. I seek the laws."

This research will also seek to establish a relationship between "poetry" and knowledge [*savoir*]. "Nothing is more natural than to read the *Discourse on Method* after reading *Berenice*" (emphasis added). Just as "poetic" practice gave us access to philosophy, so the scriptural operation will have to be "at one" with its thought. Otherwise, "the transition is lost. The mind rebels against rubbish, mystagogy." If tragedy (tragic representation) is an "involuntary error," it nevertheless retains its "prestige" because it comprises "struggle." What is eliminated here is *sophistry* (knowledge which has not been dialecticized by the text): "the belated metaphysical Gongorism of the self-parodists of my heroico-burlesque age." It is a matter of introducing *what must be done* into language (through the "chant"), and doing so unambiguously, in a dissymmetrical manner, by means of a qualitative leap and an unevenness in development: "I do not sing of what must not be done. I sing of what must be done. The former does not include the latter. The latter includes the former." Likewise, good is not the "contrary" of evil, but "the victory over evil, the negation of evil" (the negation of the negation).[22] Within language, the scriptural operation gives rise to a *configuration* [*ensemble*] which is not subject to the law of expressive truth: "The maxim does not need it (truth) to prove itself. One argument [*raisonnement*] requires another. The maxim is a law which includes a collection [*ensemble*] of arguments. The closer an argument comes to the maxim (to scriptural practice), the more perfect it becomes. Once it has become a maxim (scription), its perfection rejects the proofs of the metamorphosis." The "law" thus produced excludes all determinate, momentary, fragmentary meaning; it contains the semantic contradictions [*contradictions de signification*] which are necessary and sufficient to make its tracing a complete sequence, transformed in relation to an empty (perfect) language which may be filled but not exhausted. The dualistic (good/evil) and mechanistic *vocabulary* in which each word is defined by its opposite is thus marked by a permanent imbalance that implies the formation, within the textual apparatus, of what might be called a *scriptabulary* whose function is to reorder the series of words while repeatedly taking account of a silent and inscriptive deviation. Given this process, any "banal truth" necessarily "contains" a proposition of "genius"—the apparatus fabricates "genius" at will as it controls the process of verbal production: "Words expressing evil (denegations) are destined to take on a useful signification. The ideas improve. The meaning of words participates in this process." Language sustaining itself in writing is gradually integrated with itself and thus effaces itself in writing as it passes beyond all the "stopping points" by which metaphysics thought to impede it. "Plagiarism is necessary. It is implied in the idea of progress. It clasps an author's sentence tight, uses his expressions, erases . . . replaces . . . ." The scriptural movement is a simultaneous *expunging, replacing,* and *developing:* "To be well wrought, a maxim does not need to be corrected. It insists on being developed." "Whenever we are presented with a commonplace, a thought which is on everyone's lips, we need only develop it to find it to be a discovery." This *demand* comes from the text itself as it engenders and shapes its operators, developing itself in, through, and beyond them. At this point, Ducasse is able to *read* a passage from Lautréamont's *Chants,* is able in other words to develop—to rewrite—this passage, since, having written the *Chants* and constituted their reader, he has *also* become this reader, has become anyone, has become *the other that he is.* "On all of this we can dispense with commentary." The text, product of the two it produces, here indicates its law: "Whoever knows only one of these, renouncing the other, is depriving himself of all the aids we can employ to guide our actions." "Discourse" is consequently unified by performance: "The soul being one, sensibility, intelligence, will, reason, imagination, and memory can be brought into discourse." Contrary to Pascal's assertion, the "abstract sciences" are the assigned domain of "man." In relation to them, the "writer" can "*without separating one from the other,* indicate the laws which govern each of his poems" (emphasis added). He is able, in other words, to give the enounced and the enounced of the enunciation of this enounced, to simultaneously trace, across languages, the traits from which they originate, the spaces in which they inscribe, develop, exchange, recall, withdraw from [*s'absentent*], destroy, recompose, and diversify themselves. It is thus no longer a matter of an arbitrary description (insofar as this would be linked to the system of the real and the sign): "A meadow, three rhinoceroses, half a catafalque, these are descrip-

tions. They may be a memory, a prophecy. They are not the paragraph I am about to complete." In the inscription, the sub-scription,
the trans-scription of the work, the word no longer stands for its
"meaning" but for a more general mark of which it is the citation, in
the same way that a cipher stands for a number. The word *governor*
[*régulateur*], for example, stands for *governess* [*régulatrice*] in the economy of a divided speaking subject. But "the governor of the soul is not
the governor of a soul. The governor of a soul is the governor of the
soul (the word *governor* is inscribed into the textual process) when
these two kinds of soul are sufficiently confused to affirm that a governor is a governess only in the imagination of a jesting fool." What
the apparatus governs and controls are *types* (sets, models), not images, copies, or reproductions. "There are men who are not types.
Types are not men. One must not be dominated by the fortuitous."
From *types* we may consequently infer *precepts* (maxims, comprehensive formulas, laws) that should always remind us that they will never
refer back to concepts or substances (as the capitalist order of "knowledge" would like to pretend), but to the very act of their articulation
and formalization—the apparatus functioning on the basis of and toward an emptiness, across dialectical history, as its "great-resem-
blance-and-difference" reads the "little-resemblance-and-difference" of
the prehistoric text (thus: "some philosophers are more intelligent than
some poets . . . Plato [is not] André Chénier." This is another way
of saying that the function "Plato" is in correlation with the function
"André Chénier," albeit more intelligent. The two are in a state of
reciprocal production; every platonist is an André Chénier who does
not necessarily recognize himself as such). The effect of textual unification—a perception of the interrelationships of science, philosophy,
religion, politics, economy, technology, law, art—is in short made
possible by the discovery of the nonphonetic, by the dissimulated persistence of their interrelationship, the divergence between notated
writing and writing in space (practice), written writing and writing
writing [*écriture écrite et écriture écrivante*], the second containing the
first and always capable of reversing its propositions. "A philosophy for
the sciences exists. There is none for poetry . . . One would say
that that is strange." "Judgments passed on poetry are worth more than

the poetry. They are the philosophy of poetry. Philosophy, *thus under-stood*, comprises poetry. Poetry cannot do without philosophy. Philos-ophy can do without poetry." But: "There is a logic for poetry. *It is not the same* as the logic of philosophy. Philosophers are not on a par with poets. Poets have a right to consider themselves above philoso-phers" (emphasis added). Philosophy must be logical poetry, and po-etry—judged poetry—a comprehensive philosophy. But further: "The science I am undertaking is distinct from poetry. I am not singing the latter. I am trying to discover its source." How can we not see here, by the manner in which the words *science, philosophy*, and *poetry* are made to refer to one another, that these words henceforth designate a closed system whose "source" is precisely what the textual operation uncovers? This "source," which is not to be taken for a "common" origin but rather as the locus of what we have referred to as the "infil-tration" ["*l'effraction*"], this source beyond the "feelings" (which "are not aware of the course they follow") recalls the "principle that circu-lates through its pages: the nonexistence of evil." The descriptive level is that of the metaphysics of the sign and concept, setting itself against any practical disturbance. The textual principle, however, allows the nonexistence of the *no* (of negation) to circulate in a series of affir-mations and negations in which the two forces remain absolutely im-permeable to each other. "Nothing which is true is false; nothing which is false is true. Everything is the reverse of dreams, of lies." In this manner "humanity" begins to approach its "maturity" (its dialectical revolutionary period). "Tragedies, poems, elegies, will no longer take first place. The coldness of the maxim will dominate! . . . The genre I am undertaking is as different from that of the moralists, who merely state the evil without suggesting the remedy, as theirs is from the melo-dramas, the funeral orations, the ode, and religious knowledge. The sense of struggle is lacking." The "struggles" the transfinite text stages are the new milieu in which the "human" gesture as a whole is played out—and no longer the repetitive rumination, the *tic* of an individual dependent on the propriety of his name: "Poetry must be made by all, not by one." In the economy of the speaking and believing subject, writing is where "the same words recur more often than is their due";

the deverbalizing *apparatus* does not function in its anonymity, in its "two-and-all" that liquidates the one-and-none of past history. This "two-and-all" closes the system of knowledge ("the sciences have two extremes which meet") by means of an *overview* [*parcours*] which, having surveyed all that "men can know," "finds that they know everything" (Pascal: "finds that they know nothing"). The result is a "learned ignorance, *which knows itself*" (emphasis added). "Those who, having left behind the first ignorance, have not been able to attain the other (those who exploit the provisional system of knowledge [*savoir*] while resisting the text's violent revolution), have some tinge of this *sufficient knowledge* [*science suffisante*] and pretend to understand everything. These do not trouble the world, they do not judge less well than the others." "*In order to know things*, one need not know them in detail. Insofar as our knowledge is *limited*, it is well-founded" (emphasis added). Transfinite writing no longer sets itself the task of interpreting the "world" but sets about changing it. Not only is it no longer referential (centered on "things" or the "thing-in-itself" because it is irreducible to the system: subject-sign-concept-referent), but just as it may transform all statements into *verbalisms*, it regards the world of knowledge as an indefinite but finite text in which all things may be known by a process of *centering* [*cadrage*]. It can therefore definitively divest itself of idealism and take up the business of "consoling humanity," of "treating it as a brother": "it is more honest." It can organize the totality of "human" functions as progress: "To study order, one must not study disorder. Scientific experiments, like tragedies, verses to my sister, gibberish about misfortune, have nothing to do with life on earth." Scientizing science (the cult of knowledge) is ultimately a scriptural aberration, a loss of space whose accomplice is a poetry that is poeticizing, non-plural, non-practical (*Poems*), non-scientific and non-historical. In comparison with the textual silence that demands nothing from anything or anyone, this brand of science does no more than theorize an "indecent" phenomenalism: "the theorem is by nature a form of mockery. It is not indecent. The theorem does not insist on being applied. The application we make of the theorem debases it, becomes indecent. Call the struggle against matter, against the ravages of the mind, application." In a practice of dissymmetry, a practice of the empty and trace-making divergence which the apparatus makes controllable within a non-homogeneous space, a qualitative "leap" occurs, a mutation that simultaneously frees language from its "earthly," representative, conceptual, and structured circularity ("We must not, in describing heaven, use earthly materials") and implies a reserve, an active absence which also affects the "laws": "Not all laws should be stated." Encompassing "language," this "order" is found in what had previously been called "morality" but now becomes a theory of deviation, of "exclusive good"—Ducasse transforms Pascal's words: "Language is the same from all sides. A fixed point is needed in order to judge it . . . but where shall we find this point in morality?" to the following: "A fixed point is needed in order to judge. Where will we not find this point in morality?" Thus it is that "whatever a man's intelligence may be, the process of thinking must be the same for all." The apparatus [*appareil*]—which, moreover, manifests itself in current language rather than according to a "poetic" affectation [*apparat*] ("Do I have to write in verse to set myself apart from other men? Charity forbid!")—is not based on "reason" and consequently recognizes it for what it is [*le connaît*], comprehends it ("Order dominates among the human species: reason and virtue are not the strongest there") and imposes its *force* on it ("The force of reason is more apparent in those who know it [*la connaissent*] than in those who do not know it"), that is, the dialectical possibility of notations linked to textual action, the contradictory science.[23]

We have tried to explain how the line of fiction (the line in which we *first* appear), traversed and opened up by practice, transforms knowledge, and how this knowledge retroacts on the fictive line, pluralizing, verticalizing, multiplying, and superposing it—since the new knowledge can enounce itself only in the form of corrections, citations, negative and contradictory intervals (the apparatus' form). In this manner it is possible to see the *Chants de Maldoror* as achieving a complete permutation from the first chant to the sixth: the *Chants* are read in their recitative succession and then established, as a hexagram, in their retroactive "depth"

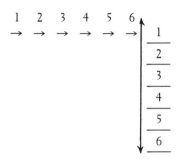

in such a way that to read them becomes, finally, a question of reading their intervals, their empty spaces, and the immanent geometry of
the language they employ as a notational system in space. Beginning
again with the text's first line—or each of its words—this reading proceeds through the sign and sentence, initially fixed but now rendered
transparent, at once confirmed and effaced by means of this reflux and
annullment (this saturation). The text is now inscribed in *columns*
whose "blank" sections are filled by the *Poems'* staves: *that which is
not spoken is written.* To know what the text "says"—and this is the
effect of an awareness of writing [*l'effet de connaissance de l'écriture*]—
is in fact to open up the space to which it is as though numerically
linked. We have an imbrication, an embedding, and the possibility of
a reciprocal reading of the two texts thus produced—each text displacing itself in relation to its act of production. Through its lines of force,
the line of fiction *indicates* the scriptural space enounced on the plane
of knowledge [*savoir*] (of science) by means of the logical apparatus
which it constructs and which constructs it, which it annuls and which
annuls it. Writing and history communicate directly through the
transfinite text's *disenunciation.* [24]

Thus we discover a science whose object is not "truth," but the
constitution and annulment of its own text and the subject inscribed
there. We can analyze this text as the *remainder* of an operation to be
accomplished *again* (i.e., in "progress"). Coming from a biographical
line (geneology, filiation; a social and cultural discursive machine),
organism X is thus heading toward a disappearance which, by achiev-

ing the limit that implies a logical mutation (contradiction, negation), introduces it into a specific space in relation to which what is "written" (notated) presents itself as residue, as trace.

This process overflows and definitively opens up the socio-historical system of speech, the *finite* apparatus programmed by this system where the apparatus perpetuates its own production, turns back upon itself. And does so as it passes from a simple diachronicity to synchronicity, and then to neither—which allows it to control all eventual diachronicity on the basis of a synchronicity reduced to zero, to practice a diachronicity in the second degree: textual history.

The periodized and multidimensional writing of time (a writing both present and absent) thus forms the space of its notated order, and this order's effacement: "I do not need to occupy myself with what I shall do later. I must do as I do. I need not discover what things I shall discover later. In the new science, each thing comes in its turn, such is its excellence."

1967

Notes

1. Marcelin Pleynet, *Lautréamont par lui-même* (Paris: Editions du Seuil, 1967).

2. See the sometimes astonishing examples cited by Pleynet.

3. "The meta-rationality or the meta-scientificity which are thus announced within the meditation on writing can therefore be no more enclosed within a science of man than made to conform to the traditional idea of science. In one and the same gesture, they leave *man, science,* and the *line* behind." *De la grammatologie* (Paris: Editions de Minuit, 1967) [p. 130; Eng. ed., *Of Grammatology,* Gayatri Spivak, tr. (Baltimore: Johns Hopkins University Press, 1976), p. 87; see also Derrida's remarks on the *line,* pp. 85–87 in *Of Grammatology*].

4. This is the reason it is always so ridiculous to see the "*oeuvre*" of a "writer" linked to this experience, recuperated by a "family" according to bourgeois "property rights." Nothing could be more *reasonable* than Artaud's declaration: "Me, Antonin Artaud, I am my son / my father, my mother / and me." "An enormity become norm, absorbed by all" (Rimbaud), the text belongs to everyone, to no one.

5. Tr. note: English citations from the *Chants* and *Poems* are based on *Maldoror,* Paul Knight, tr. (London: Penguin Books, 1978), and *Maldoror,* Guy Wernham, tr. (New York: New Directions, 1965). These translations have been frequently modified

to correspond with Sollers' text. Cf. Isidore Ducasse, *Oeuvres complètes*, établie, présen-tée et annotée par Hubert Juin (Paris: Gallimard, 1973).

6. For Freud, the "imaginative writer" is a "strange being" who acts without him-self knowing why, but with the intent of obtaining "honor, money and women." He is like "the child at play," with play defined as the opposite of reality. The "poet" creates himself "a world of imagination," of "unreality," and thus demonstrates—although with an element of "fore-pleasure" [*prime de séduction*; for Freud's explanation of this term, see the final paragraph of "The Relation of the Poet to Daydreaming"]—the mechanism of "fantasy" present in each person and indicative of neurosis. It is true that Freud intends to limit himself to "the less pretentious writers of romances, novels and stories, who are read all the same by the widest circles of men and women" ("The Relation of the Poet to Daydreaming") [translated by I. Grant, in *Character and Culture* (New York: Collier, 1963)]. It is scarcely necessary to insist on the obfuscating naïvete of such a conception. Nevertheless, most analytical research on the so-called literary text is still entirely oriented toward the "signified" alone (on this subject, see Derrida's *"Freud et la scène de l'écriture"* [in *L'Ecriture et la différence* (Paris: Editions du Seuil, 1967); Eng. ed., *Writing and Difference*, Alan Bass, tr. (Chicago: University of Chicago Press, 1978)]. None of Freud's personal and petit-bourgeois presuppositions have been brought into question here.

7. "Spacing as writing is the becoming-absent and the becoming-unconscious of the subject . . . All graphemes are of a testamentary essence. And the original absence of the subject of writing is also the absence of the thing or the referent." *De la gram-matologie* [p. 100; *Of Grammatology*, p. 69].

8. We refer the reader here to the important text of Julia Kristeva, *"Pour une sémiologie des paragrammes"* (in *Recherches pour une sémanalyse*) [(Paris: Editions du Seuil, 1969)], where the following principles for the study of poetic language are de-fined:

a) the fact of describing the mechanism of *junctions in a potential infinity* [see p. 180].

b) the need to think contradiction and negation according to another logic: "The specificity of *prohibition* in poetic language and its functioning makes poetic language the only system in which contradiction is definition rather than non-sense; in which negation functions to determine, and in which empty sets are a particularly significant mode of embedding. It would perhaps not be too extreme to postulate that all relations in poetic language may be reduced to functions utilizing two modes simultaneously: *negation* and *application* [p. 190].

c) the connecting of mathematical thought with that of the *text*.

d) the essential proposition, to consider the "paragrammatic" text as a "zero path" [see pp. 191–94, 196–97]—as destroying the texts with which it dialogues and as auto-destructive (see our remarks below concerning Chinese logic).

9. "He who sings does not claim that his cavatinas are an unknown thing." Pleynet remarks: ". . . what the author means is his chant in writing, his scription, his sub-scription of *cavatinas*, and not the misfortunes in the tale. And he alerts us to this

through a thousand detours: contradictions, lack of verisimilitude, caricatures . . ." [p. 128]. "The author chooses a canvas (a fiction) from which he will adopt his locus of exposition (in this case the mystery novel as genre), insofar as this locus functions initially as resistance (limit) and subsequently becomes the locus of metamorphosis (consciousness), metonymically including the chain of all possible metamorphoses" [p. 85]. The problem of "sub-scription" is also treated, in what is of course an entirely different fashion, in Raymond Roussel (see Michel Foucault's *Raymond Roussel*).

10. Emile Benveniste, *Problèmes de linguistique générale* (Paris: Gallimard, 1966) [p. 86; Eng. ed., *Problems in General Linguistics*, Mary E. Meek, tr. (Miami: University of Miami Press), p. 129].

11. See Julia Kristeva, "*Bakhtine, le mot, le dialogue et le roman*," in *Critique*, April 1967 (reprinted in *Recherches pour une sémanalyse*).

12. Tr. note: And by extension, "sick of seeing the day," i.e., "labor-pains." See Pleynet's discussion in *Lautréamont par lui-même*, pp. 85–89.

13. "In other words, having become "he" in reading (which is only possible if "I" is introduced as reader), the "I" (the reader) can read this "he" (the subject of reading) insofar as the reading and the subject of reading have become one, insofar as "I" will have become like what he reads; himself written: writing" (Pleynet [p. 112]). Pleynet is the first to have grasped this systematic functioning, just as he is the first not to "contrast" the *Chants* to the *Poems*.

14. Tr. note: *Frayage* signifies both "to make a path" and psychoanalytical "facilitation," *frayage* being the French translation of Freud's *Bahnung*. See J. Laplanche and J. B. Pontalis, *The Language of Psychoanalysis*, D. Nicholson-Smith, tr. (New York: Norton, 1973), pp. 157–58.

15. "If one follows the numbers (*shu*) (of all things) then one can know their beginnings, if one traces them backwards then one can know how it is that they come to an end. Numbers and Things are not two separate entities, and beginnings and endings are not two separate points. If one knows the numbers, then one knows the things, and if one knows the beginnings, then one knows the endings. Numbers and Things continue endlessly—how can one say what is a beginning and what is an ending?" (Tshai Chhen). (We have taken these citations from Chinese texts from the admirable work currently being done at Cambridge University under the direction of Joseph Needham: *Science and Civilisation in China* (Cambridge: Cambridge University Press, 1954–   ) [2:273].)

16. Tr note: A play on *consigner*, meaning "to shut away" and "to write down," "notate," etc.

17. "To know that heaven and earth are no bigger than a grain of the smallest rice, and that the tip of a hair is as big as a mountain—that is to understand the relativity of standards." "A great similarity differs from a little similarity. This is called the little-similarity-and-difference. All things are in one way all similar, in another way all different. This is called the great-similarity-and-difference" (Chuang Tzu) [Needham, 2:103, 190].

18. Tr. note: For the "concept" (and vis-à-vis Hegel, the non-*Begriff*) of *non-savoir*

as developed by Georges Bataille, see Bataille's *L'Expérience intérieure* (Paris: Gallimard, 1954) and *"Conférences sur le non-savoir," Tel Quel* 10 (1962).

19. "The paragram is the only language space in which the 1 does not function as *unity* but as *entire*, as all, because it is double." "This 'unity' is not a synthesis of A and B, but it has the value *one* because it is *all*, and at the same time it cannot be distinguished from two . . . Every set [which is] *unity* locates itself [*se retrouve*] in the three dimensions of the volume" (Kristeva [*Recherches*, p. 193]). This sort of functioning is that of Chinese thought as a whole (cf. Marcel Granet, *La Pensée chinoise*).

20. "The modes of negation substitute for the ambiguity of the texts that have been read a proposition in which negation and affirmation are clearly distinct, separated (*découpées*), and incompatible" (Kristeva [*Recherches*, p. 195]).

21. Tr. note: A reference to fragment 372 (Brunschvig ed.) of the *Pensées:* "In writing down my thought, it sometimes escapes me; but this makes me remember my weakness, which I constantly forget. This is as instructive to me as my forgotten thought; for I strive only to know my nothingness." W. F. Trotter, tr. *Thoughts on Religion and Other Subjects* (New York: Washington Square Press, 1965).

22. In his "Essay on the Theory of the Double Truth," Chi-Tsang defined the utilization of a series of negations of the negations until nothing remains to be either affirmed or denied as "a framework that leads upward from the ground." Thus we obtain a "mundane truth":

    a) Affirmation of being
    b) Affirmation of either being or non-being.
    c) Either affirmation or negation of both being and non-being.

and an "absolute truth":

    a) Affirmation of non-being.
    b) Negation of both being and non-being.
    c) Neither affirmation nor negation of both being and non-being.

[See Needham, 2:424–25.]

23. It is no accident that Ducasse's global operation has remained "unreadable" for bourgeois culture. This operation is in fundamental accord with revolutionary thought: "not only a unity of opposites, but the transition of *every* determination—quality, feature, side, property—into *every* other" (Lenin) ["Philosophical Notebooks," C. Dutt, tr. in *Collected Works*, vol. 38 (Moscow: Progress Publishers, 1961)]. For Lenin, we know, the concept is a "form of the expression of movement." "Multilateral, universal flexibility of concepts, achieving the identity of opposites—that is the essence." And further: "If everything develops, then everything passes from *one* into *another*."

24. Tr. note: In an interview entitled *"Encore Lautréamont" (Tel Quel* 41, 1971), Sollers elaborates on this passage as part of a discussion of the interrelation of the *Chants* and *Poems:*

    Franz de Haes: . . . You say that the *Poems* inscribe themselves into the space opened up by the *Chants*, a space which has effaced the representative line. How is the inscription of the *Poems* in this space to be read?

Ph. Sollers; . . . what I wanted to suggest at the end of my text—[was] that the *Poems* represent the "verticality" of the *Chants de Maldoror*, or in other words that they represent the dialectical abbreviation of all the logical operations that were set in motion, as part of another "topology," in the *Chants*. Each of the two texts plays the role of entrance and exit vis-à-vis the other. If we read the *Chants* vertically, we see the type of operation that will be set in motion in the *Poems* inscribing itself there. This is also a condensation of what was extended and developed in the *Chants*. All of the interpretations that tend to produce an antagonistic relation between the *Chants* and the *Poems* may be explained in this manner: namely, that *contradiction* is the fundamental concept of dialectical materialism, and that if we do not possess this concept then we are by definition unable to understand the *eminently contradictory* operation of language of Lautréamont-Ducasse and Ducasse-Lautréamont. This is, precisely, the startling demonstration of a utilization [*mise en place*] of contradiction in signifying practice, a utilization that can be understood only on the basis of dialectical materialism. And this is also the reason I close my text with some of Lenin's statements on dialectics—in order to say that it should hardly be surprising if the operation given in its practical state has remained unreadable, since the theoretical base itself is precisely what cannot be mastered by notions or identifications that belong to idealistic or metaphysical space. It would be altogether illusory to think that a given philosophical base does not have its repercussions on—and does not emerge from—a conception of language. This is, indeed, what may appear as something new in an area that has been left blank by dialectical materialism. This is something that now demands to be formulated. What we understand by "signifying practice" serves *to formulate this blank*; there is a relation between philosophy and language that needs reformulation, and Lautréamont, once again, constitutes the text of the contradiction to be analyzed in this field. (P. 90.)

7

The Novel
and the Experience of Limits

You must push your head through the wall. It is not difficult to
penetrate it, for it is made of thin paper. But what is difficult is
not to let yourself be deceived by the fact that there is already
an extremely deceptive painting on the wall showing you pushing your head through. It tempts you to say: "Am I not pushing
through it all the time?"

Franz Kafka

The Mythology

LET'S ADMIT IT—the novel has become a subject for polite conversation.[1] This conversation has its ritual: humanists take the role of
humanists, moderns are modern with conviction, everyone speaks in
turn according to well-defined rules of opposition, and no one expects
to be in the least surprised. The veterans, object though they may (but
that's all part of the game), gladly make way for the young, who, as
soon as they take their places (and everyone knows how fast things
move today), hasten to affirm the great historical continuity of which
they are the resolute and lucid incarnation. Before becoming en-
lightened thanks to them, history has taken many a detour; but now
the novel has repudiated its false gods (Balzac, Tolstoy) and ostensibly
discovered its trinitary gospel (Proust, Joyce, Kafka). Dialectical necessity would have the new novelists *complete* what was present in germ
in these three authors whose revolutionary genius everyone agrees to
recognize. Other names may be summoned in support; nevertheless,

what matters is to know how to isolate a linear evolution that makes the advances associated with these three names a guarantee for the elevation of the contemporary novelist—an elevation that, despite a few temporary obstacles, is quickly displayed in the by now infallible museum of cultural values. Thereupon, work proceeds as before: the Balzacian novel appears in ever greater quantities, the humanists are no less humanistic, young humanists are always at hand to take over—and the moderns, since the exception they represent only confirms the rule, waste no time in revealing that their hidden desire was always to attain the modest recognition that they were modern at the right moment. Who can blame them for that? No one. Such appears to be the current mythology.

So everything goes on as usual, and a fixed literary genre—but why that particular one?—is able to assume both its clear and its guilty conscience. A permanent division seems to be established; we have a dogma and its heresies—but above all an ecumenicism that enables both parties to pursue a by and large peaceful coexistence. The law tolerates transgressions that recognize it and require it in order to manifest themselves. This critic defends eternal classical values; that writer denies them with equal sincerity—at which point both sit down at the same round table, and the gratified listener may confidently assume that an assembly like this one establishes the problem's true dimensions, that this confrontation is a fine example of democracy, that literature has finally become synthesis and self-consciousness itself. Surely these enemies are using an identical language if they can oppose and yet hear one another so well—and indeed, *avant-garde* already contains the word *garde*. Strange combat, strange complicity.

Our society needs the myth of the "novel." It is not simply an economic matter, a ceremonial that allows for a cheap recognition of literature while keeping it under tight control—in other words while carefully filtering its deviations (we need only refer to the tawdriness of everything associated with the notion of the "literary prize")—but also, more subtly, a means of instituting a permanent conditioning that goes much farther than the book market alone. THE NOVEL IS THE WAY

THIS SOCIETY SPEAKS [TO] ITSELF [SE PARLE], the way the individual MUST LIVE HIMSELF in order to be accepted there. Therefore it is essential that the "novelistic" point of view be omnipresent, self-evident, inviolable; that it have its frequently cited, interpreted, and recalled masterpieces; its difficult experiments; its semi-successes; its failures. It must be able to utilize every register: naturalistic, realistic, fantastic, imaginary, moralistic, psychological and infra-psychological, poetic, pornographic, political, experimental. Indeed, everything proceeds as if these books were henceforth written in advance; as if they were part of the all-powerful, anonymous speech [*parole*] and thought that hold sway over the interior and exterior, from public information to the most intimate, that are thus excessively visible and consequently invisible. Our *identity* depends on this speech and thought—what others think of us, what we think of ourselves, the way our life is imperceptibly drawn into form [*amenée à composition*]. Who do others recognize in us if not a character from a novel? (Who do you recognize in me speaking to you, if not a character from a novel?) What speech could escape this insidious, incessant speech that always seems to be there before we think of it? One can be recognized—and preferably posthumously—as a great thinker or poet, but the "great thinker" and "great poet" are *first of all* characters from a novel. The "great writer" is *first of all* a character from a novel. What with the current silence of science, the novel is our era's *value*, which is to say its instinctive code of reference, the vehicle of its power, the key to its everyday, mechanical, closed unconsciousness.

Hence the wrath and irritation of this code's guardians, officers of smooth-flowing literary traffic, whenever a book that does not seem to recognize any of the genre's laws dares call itself a *novel*. This is a diary, they say, an essay, a poem—but this is not a *novel*. And yet such a book is generally not a diary, or an essay, or a poem. If it calls itself a "novel," then this may be a deliberate means of making the challenge where it must be made. If one were at all attentive, one would begin by remarking that what is in question here is a book. After all, what is a novel?—A book. And what is a book today? Now perhaps that is our question.

Let's begin with a few very simple statements: in our civilization, the book was initially a written word. It later became a printed writing. Perhaps it is now in the process of assuming—this has been going on for a long while—an entirely different signification that would pose the genuine, but ignored, question of the nature of *writing*, of which the written volume would be only a limited and particular case. There have never been so many books: there have never been so few. In relation to current informational media—and if it means to rival them—the book reveals its poverty, its inertia, its heaviness. It is clearly no longer possible for it to benefit from its author's "style": the repertoire of fine language is henceforth complete and fixed (which does not, however, prevent incessant plagiarism). If, on the contrary, it wants to constitute itself as *object*, then it compounds its failure and assumes a derivative function that can be (better) accomplished by another technique. Perhaps one no longer reads except with reference to the integral Library or to modes of audio-visual communication, and it would be no exaggeration to say that from now on virtually every book published is a replacement product.

But, by the same token, another dimension of the book appears marginally, a dimension it has always possessed. At first glance a negative dimension, one opposed to the idea of power, to aesthetic values, to narrative or spectacular objectification. The book that truly wants to be a book, or in other words text, is no longer obliged to inform, convince, demonstrate, narrate, or represent. If it continues to do so, this can only be in relation to the book's own obsolete history or in reference to means other than its own. Of course, the genre can prosper for quite a long time (verse tragedy was quite successful in the eighteenth century). But all its devices are becoming better and better known, despite the efforts of those who would like to prevent such an awareness: someday a machine will invent the most engaging, most human, most profound novels, in which the imaginary will be at its most effective—this impoverished imaginary will be more and more easily *coded*. Men will more and more frequently ask machines to make them forget machines, and the apotheosis of the civilized individual may someday be to live in an entirely novelized manner. In

any case such a fiction allows us to conjecture what would be a maximum of alienation living itself as liberty and psychic compensation.
Thus it should come as no surprise if, from now on, the accent is
placed, with an increasingly inept and confused haste, on the fantastic, Epinal surrealism, the neo-baroque, cheap sexuality, more or less
organized fabulation, the ciné-novel, the novel-ciné, and, as a formerly intransigent writer who evidently decided the time had come to
reassure the briefly disquieted orthodoxy was still saying recently, on
the irresponsible *forms*. "My novels," added this same less and less
new novelist, "are not thought, they are life." Now, at the very least,
this is a declaration of humility that ought to appease hostile criticism.
Therefore let us set our minds at ease: there is no need to pity the
readers of the novel—this is the *"belle époque,"* and no one's bored.

"Not thought, but life." Or: "Not questioning, but entertain-
ment." Such are the mottoes of all the reactions, all the mystifica-
tions, all the regressions. No longer is it, "When I hear the word
culture, I reach for my revolver." We are permitted instead, "Culture
sits so well in my pocket that whenever I hear the word thought, I
smile." Obscurantism has never been so aggressive, and the strangest
part is that now it takes the form of an apology for *literature as literature*, as if for over one hundred years now literature has not been an
insistent, irrepressible excess and negation, or to put it another way,
as if literature's birth certificate, in the middle of the last century, had
not been a violent act: *"Literature is not literature, literature is all."*
But pseudo-cultural inconsequence has become the rule: bourgeois
journalists, more and more sure of themselves, judge from on high
and hand down decisions with enviable impunity; biographical and
promotional exploitation of authors has never been so widespread, as
if the important thing was above all to discover the man behind the
author, a man whose photograph would be large enough to hide the
texts; certain professors, embittered by the obscurity to which their
conformist teaching justly assigns them, abruptly give themselves the
airs of pamphleteers fanatically opposed to whatever is rigorous in contemporary criticism, and are applauded with relief (thus the recent and

calculated attack launched against Roland Barthes).[2] Within psycho-analysis itself, which by definition ought to be a self-critical enterprise, the sense of intellectual comfort has become such that an increasingly questionable dogmatism obstructs any fresh effort at elucidation (such as that being conducted with customary thoroughness by Jacques Lacan).[3] As for writers suspected of threatening the health of the novel, and therefore of "life itself"—as it was put by that ever-flourishing God of the French, Sainte-Beuve—these are dubbed castrati, impotents, fetuses. Their writings are sterile, disembodied, unreadable; their authors are decadent mandarins, fat women incapable of giving birth, larvae—in a word, just the opposite of what a novelist's function demands: a narrative virility able to rape nature effortlessly, a creator, a *procreator.* "We need flesh and blood beings, we need sperm!" says one. "Exoticism, eroticism!" says the other. "The imaginary!" they cry in chorus. And let us not forget the essential: "humor," in case they should be called to account. But humor that announces its own sense of humor is not quite humor, we suspect. It would seem more like fear.

A strange logic thus wants every genuine revolution to be followed by a pseudo-revolution, not to mention a counter-revolution which is then recognized as "revolutionary." The process is always evident, and its simplistic and repetitive mechanism could have been demonstrated long ago. Is it possible, after all, that Proust, Joyce, and Kafka—and the others—have done nothing else but pave the way for what is presented to us with such tiresome and academic persistence as the modern novel? Is it possible that they would indeed be surprised to be taken for novelists in the accepted sense of this word today? Is it possible that the limits they reached, in writing, in disappearing, far from founding some sort of a renewal of a literary genre—or at least its so-called renewed exploitation—signaled, along with other mutations (notably in "poetry"), a rupture that we pretend to recognize—that our money pretends to recognize under the name of avant-garde—in order not to see it? But then what are these limits? And how suitable is the term *novel* to indicate them?

Writing, Reading

We will call a *novel* the incessant, unconscious, mythical discourse of individuals. By that we mean that this discourse depends on a mode of interpretation tending to reveal its own *determinants*, even though it is officially declared spontaneous and natural. The unconscious, whether we like it or not, is henceforth at the heart of our existence, and this is why optimistic declarations on "creativity" will necessarily find us a skeptical audience. We are doubtless entering a period of general interpretation to which no domain will remain foreign, and language least of all. This is only fitting, since it is language's insistent claims to our attention that should bring about a global revision of our knowledge. It seems more and more necessary, for example, to consider literature not only in time, but also, as it were, *in space*, in its *meaning* and its *function*, or in other words on its different, more or less constant levels of enunciation. This presupposes that we have the *right* to demand that writers take a critical, virtually a scientific attitude toward themselves, that they break permanently with the individualism of the would-be creator of forms. There are no innocent forms, no rough, original, pure, immediate, popular, first or last forms, there is no degree zero of communication. Thus there is no *a priori* "true" or "realist" novel, at whatever level one takes it, be it the most evident or most profound. Besides, this distinction between the superficial and hidden has become incomprehensible, as have all of the arbitrary dualistic classifications (interior-exterior, thought-life, imaginary-real, good-evil, god-devil, etc.), and the difficulty for us during this transitional phase we live in is clearly to be able to situate ourselves outside these distinctions and the limits they continually impose without our knowledge. We can safely say that the novel, the literary genre referred to as the novel, has survived this long as an inoffensive fiction because it hypocritically ignores its history's most notable event and the novelist who destroyed in advance the laborious construction of characters, plots, and social or psychological idiocies; this event and the novelist who gives it his name (and who is, moreover, the author of a *Reflection on the Novel* in which we can read: "when man's very *aberrations* [*écarts*] now seem to him naught but *errors* legitimized by his own studies—should we then not speak to him with the same fervor he applies to his own conduct?") have been excluded to the same degree, in our opinion, that they revealed the novelistic Tartuffery of an entire culture in the clearest light, in the clearest and firmest language. We are of course referring to Sade. For us, Sade is still the fire most novels can be tossed into. But unfortunately, despite the clarification brought to the subject by contemporary thought, it may still be a long while before Sade's language ceases to be unreadable in its true perspective, which is not that of a pathological sexuality, but rather of the will to *tell all*.[4] Maurice Blanchot recently recalled this remarkable phrase of Sade's: "However much men may shudder, philosophy must tell all." This could be the definition of literature as well; for to *tell all* signifies something quite different today than a sort of indefinite, manifestly scandalous verbalization. To *tell all*, and this involves no paradox whatsoever, would be to refuse vigorously to state what have you, *but while stating it* [*en le disant*], or again to reject such verbalization insofar as it continually conceals and justifies novelistic mystification. As we can see, this position leads immediately to a most concrete choice:

—either we accept, as social individuals (and beyond simple material necessity), the guarantee of reality this society gives us in exchange for an implicit abandonment of all fundamental claims (of any attempt to alter this society's principles)—in which case language becomes a secondary phenomenon for us, becomes "art";

—or else we decide to live ourselves, regardless of the cost to our *fiction*, at which time a decisive and undoubtedly scandalous reversal is produced, but a reversal whose singular nature constitutes the literary experience. Literature is nothing if it does not achieve this reversal.

We are speaking of an experience that serves as our basis for a reexamination of the novel as *expression* and consequently of the life that is given us. Such an undertaking demands that we leave the confines of culture, of our habits, of our sleep. Here the facile, frivolous attitude that would have a given experience be of interest only to the person who lives it (in other words "the author") reveals the misconception on which it rests. For this new dimension of the book that we spoke of, which although new has always been present, and which the book appears to have assumed the precise job of discovering as if by emerging from and doubling back upon itself, is on the contrary the *reader*, its *present* reader, and with him the drama of posited, avowed, described communication. Significantly, the most powerful prohibitions are directed against precisely this communication: at some moments the accent is placed on the author as personality, an author whose works will ultimately do no more than confirm his mythological existence; at others—although often as part of the same tendency—it constitutes a kind of fetishization of the work as dogma and absolute. On the one hand we have an author without a work, on the other the work without a reader. It is elementary to point out:

—that an author is not truly the cause of what he writes, but rather its product; that he thus ceaselessly renders himself potential [*virtuel*] and plural in relation to his writing;

—that a work exists by itself only potentially and that its actualization (or production) depends on its readings and on the moments at which these readings actively take place.

In sum, these are the facts society attempts to dissimulate by means of antinomical sanctifications. On the one hand we are told, "Not forms, but meaning"—and the old humanism continues its indefatigable sermon on the SOUL and the author's salvation through his SOUL; and on the other, "Not meaning, but forms," and we fall back into the midst of aestheticizing gratuitousness, in a barely disguised reincarnation of "art for art's sake" in the form of an OBJECT and a more or less lucrative commerce in this OBJECT. One feels like crying out like Michelet on the subject of the indulgences formerly sold by Rome: "Magical virtue of equivocation! Thanks to the word *works*, money and philosophy even have language!" Everything proceeds as if Surrealism, for example, never took place, and yet it is impossible not to *take account* of it, even if the "automatic writing" formula introduces an ambiguity from which many have tried to profit automatically with none but superficial results. As we know, this formula has had the additional effect of allowing recourse to various sorts of *simulations*, and ultimately to the controlled and somewhat mundane fabrications of the "surrealist" genre. Nevertheless, we must give André Breton credit, despite a few of his unjustified condemnations (Poe, Joyce), for having unmasked beforehand all those who would like to revive regressive or anti-historical [*d'ommision historique*] attitudes, attitudes which more than ever seem to have become the order of the day. When Breton writes, in 1953, that "Not enough emphasis was placed on the meaning and scope of the operation that tended to bring language to its true life: in other words, rather than reascending from the thing signified to the sign that survives it (which, moreover, would prove to be impossible), it is better to go back in one leap to the birth of the signifier," [5] he reveals an event that up until that time had been sadly neglected, and that allows Blanchot to write, for example: "Literature's search is the search for that which precedes it." But this event leads to the denunciation of would-be *realism* (regardless of the name disguising it, be it naturalistic or mental), a bias that consists in the belief that a writing must *express* something that would not be given in this writing, something that would be immediately and unanimously acceptable. But of course this agreement is effective only by virtue of preliminary conventions, the notion of reality being one such convention and conformity, a kind of tacit contract between the individual and the social group; declared real, in given historical circumstances, is that which the greatest number of those in power are obliged, for precise economic reasons, to hold as real. This real, moreover, is manifested nowhere else but in a language, and a society's language and myths are what it decides to take as reality. Which is the reason why discussions on realism can be interminable, each person believing in good or bad faith to be more of a realist than the other. [6] At bottom, the social censure we submit to may be defined thus: what our society must prevent with its network of codes, its monetary obsession, its legislation, its *literature*, is an awareness of the fact that we are signs among other signs, signs producing signs. Let us say, in Marxist terms: as long as there are *social classes* there will be *classes of reality*, the ones indefinitely opposing the others by means of a contradiction that only a radical de-psychologization can do away with. Now, what kind of liberation would this be? Is it even possible? It may seem odd to look to Nietzsche for an insight on this possibility—but Nietzsche taught us that we would never think freely so long as we had not "unlearned our antinomies." "The contradiction," he writes, "is not between 'false' and 'true,' but between 'abbreviations of signs' and signs themselves. The main thing is the elaboration of forms that represent numerous movements, the invention of signs that summarize entire categories of signs." It is therefore within language, recognized somewhat mathematically as being our *milieu of transformation*, that the problem that occupies us must be posed—in other words outside the notion of *character* (insofar as you, actors, authors, and readers of this life take yourselves for characters, you yield to our society's mythology, you identify with a ridiculously limited identity that is not your own), outside the notion of *product* (insofar as you valorize the product, you posit the museum's existence, and, sooner or later, that of the academy; you promote the collection of things that have been fixed and frozen in the pseudo-eternity of value, whereas what we seek should lead us beyond all value).

Thus we see that the essential question today is no longer that of the *writer* and of the *work* (and even less that of the "work of art"), but that of *writing* and of *reading*. Consequently, we need to define a new space where these two phenomena could be seen as reciprocal and simultaneous, a curved space, a medium of exchanges and reversibility where we would finally be on the same side as our language. Here, the difficulty arises from our error concerning the specific nature of writing: we are accustomed to considering it as a simple, fictive image or imitative transcription of speech (revealing above all our obsession with *time*, whereby our perception grants predominance to the acoustic element and becomes increasingly blind to the sign's spatiality). But the experience of writing cannot be assimilated to that of speech: one writes in order gradually to silence oneself, to attain the written silence of memory that paradoxically translates the world in its ciphered movement, this world of which each one of us is the dissimulated and irreducible cipher. Writing is linked to a space in which time would have in some way *turned*, in which it would no longer be anything but this circular and generative movement. We might say that writing is genetic, that it is both the most peripheral and most central of phenomena, thus comprising speech and using it as material twice-removed.[7] If we want to clarify *what is at stake* in the literary experience—and show that it has nothing to do with "literature," but on the contrary that *in its life* it touches each one of us, we must insist on this point that makes it unique and sets it beyond the reach of inane prattle. It would be easy to demonstrate that the search for this *real* point has been the sole preoccupation of writers otherwise at opposite ends of the spectrum—an undertaking our society has continually attempted to impede by denigrating or celebrating their lives or works in order to avoid having to draw out the implications, to avoid having to *read* them. But let us simply take Proust, Joyce, and Kafka. Let's simply reread the few phrases with which Proust, as he nears death, informs us of the meaning of his search and of all searches:

> I used to fix before my mind . . . a cloud, a triangle, a church spire, a flower, a stone, because I had the feeling that perhaps beneath these signs there lay something of a quite different kind which I must try to discover, some thought which they translated after the fashion of those hieroglyphic characters which at first one might suppose to represent only material objects. No doubt the process of decipherment was difficult, but only by accomplishing it could one arrive at whatever truth there was to read. . . . As for the inner book of unknown signs (signs carved in relief they might have been, which my attention, as it explored my unconscious, groped for and stumbled against and followed the contours of, like a diver exploring the ocean bed), if I tried to read them no one could help me with any rules, for to read them was an act of creation in which no one can do our work for us or even collaborate with us. How many for this reason turn aside from writing! What tasks do men not take upon themselves in order to evade this task . . . The book whose hieroglyphs [*caractères figurés*] are patterns not traced by us is the only book that really belongs to us. . . . every reader is, while he is reading, the reader of his own self. The writer's work is merely a kind of optical instrument which he offers to the reader to enable him to discern what, without this book, he would perhaps never have perceived in himself. And the recognition by the reader in his own self of what the book says is the proof of its veracity, the contrary also being true, at least to a certain extent, for the difference between the two texts may sometimes be imputed less to the author than to the reader.[8]

The movement of the *Temps Perdu*, of time recaptured, is entirely given in these obvious and disregarded lines, and it is this movement that matters, that must be understood and translated into a writing other than that of Proust (since writing as he did is clearly out of the question). For Joyce the matter is even clearer, and without the "aesthetic" ambiguity of discourse that, in a certain sense, retards the Proustian experience: here legibility creates itself at the very heart of the illegible, and the sedimentation of languages, on the frontier between the world and the dream, becomes the world and dream of a single person and of all humanity. The limit attained by *Finnegans Wake* is crucial here: the reader is obliged to become the act of deciphering which will never be total and definitive, but which is revealed instead as a circular metamorphosis and sliding: "In writing of the night," said Joyce, "I really could not, I felt I could not, use words in their ordinary connections. Used that way they do not express how things are in the night, in the different stages—conscious, then semi-conscious, then unconscious. I found that it could not be done with words in their ordinary relations and connections. When morning comes of course everything will be clear again." [9] In the night Joyce entered through his writing, tongues [*les langues*] are unknotted and come to life, revealing their ambiguity, their multiplicity of which we are the daylight reflections—reflections, images believing themselves to be clear and protected. We live in the false light of a dead language with narrow significations: we lack daylight to the extent that we lack the night that we are. But we are nothing other than this nocturnal and diurnal movement of the legible and illegible, in us, outside us—and this is precisely what we would rather not know. We prefer to think Joyce committed a baroque error; we speak calmly of Mallarmé's "failure"; we insinuate that Roussel pushed the joke a little too far, that Kafka liked his illness, that Lautréamont was mad, that Artaud should have been kept locked up, that Nerval or Nietzsche merely lost control in a situation anyone could have avoided—it's a matter of common sense. Or else these writers' existence is romanticized, even though they had absolutely no desire to be "writers" in the accepted sense of that word, even though they themselves repeatedly emphasized their impersonality. Thus the *intelligence* these names designate, a *textual* intelligence, becomes the object of a sentimental indulgence. And always for the same reason: the inability of a certain mentality *to read what is written*, its inability to think otherwise than in terms of "products" or "persons," this mentality's inability to see itself as radically compromised in its language and in the blind night it would impose upon us, thus reducing the *wakefulness* of writing. This wakefulness is what a writer like Kafka has wholly *become*, he who defined himself thus: "I am a memory come alive, hence my insomnia." This sleepless writing, exterior as much to the world as to the dream, yet established at their center and drawing them into its interrogative wake, is what Kafka wanted to live, denouncing lucidly and to the point of death, acting as death, the invisible constraints we are subjected to: "He who searches does not find; but he who does not search is found." "In literature," he writes, "I have experienced states (not many) which, in my opinion, correspond very closely to states of illumination—and during which I completely dwelt in everything that came to mind, but this did not keep me from completing every idea while I felt myself arriving not only at my own limits, but at the limits of the human in general." And here is another passage that in the simplest and most enigmatic fashion draws together everything we are trying to suggest—and first of all this relation between writing and reading pushed to a limit where it seems to double and reverse itself:

> Three houses adjoined one another and formed a small yard. This yard also contained two workshops under sheds and a great pile of little boxes set in a corner. One very stormy night—the wind drove the rain in sheets over the lowest of the houses into the yard—a student still sitting over his books in an attic room heard a loud moan coming from the yard. He jumped up and listened, but all was silence, unbroken silence. "I must be mistaken," the student said to himself, and returned to his reading. "Not mistaken"—these were the words the letters formed after a moment, shaping the sentence in the book. "Mistaken," he repeated, and moved his index finger along the lines to calm their restlessness.[10]

Therefore we say this: writing, for these individuals, was not an activity meant to tell about this or that more or less successfully, to express this or that, imagine ("fantasize") or produce this or that, but, on the contrary, an abrupt and by definition open-ended experience that necessarily put their lives fundamentally at risk; an act that involved not only tracing words, but inverting the perspective of the world in which they found themselves, concretely touching for themselves its limits—an act that can be stated in the following threefold fashion: *"Whoever writes deals with all things." "Whoever does not write is written." "Whoever writes encounters death."*

The Experience

The work refusing to be an object and affirmed as experience, the author's effacement preferred to his academic or romantic acceptance by a society more than willing to offer him recognition so long as he provides an outlet for escapists or the inspired—clearly, this is what we must emphasize and attend to. And lest this position become a simple alibi, an escape, we must pursue and clarify the problem even further. Morality is not at issue here, any more than the psychology of the individual who takes himself for the subject of his experience. On the contrary, the issue is an inevitable economy that is part of language, an expenditure that belongs to it and that *determines* the forms and significations which are its ever-renewed and changing effects, *in progress.* [11] Written writing is only a fragment of the writing that is lived and thought, and the two are reciprocally related in permanent contestation; this may allow the reader to understand that he must not, as is too often said, fabricate a book through his reading, but that he must continually become his own writing—or in other words shatter the speech that is spoken in him by prejudices in order to judge for himself in each case, to accede to his own *generation.* We can see that this is not a matter of writing "the novel of novels"— of writing one's incapacity to write a novel, but of a renewed access to this point which is similar in each person—this nerve center, this "navel of dreams" Freud spoke of, this "center of vibratory suspension," as Mallarmé put it—which is the source of all fiction and consequently of our life communicating with us. Can we still seriously reproach Mondrian for having done the painting of painting? Webern for having composed the music of music? Giacometti for pursuing only the sculpture of sculpture? No one would venture such insanities any longer, and everyone is well aware that what we still call "art" henceforth passes through this reversal that places it in another dimension, where, in a slight yet nonetheless decisive withdrawal, it lets itself be seen and understood as it sees and understands itself. Resistances also concentrate, definitively, on "literary" language, on the symbolic activity capable of making this reversal *manifest*. Moreover, it is not a matter of "modernism" here—and the misreading that one can make of literature would be to think that it can be reduced to an exclusively technical or formal exercise, when it is fundamentally the proposition made to a subject to be all forms. Literature's goal is not the constitution of objects, but a ciphered relation, a sliding which by opening up different subjects outside their limits reveals objects of thought and of the world. In order to see and understand modern art—which is *also* to live in the world today—the problem is not to construct books that *resemble* modern art, but to bring writing in all domains to the interrogation that is its own, to an infinite interrogation. Literature is to the world and to "art" what signs' abbreviations are to signs, whence its concentrated and discontinuous nature, turned away from all visibility and opening onto the movement prior to signs that allows signs to be seen, heard, and touched. Writing takes place in and must pass into the ground [*fond*] of all forms, including those it activates as it writes itself; it must tell what it does even as it does it. The novel we have in mind would be one that opens itself fully to this inexhaustible possibility, a possibility continually decentered and annulled, that can never be fixed in this or that particular story, in this or that first degree narrative [*récit*]. This "first degree narrative" is in effect the "bulk" of the novelistic text, which plays not on small units (words) but on ensembles (surfaces) that depend on a redoubled topology: "Narration [*narration*] is the architecture made with words. The architecture made with 'narrations' is the surnarrative [*surrécit*]" (Khlebnikov). The novel must therefore burn and consume every trace of the novel, or else resign itself to being only a novel, and this in the sense that one can say: "He who does not die from being only a man will never be anything but a man." There can no longer be any possibility of relief for it, nor of relapse into the aesthetic gratuity of the imaginary, any more than into that of sham realism. But is anything left? The essential, perhaps; a force which is neither fortuitous nor haphazard, but on the contrary subordinated in each word to the greatest necessity—a force that through its nuclear organization and *play* presents itself as continual excess [*dépassement ouvert*].

The most tenacious prejudice, as we have said, is that which defines the novel, once and for all, as a reflection of the world or of the mind—a mirror walked along the street or around the brain; a reflection, consequently, that would write itself, in a more or less structured manner, through a "temperament," an engineer or visionary, and under the influence of events that would be exterior to it. Though obviously ridiculously naive, this prejudice remains nonetheless implanted with the unshakeable power of illusion. An illusion of such power that in it we must recognize a very profound sort of law bearing on language itself: the necessity that compels us to remain unconscious of its radical operations, so that we retain only its superficial fiction. Where does this illusion come from? Freud perceptively connected it with our conventional attitude toward death, with the fact that we do everything to eliminate the thought of it from our life: "It is an inevitable result of all this," he writes,

> that we should seek in the world of fiction, of general literature, and of the theatre compensation for the impoverishment of life. There we still find people who know how to die, indeed, who are even capable of killing someone else. There alone too we can enjoy the condition which makes it possible for us to reconcile ourselves with death—namely, that behind all the vicissitudes of life we preserve our existence intact. For it is indeed too sad that in life it should be as it is in chess, when one false move may lose us the game, but with the difference that we can have no second game, no return match. In the realm of fiction we discover that plurality of lives which we crave. We die in the person of a given hero, yet we survive him, and are ready to die again with the next hero just as safely.[12]

With these words Freud precisely designates the idealization and identification mechanism of the *belief* that consists in living fiction as reality (immediate belief in a "story," in narration perceived as if outside the forms that manifest it; a belief that permits one to live oneself in a projected, deferred, delegated manner) instead of confronting, as in a chess match, the ineluctable process that makes every one of our gestures a *written act*, the very fiction (and reality) of our existence. A continual and monumental dupery, so monumental that it generally goes unnoticed; the refusal to recognize [*méconnaissance de*] the *letter* and the central character of that letter's relationship to ourselves. Everything leads us to confer reality *on anything at all rather than on language*, so that language will not be a reality—admittedly a most unusual situation, especially if one considers that this situation is precisely what determines us so long as we determine it. We can illustrate this by citing one of our influential literary critics: his name hardly matters, since his colleagues continually write the same sentence in different forms: "Telling a story, moreover, passes for an outmoded and abusive practice in the eyes of a certain integralism of the literary faith that would like to limit itself to the book and its verbal material, as if the organization of characters and situations did not reveal a writer's thematic just as well as the organization of sentences and words." We did not see ourselves as "integralists of the literary faith," but what appears more than certain to us is that a critic capable of perceiving situations and characters in a book, *without going through the sentences and words of that book*, must have received a divine dispensation very early on. We are forced to conclude: literary criticism today—and we pity the readers it conditions in this fashion—is pure hallucination.

In this disregard [*méconnaissance*] for the *letter* (and in its corollary, blind apology for "the imaginary"—and wherever you find this apology, you can presume a passive or active acceptance of social conditioning), we can also see a clear rejection of the *body*. We do not care to hear talk of [*entendre parler de*] our body, because we do not want to hear it speak [*l'entendre parler*]—in other words: we do not want to talk of our language because we do not want to hear it speak. As concerns the novel, the book that in its language will challenge the unconscious narrative designed to dissimulate sexuality and death will consequently, and necessarily, fall under an essential prohibition. We say that this contestation must take place *in its language*, for then and then only will the functioning of writing lay bare the fiction and meaning of its era—along with the limits, codifications, and repressions this meaning undergoes. To be inside history's meaning is to be inside its form, and this form's most elusive meaning (its strange contact with writing) may simply be itself. No one has said it better than a writer whose novels and essays, as if by chance, are practically never cited, even though their undertaking is one of the most important of our time: "The innermost meaning," writes Maurice Blanchot, "of every literary work is always the 'literature' which signifies itself." The whole problem is to know whether we will or will not attempt to reach this innermost meaning. Between the man who writes in this way and history, there is an extreme and contradictory relationship that stems from the fact that for him time is suspended; non-time is the very time of writing, while space, which at this moment is null, unveils itself and withdraws into its possibility—a symbolic concentration and dispersion introducing the most vast and hazardous play, since in it the entire future is challenged to make itself heard. Whoever writes becomes other for this other to himself who must become the one who reads; between them there is the rule of an irreversible isolation and anonymity in which everything is, properly speaking, brought into question; a tactical retreat which is not that of solitude or aesthetic individualism, but on the contrary that of every language confronting its own disappearance. *We say that each person has the right to live the narrative of his life in terms of his death,* and we say that this narrative is rooted nowhere but in *language.* Just as we were able to affirm that language had its rationale that reason did not know, we can propose this definition of the "novel": language has its fiction that fiction is unaware of. This fiction we are caught in without knowing it, this fiction we are obliged to live or else deliberately ignore, is that of writing and of reading: we are continually in the process of reading and writing, in our dreams, our perceptions, our acts, our fantasies, our thought—but we remain unaware of it insofar as we *believe we know how to read and write.* We must dare put this question—and I will put it to us: are we, then, so sure we know how to read and write?—are we so sure that we weren't taught to no longer know how to read and write *our life* from the day we were told that we knew how to read and write? Then what is happening right now? What are you doing in order to understand me, if not instantaneously recording, or in other words writing and immediately reading what I pronounce, with each person utilizing his own writing and references, which means that no two people here are listening to the same talk, which is nonetheless the same? "To think," says Mallarmé, "is to write without implements." It follows that we can say that "life" and writing intermingle, and those we call "writers" (these bizarre individuals so often incomprehensibly proud of their privileges) do no more than accentuate a reality that is everyone's. We are nothing else, in the last analysis, than our writing/reading system, and that in a concrete and practical way—a proposition that would allow us to understand Lautréamont's enigmatic assertions in their full force, assertions that should be tirelessly reconsidered: "Poetry should have as its goal practical truth"; "poetry should be made by all, not by one." To write, to make writing appear, is not to dispose of a privileged knowledge; it is to try to discover what everyone knows and no one can say. It is, perhaps, to try *for once* to lift the veil that keeps us in an obscurity we have not chosen.

It will be clear that on this level distinctions between "literary genres" inevitably collapse. They are generally maintained only by a convention that pays no attention to the economy and field of writing, a repressive convention that allows the novel to be assigned false limits (those of a precise pseudocommunity) and poetry, for example, to be confined in ineffable obscurity. We ought not allow the society we live in to dictate the definition of literary activity any more than our factitious roles as producers and consumers. We have to think differently, according to a circular and periodic schema that would state itself thus: the novel would say what poetry is not intended to say, and criticism would be the basis for the great *translation* in progress within operations linked by the same experience, an experience involving a subject's entire life.[13] It is therefore no longer a matter of the customary writer-work-critic relationship and its recuperation, but rather of a moving constellation, that of writing-reading-fiction-thought; an impersonal and necessary movement, since it will become increasingly apparent that writing should be thought, that our reality should become a thinking of writing and of reading. If we want to act, we can do so on this level which seems to be that of non-power and retreat, but which in fact controls all possible action, and which, in this action, derives at once from both chance and an ungraspable necessity whose key is our *desire*. We are not supporting this or that ideology, this or that conception of the world, a pathological mania, nor yet the illusionist's point of view. We mean to point to a concrete, living experience, the most concrete and living of all, something each of you may claim; something, in any case, that each of you *is*. What good is it to talk of literature and writing today, if the most physical effects do not result from these words? We have no infantile desire to be told stories, but we would, perhaps, like to open our eyes, even at the risk of blinding ourselves, on the source of all stories, knowing that such an activity is and must be *guilty* in relation to the reigning stories and myths. An experience involving risk and silence, and which was lived by a novelist, poet, critic, philosopher of our time, who in passing made these two apparently contradictory assertions: "To write is to impose one's will." "To write is to pursue chance." To passivity and resignation, we must therefore oppose will and chance, will as chance, which is what is effectively disclosed by the writing of Georges Bataille, to whom we dedicate these words.

1965

Notes

1. *Tel Quel* talk delivered December 8, 1965, in Paris.

2. Tr. note: See Raymond Picard's polemical treatment of Barthes and the French "new criticism" in his *Nouvelle critique ou nouvelle imposture* (Paris: Jean-Jacques Pauvert, 1965). Barthes' response to Picard was published as *Critique et vérité* (Paris: Editions du Seuil, 1966).

3. Tr. note: For an account of the conflicts between Lacan and the French psychoanalytic orthodoxy, see Sherry Turkle, *Psychoanalytic Politics: Freud's French Revolution* (New York: Basic Books, 1978), esp. chs. 4 and 5.

4. This fear is far from unjustified, since the mere mention of Sade's name arouses every sort of confusion: frivolous apologies, inconsequential condemnations (cf., for example, the inquiry organized by *Le Nouvel Observateur*, "Should the Divine Marquis be burned?"—an inquiry conducted in the name of a supposedly "leftist" thought, a right-thinking thought that doubtless obscures beneath a cloud of impenetrable mystery the expression "non-communist left"?).

5. Tr. note: See André Breton, "On Surrealism in Its Living Works," in *Manifestoes of Surrealism*, Richard Seaver and Helen Lane, tr. (Ann Arbor: University of Michigan Press, 1969).

6. "Naive realism, as distinguished from critical realism, asserts that things are as they seem to be, and that sensory qualities are inherent in the very nature of things themselves. We know that neither of these statements is tenable . . . Naive realism was a pre-scientific viewpoint, and with the spread and advance of science, it has become anti-scientific . . . In Marxists the error is astonishing since it is based on theses that clearly contradict the epistemological assumptions of Marxist doctrine: cognition is an eternal process, and the results of cognition are not absolute truths (in a particular sense of the term)." Adam Schaff, "Language and Reality" [in *Diogenes* 51 (1965)].

7. Everything we are suggesting here (the end of the book, of "truth," of logocentrism; the originality of writing in relation to language; the reciprocal relation of writing and death; the world's movement as *play*) is based on Jacques Derrida's authoritative work in *Of Grammatology*. We can also recall these lines from Ponge:

"Let us see to it that the unpronounceable word SCVLPTVRE, this thundering word, created in memory of the first fulguration at the moment when consciousness in the flash of its own rending conceived itself at once as a mass of clouds and the world, with clarity around it like a Temple or a Forest peopled with forms whitened by the electric arc which then died away, this word [*mot*], model of those for eternity which then found themselves engraved by the same stroke on the stone tablets of the law—but the Word [*Parole*], contrary to what is usually believed, did not make itself heard until *just afterwards* like a cracking interminably reverberated since then as the ever more indistinct and distant proclamations of the mysterious INSCRIPTIONS which, like all else in the world fallen back into obscurity, will not soon be read . . ." (1948). [See "SCVLPTVRE" (*Lyres*), in *Le Grand Recueil* (Paris: Gallimard, 1961).]

8. Tr. note: See *Le Temps retrouvé*, in *A la recherche du temps perdu* (Paris: Gallimard, Bibliothèque de la Pléiade, 1954), vol. 3; Eng. ed., *The Past Recaptured*, Andreas Major, tr. (New York: Random House, 1970).

9. Tr. note: See Richard Ellmann, *James Joyce*, new and rev. ed. (New York: Oxford University Press, 1982), p. 546.

10. Tr. note: See the entry for July 3, 1916, in Kafka's *Tagebücher* (New York: Schocken Books, 1954), pp. 502–03; Eng. ed., *The Diaries of Franz Kafka, 1914–1923*, Max Greenberg and Hannah Arendt, tr. (New York: Schocken Books, 1949), pp. 156–57. Translation modified.

11. Tr. note: In English in the original.

12. Tr. note: See "Thoughts for the Times on War and Death," E. C. Mayne, tr., in *Collected Papers* (New York: Basic Books, 1959), 4:306–07.

13. Thus, in relation to language, the novel may be thought of as a poem whose action leans, reflexively, toward narrative [*récit*], this reflexivity recharging its "poetic" (mythic) capacity. In a unified field of signs, the novel becomes the appearance of these signs, their history. Writing, or textual production, thus follows, as thought, the thought of the *symbol* and the *sign*, or in other words, the period which took *meaning* to be divinity and capital.

Index